SUPPLY CHAIN EXCELLENCE

Second Edition

SUPPLY CHAIN EXCELLENCE

A Handbook for Dramatic Improvement Using the SCOR Model

Second Edition

Peter Bolstorff
Robert Rosenbaum

American Management Association
New York • Atlanta • Brussels • Chicago • Mexico City • San Francisco
Shanghai • Tokyo • Toronto • Washington, D.C.

Special discounts on bulk quantities of AMACOM books are available to corporations, professional associations, and other organizations. For details, contact Special Sales Department, AMACOM, a division of American Management Association, 1601 Broadway, New York, NY 10019.
Tel: 212-903-8316. Fax: 212-903-8083.
E-mail: specialsls@amanet.org
Website: www. amacombooks.org/go/specialsales
To view all AMACOM titles go to: www.amacombooks.org

Library of Congress Cataloging-in-Publication Data

Bolstorff, Peter.
    Supply chain excellence : a handbook for dramatic improvement using the SCOR model / Peter Bolstorff and Robert Rosenbaum. — 2nd ed.
        p. cm.
    Includes bibliographical references and index.
    ISBN-10: 0-8144-0926-1
    ISBN-13: 978-0-8144-0926-8
    1. Business logistics—Management. I. Rosenbaum, Robert (Robert G.)
    II. Title.
HD38.5.B64 2007
658.7—dc21

                                                                    2007012167

Printing number
10 9 8 7 6 5 4 3 2 1

To those who carry out the mission of SCE each day.

Contents

Phase IV: Work and Information Flow Analysis and Design

Reference files for the Supply Chain Operations Reference Model, the Design Chain Operations Reference Model, the CCOR Process, a partial list of SCOR Model Leading Practices, Fowlers' Business Context Summary, Fowlers' Supply Chain Excellence Project Charter, a SCOR Quick Reference, and a SCOR and Six Sigma DMAIC Comparison are all available at www.amacom books.com/go/SupplyChainExcel.

Preface

When *Supply Chain Excellence, A Handbook for Dramatic Improvement Using the SCOR Model* was published in 2003, it documented a process that had been developed over the course of 30 projects, and it focused on the Supply Chain Operations Reference (SCOR) model as the key facilitator for defining, measuring, and improving the supply chain.

The second edition reflects the experience gained from still another thirty-plus projects, presenting a wider set of variables and increasingly sophisticated responses to real-life issues. Although SCOR remains the central framework for defining the AS IS and TO BE states of an enterprise, *Supply Chain Excellence*, 2nd edition, reaches further into the toolbox—seamlessly integrating Lean Six Sigma and Continuous Improvement into the process.

It also reaches further to the edges of the traditional supply chain with a new chapter on how the principles of SCOR can be applied to the outlying functions of sales and design: *the Value Chain*. In 2003, the frameworks to do this hadn't yet been written. Now, the Supply-Chain Council, which created SCOR, offers the Design Chain Operations Reference and Customer Chain Operations Reference models—both using similar language and logic as SCOR, and both applied in the Value Chain chapter of this second edition. At another level, the second edition simplifies the data collection and analysis involved through the course of a project. It does this by eliminating some painstakingly manual techniques (anyone who has struggled to build fishbone diagrams will be relieved) and replacing them with an easily accessible and affordable computer tool, ProcessWizard, that makes the arrangement of data faster and more beneficial. Metrics have been revised, practices have been honed, and processes have been updated, including the latest edition of the main tool, SCOR 8.0.

Perhaps the most significant change is the surefooted evolution of this book's primary offering: from an application of SCOR to a unique, tested methodology—the *Supply Chain Excellence method*—that uses SCOR, Lean Six Sigma, and other advanced tools to re-design your Value Chain in 17 weeks.

Introduction

At one seminar on the Supply Chain Operations Reference (SCOR) model, one of the executives in attendance opened the question-and-answer session by asking, "Most of us don't have good control of our supply chains—inside the company or with trading partners. What two or three things would you would motivate us to address the supply chain?"

"If you can *define* your supply chain—which isn't hard to do—then you can *measure* it," I answered. "Once you've measured it, you'll find the opportunities are so big that you won't need any more motivation. You'll want to drive continuous improvement in your supply chain. The potential will be that obvious."

This book is not a manifesto on the power of supply chain management (SCM). In fact, the two paragraphs that you've just read are the only argument you're going to get in this book about *why* SCM is important.

The rest of this book is about the how—how to achieve these two fundamental principles of SCM: define and measure, and drive performance improvement.

Defining Supply Chains

Like most bandwagons, SCM has been defined and redefined in many ways over the past ten years. To a large degree, the definition depends on your motivation and interest.

A technology provider trying to sell software might align SCM with the use of advanced planning functionality; a third-party logistics provider trying to sell its outsourcing capabilities will align SCM with distribution practices; and a consulting firm selling services will align SCM with its intellectual property. There really is an objective way to help SCM; it's a cross-industry standardized model called "SCOR." It's the foundation of this book.

Supply Chain Performance Improvement: Fifteen Common Scenarios

Supply chain performance issues can show up just about anywhere in a business: profit-and-loss statements, balance sheets, employee satisfaction surveys, customer report cards, analyst ratings and commentary, and new products or other indicators of innovation.

Ultimately, supply chain performance issues reach a point that pushes an enterprise to take action. The question is: How do you take action?

Leading companies in every industry have teams of skilled and motivated business managers working to build integrated supply chains. Many of these managers run into trouble; projects stall and valuable initiatives get scrapped. That doesn't have to be the case. SCOR offers a step-by-step engineering approach that can help you to analyze, design, and improve supply chain performance. Its framework is both rigorous and flexible, allowing it to work in any industry and for any supply chain issue.

In more than sixty projects I've done with SCOR, I've identified 15 general business scenarios that seem to cover just about any circumstance. Some are rare; others are present in almost every company.

Because you have come far enough in your thinking about SCM to be reading this book, you'll see yourself and your company in at least a few of the following scenarios.

1: Building a Technology Investment Plan

A chief information officer deflected pressure to install an enterprise resource planning (ERP) system before 2000—making the case that simply being Y2K compliant was not a good enough reason to put the company into upheaval. Even after Y2K, as she watched the rapid evolution of web-based applications and robust advanced planning systems, she found herself without a technology investment plan that supported the company's business strategy.

2: Searching for a Return on Investment

A company bought its ERP package during the vendor's end-of-quarter push to meet sales goals. The deal included all the latest add-ons—things such as customer relationship management, advanced supply chain planning, event management, and web portals providing self-service to customers and suppliers. Now the executive team is looking for an answer to a question that's harder to answer than it would seem: When will we start to see return on investment in the earnings statement?

3: Creating a Supply Chain Strategy

Three executive vice presidents—for sales, marketing, and operations—assembled their own strategies for developing supply chain competence within their departments. Then they invested in application technology, manufacturing processes, and product development—all with measurable success. What's missing is a comprehensive blueprint that combines their individual efforts to drive profit and performance across the entire company.

4: Implementing a Supply Chain Strategy

The company's top executive for SCM assembled a dozen of his brightest managers for a structured brainstorming process—resulting in a list of forty-five high-priority projects. But when the managers began implementation, the results were not encouraging. General managers were being asked to support multiple initiatives with many of the same financial, human, and technical resources. Goals seemed in conflict. They needed to align their objectives and prioritize projects to make good use of the available resources.

5: Improving Sales and Operations Planning

The vice president of operations had serious cash-to-cash problems and declining customer satisfaction—all resulting from raw materials shortages, mismatched capacity, poor forecasting, and inventory build-up. The challenge was to address the planning and forecasting issues, and put the balance sheet back in shape.

6: Meeting Financial Commitments

The Chief Executive Officer promised the board of directors to improve earnings per share. An analysis of competitors' balance sheets and income statements indicated that the company's direct and indirect costs were out of line, and that its cash-to-cash cycle was too long. The leadership was charged with identifying the right mix of improvements to obtain a predictable result that would satisfy shareholders. The Chief Executive Officer's credibility was now at stake.

7: Building Support and Competence

The director of a new supply chain solutions team needed a proven method for evaluating and implementing projects. That meant being able to document examples of its use and demonstrating that it was both scalable and repeatable. Then she would have to sell the method throughout the organization—requiring executive references and easy, low-cost access to the method itself. Finally, she would have to develop a team who could use the model to deliver early successes.

8: Optimizing Enterprise Resource Planning

As the ERP implementation wore on and business processes were increasingly automated, things suddenly started to go wrong. The project leader had a pretty good idea why: The company was organized in rigid, vertical functions that directed AS IS practices, but the ERP system was horizontal, organized by transaction flow for purchase orders, sales orders, forecasts, master data, and so on. How could the corporate culture shift from functional management to process management?

9: Maximizing Use of Existing Technology

The vice president of administration was being pressured by her colleagues to replace a two-year-old transactional system with a new, name-brand system offering advanced supply chain planning, but the return on investment analysis just wasn't adding up. A more detailed investigation revealed that not all of the business leaders were complaining about the old system. In fact, the vice president found a direct correlation between a business leader's satisfaction and the effort he or she had exerted to learn the system. Those who were least satisfied hadn't handled implementation very well and as a consequence were using few of the available modules. The challenge was to motivate business leaders to use existing functionality better.

10: Achieving Operational Excellence

The executive team agreed that it would differentiate the company through a strategy of operational excellence. The other choices had been customer intimacy and product innovation. Now that the decision was made, the team had to define—at tactical levels—the characteristics of an operationally excellent supply chain.

11: Performing Mergers and Acquisitions

The executive teams from the acquiring and purchased companies needed the acquisition to go smoothly and yield short-term synergies. The challenge was how to leverage efficiencies in material flow, technology platforms, work and information flow, and capacity in the due diligence, integration, and stabilization stages of the merger.

12: Standardizing and Managing Business Processes

Five years after a successful ERP implementation, 15 plants had turned off select pieces of the system in the name of continuous improvement and "leaning out" their processes; three business units independently redefined how date fields were used by customer service to promise-date orders for customers; corporate logistics added a transportation optimization tool that made the promised ship date subordinate to efficient truck load; and the business rules to manage planning data were changed, ignored, or forgotten by new employees not having the benefit of the original training. The net result was poor delivery performance, extended order cycle times, and seemingly routine feast-or-famine mismatches between capacity and demand. The executive team realized it needed to get a handle on defining and managing supply chain process performance.

13: Extending the Value Chain to Solve Tough Issues

The operating committee challenged the supply chain executive with some difficult improvement pairings: support the increased pace of new product introduction while making material acquisition more efficient; support increased sales productivity while making pre- and post-sale customer service more effective; make global distribution more flexible while increasing the efficiency of warehouse and transportation costs; and implement planning for his supply chain AND the customers' supply chains, even while improving his own planning efficiency. In each case, these improvement pairings move beyond the four walls of the company and include more than just supply chain processes—requiring a clear definition for the concept of a "value chain" along with skills to improve it.

14: Integrating Lean Six Sigma and SCOR to Build a Better Project Portfolio

After five years of using the annual "brainstorming" technique, the Lean Sigma Executive Steering Team concluded that corporate impact on operating income achieved its peak last year; all new projects seemed to be aiming at inventory; many project scopes seemed to compete for the same resources and have contradictory impact on metrics (supply chain cost vs. service-level improvement); and the scope of projects still seemed to be exclusively manufacturing. The steering team's challenge was to broaden the scope and increase the effectiveness of projects.

15: Defining and Building an Effective Supply Chain Organization

A Chief Executive Officer looked at his organization and complained: "We've got five business units, six high-level P&Ls, two headquarters, four global regions, 26 regional distribution centers, 18 plants, the requirement to implement Collaborative Planning, Forecasting, and Replenishment with our largest accounts, and about five-thousand active suppliers. We need a forecast that supports the corporate financial plan and a set of supply chain plans to support the regional service levels and cost commitments. How?" Nothing more needs to be said about this challenge.

A common thread connects these situations. In every case, SCOR helped define the supply chain challenge, define strategic requirements, measure the size of the issues, and identify necessary changes to improve performance. Beyond the tactical focus, SCOR also helped transform organizational thinking from event-driven reflexes to strategic, integrated team behaviors that balance customer requirements with the internal need for cost and asset management. In other words, SCOR helped these companies to achieve a core competency in solving supply chain problems and achieving goals.

■ Why *Supply Chain Excellence?*

By using experience gained from 65 supply chain improvement projects, *Supply Chain Excellence* is an instruction manual for anybody who seeks a rigorous and proven methodology for systematic supply chain improvement. Whether it's a system selection or implementation, an adoption of supply chain process best practices, an alignment of dysfunctional organizations, or a creation of a culture of continuous supply chain improvement, *Supply Chain Excellence* provides a step-by-step framework to use the leading methodology.

In short, this book tells how an organization can achieve core competency in the process of supply chain improvement. The standardized tool for this achievement is the SCOR® model. It is a handbook for anybody who is motivated to improve and wants to rely on a rigorous, proven methodology to make sure supply chain improvement is done right.

This book is built on the story of how one company, Fowlers Inc., started its journey toward supply chain excellence using SCOR.

It tells how Fowlers navigated around such difficult issues as educating the enterprise about supply chain improvement to gain support; building consensus where to begin; organizing the effort for success; conducting competitive analysis to define business opportunity; building the burning platform for change; aligning strategy, material flow, work flow, and information flow to focus on the right changes; putting hard numbers to the financial value of change; and implementing those changes to achieve sustainable competitive advantage.

This book is a working guide for using SCOR as a tool to help senior managers at every step as they undertake supply chain initiatives.

■ How This Book Is Structured

Supply Chain Excellence is built around a simple project timetable, providing achievable action plans to navigate the SCOR project road.

Each chapter represents a week's worth of work. Each week is conducted in two days of meetings, with follow-up assignments (or "homework," which many clients have learned to love). Included are sample deliverables, summaries of tasks, tables, and figures to illustrate the step-by-step processes.

The case-study company, Fowlers Inc., is not a real company, and its employees are not real people. Fowlers is a conglomerate, with diverse products and operating divisions that face their own unique circumstances. The idea was to provide a case-study subject that would seem at least a little familiar to everyone, and that would offer a variety of the real-world issues found in real projects with which I've been involved. Most important, it serves to maintain continuity to help readers follow the logic of the *Supply Chain Excellence* approach from beginning to end.

Acknowledgments

We would like to acknowledge those companies and individuals who have directly (and indirectly) contributed to this book. First and foremost, we would recognize our supply chain colleagues at Access Business Group, Kohler Co., McCormick and Company, and Nortech Systems, who committed themselves to the approach and applied it again and again—bringing new ideas and suggestions to bear each time and pushing us to make Supply Chain Excellence easier, more effective, and more relevant to their current business challenges. This second edition is a tribute them. Specific thanks are in order to Denise Layfield, Don Horne, Mike Degen, Davor Grgic, Joe Hnilicka, Gerard Gallenberger, Dave Strach, Tom Manoni, Chris Kozak, Brad Rick, Chris Wilson, Chuck Kerr, and Kelly Jasperse.

Second, we would like to recognize Xelocity, which has rapidly made ProcessWizard a work flow management tool for the Supply Chain Excellence approach. Specific thanks go to Mike Stobbs, Will Polese, Laurence van Camp, Nikhil Ravishankar, Robert Assink, and David Laurence for the "24 hour" software and graphics support needed to complete this project. Thanks also go to the Xelocity management consulting team who perfected the approach for use "Down Under."

Third, we would thank The Supply-Chain Council. Its dedication to improving SCOR and introducing new tools like DCOR, CCOR, and the APQC Benchmark Survey has provided the platform for all of us to experiment. Specific thanks are in order for permission to use the process models in this project and a commitment to education through the SCOR Implementation Workshop.

Specific thanks go to Joe Francis, Caspar Hunsche, and Douglas Kent.

Fourth, we acknowledge the teams at Penton Media's *Logistics Today, IndustryWeek* and *American Machinist,* all of whom lent an invisible hand in this book by offering a wealth of insights and perspectives from the fast-changing world of manufacturing and supply chain management. Specific thanks are due to Dave Blanchard, Bruce Vernyi, Sarah Harding and Teri Mollison—all of whom provide a never-ending source of inspiration in their energetic pursuit of continuous improvement.

Last, and most important, we would offer our heartfelt gratitude to our families.

From Peter: To Cary who, as a full time teacher, endured 25 third graders, provided taxi service for after school activities, and managed the home front during many a coaching assignment; to Kristi who, as a senior, managed school, home, work, and admission to college; to Jenni who, as a freshman, keeps us all on our toes with her wit, energy, and activities; thank you! Thank you for the time, thank you for the support, and thank you for your prayers. I couldn't have completed the project without you!

From Bob: Unlimited thanks to Barb, who manages to run the world while others just manage to run in circles; to Nicky and Kelly, wise beyond their years and secure in their knowledge that nothing is more important than passion; and to Adam, Lego engineer and a constant source of a better perspective. Thank you for your support, your admiration, and for sharing the computer long enough for me to finish this project.

1

About the Supply Chain Operations Reference Model

Peter was introduced to the Supply Chain Operations Reference (SCOR) model in the fall of 1996 as part of a newly formed corporate "internal consulting" team for Imation, which had just been spun off from 3M. He's been using it in supply chain project work ever since. He has also been active in the Supply-Chain Council, involved in the process of improving SCOR, and teaching others how to use it.

So he's heard all the questions. Among those most frequently asked are: What is the Supply-Chain Council? What is SCOR? How do I use SCOR? What is the value to my organization? How do I learn more about SCOR?

▓ The Supply-Chain Council

The Supply-Chain Council (www.supply-chain.org) is an independent not-for-profit corporation formed in 1996 as a grassroots initiative to develop a supply chain process model. Among those involved at the start were individuals from such organizations as Bayer; Compaq; Procter & Gamble; Lockheed Martin; Nortel; Rockwell

Semiconductor; Texas Instruments; 3M; Cargill, Pittiglio, Rabin, Todd, & McGrath (PRTM); and AMR Research, Inc. In all, 69 of the world's leading companies participated in the council's founding. Its mission today is to perpetuate use of the SCOR model through technical development, research, education, and conference events. By the end of 2006, the council's technical community had released eight subsequent versions of SCOR, providing updates to process elements, metrics, practices, and tools.

The council maintains about 750 corporate members worldwide, with chapters in Australia/New Zealand, Brazil, Europe, Japan, North America, Greater China, and Southeast Asia. Membership is open to any organization interested in applying and advancing principles of supply chain management. There are six special-interest industry groups within the council: Lean Six Sigma convergence, aerospace, defense, automotive, electronics, and chemicals. Members work in private-sector companies, academics, government, consulting firms, and technology services. In 2006, a corporate membership cost $2,500 per year and the educator's fee was less than $300.

The SCOR Framework

SCOR combines elements of business process engineering, metrics, benchmarking, and leading practices into a single framework. Under SCOR, supply chain management is defined as these integrated processes: PLAN, SOURCE, MAKE, DELIVER, and RETURN— from the suppliers' supplier to the customers' customer, and all aligned with a company's operational strategy, material, work, and information flows (Figure 1-1).

Here's what's included in each of these process elements:

PLAN: Assess supply resources; aggregate and prioritize demand requirements; plan inventory for distribution, production, and material requirements; and plan rough-cut capacity for all products and all channels.

SOURCE: Obtain, receive, inspect, hold, issue, and authorize payment for raw materials and purchased finished goods.

Figure 1-1. The SCOR framework.

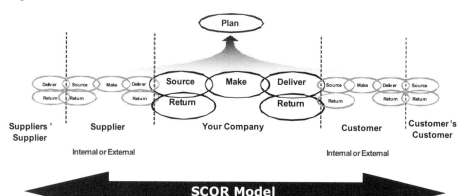

MAKE: Request and receive material; manufacture and test product; package, hold, and/or release product.

DELIVER: Execute order management processes; generate quotations; configure product; create and maintain customer database; maintain product/price database; manage accounts receivable, credits, collections, and invoicing; execute warehouse processes including pick, pack, and configure; create customer-specific packaging/labeling; consolidate orders; ship products; manage transportation processes and import/export; and verify performance.

RETURN: Defective, warranty, and excess return processing, including authorization, scheduling, inspection, transfer, warranty administration, receiving and verifying defective products, disposition, and replacement.

In addition, SCOR 8.0 includes a series of enable elements for each of the processes. Enable focuses on elements such as process performance, information, policy, inventory strategy, capital assets, transportation, physical logistic network, regulatory, and other management processes to enable the planning and execution of supply chain activities.

SCOR spans all customer, product, and market interactions surrounding sales orders, purchase orders, work orders, return authorizations, forecasts, and replenishment orders. It also encompasses material movements of raw material, work-in-process, finished goods, and return goods.

The SCOR model includes three levels of process detail. In practice, Level One defines the number of supply chains, how their performance is measured, and necessary competitive requirements. Level Two defines the configuration of planning and execution strategies in material flow, using standard categories such as make-to-stock, make-to-order, and engineer-to-order. Level Three defines the business processes and system functionality used to transact sales orders, purchase orders, work orders, return authorizations, replenishment orders, and forecasts. Level Four process detail is not contained in SCOR but must be defined to implement improvements and manage processes.

Value Chain Processes

In 2004, the Supply-Chain Council introduced two new frameworks that help piece together more of the detailed mosaic of enterprise Value Chains. The Customer Chain Operations Reference (CCOR) model defines the customer part of the Value Chain as the integration of PLAN, RELATE, SELL, CONTRACT, SERVICE, and ENABLE processes.

The Design Chain Operations Reference (DCOR) model defines the design part of the Value Chain as the integration of PLAN, RESEARCH, DESIGN, INTEGRATE, AMEND, and ENABLE processes (Figure 1-2).

Chapter 20 will discuss how these process models can be used with SCOR to drive overall Value Chain performance improvement.

"Operationalizing" the Definition of Value Chain

To put Value Chain in the same frame as SCOR, let's define it as the integrated macro processes of Marketing, Design, Supply, and Customer. A Value Chain spans the three essential constituencies of a business: Markets (of supply and demand), Your Company, and Your Customer (ultimate buyer of your products). A Value Chain is

Figure 1-2.   Value Chain frameworks.

composed of four dimensions: Strategy, Product Flow, Work Flow, and Information Flow. As with SCOR, a company must align all four dimensions in an improvement effort. Figure 1-3 attempts to put the four frameworks together in a high-level process relationship map. As illustrated in the diagram, each process relates to its Markets, to other macro processes in Your Company, and to Customers through key inputs and outputs. The picture is far from perfect; the process relationships are more complex and dynamic than the series of inputs and outputs suggest, but it is a place to start.

Integrated Level One Processes

"Integrated" in this case describes how the macro level Value Chain processes interact in planned, directive, and yet adaptive ways that satisfy your customer requirements and help your company grow profitably. "Integrated" does not imply that the processes are serially executed. We all know that at any given moment of the business day, new channels are targeted, new products are introduced, salespeople win and lose contracts, suppliers miss deliveries, customers change their orders, and warranty claims are acted on. Figure 1-4 portrays the parallel nature of the Value Chain illustrating the Level One processes. The "so what" of this diagram is the ability to describe the complexity of your Value Chain using simple, common language and, more important, determine through analysis which processes are working well, which need improvement, and which are completely broken or absent.

Figure 1-3.   Value Chain process relationship map.

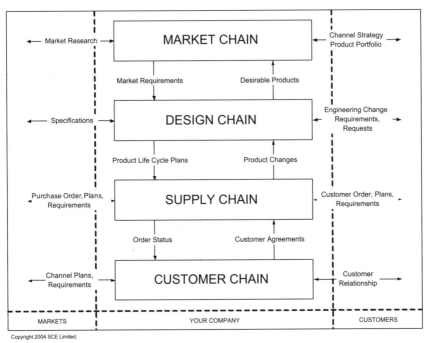

Copyright 2004 SCE Limited.

For example, if the Big Question is "Why is revenue not growing at the expected rate?" this Value Chain framework provides a context for finding the answer that's better than simply pointing the finger at sales. As with SCOR, underneath each Level One process are two more layers of process detail, definitions, suggested metrics, and leading practices.

■ Using SCOR to Drive Supply Chain Improvement

For all its power and flexibility, the SCOR model is still just a noun-a series of definitions for processes, metrics, and leading practices. Simply having the dictionary doesn't do any good for the business. To make it a verb, you need to add effective change management, problem-solving techniques, project-management discipline, and business-process engineering techniques. Supply Chain Excellence attempts to

Figure 1-4.   Value Chain Level One processes.

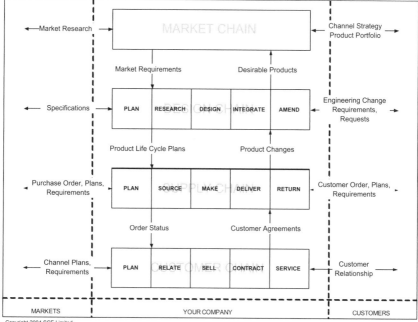

Copyright 2004 SCE Limited.

fill this void with a documented 6-step formula that has been tested and proven in the course of more than 60 projects (Figure 1-5).

The phases of the Supply Chain Excellence approach as detailed in this book are as follows:

❑ Educate for Support
❑ Discover the Opportunity
❑ Analyze Basis of Competition
❑ Design Material Flow
❑ Design Work and Information Flow
❑ Implementation Planning and Project Portfolio Development

Educate for Support

Chapter 2 examines this phase of a SCOR project. The focus in this initial phase is to build effective organizational support. The chapter explores four important roles: the "evangelist," the person in the company who has the passion, experience, and talent to lead a supply chain

Figure 1-5.   The Supply Chain Excellence approach.

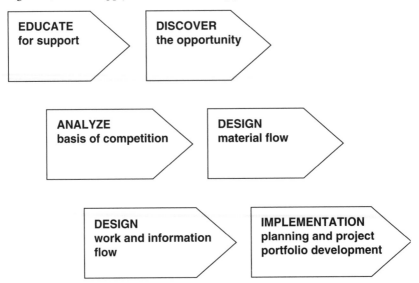

project; the "active executive," the individual who is accountable as sponsor of a supply chain project through modeling, influence, and leadership; the "core steering team," which has the champion role to review and approve recommendations and ultimately lead the implementation efforts; and the "design team," which analyzes the supply chain from end to end and assembles recommendations for change.

Discover the Opportunity

Chapter 3 helps to define and prioritize the organization's supply chains using a combination of data and strategic assessment. One of the primary outcomes from the discovery step is a Project Charter, which helps define a project's scope, approach, objectives, schedule, milestones, deliverables, budget, organization, measures of successes, and communication plan.

Analyze Basis of Competition

This analysis stage (Chapters 4 to 7) is where the metrics are defined, data are collected, benchmarks are tallied, and gross opportunity is calculated. Frequently used SCOR metrics include cash-to-cash cycle time, inventory days of supply, perfect order fulfillment, order fulfillment cycle time, total supply chain management cost, and upside supply chain flexibility. This phase also helps the team to prioritize and balance customer metrics with internal-facing metrics: delivery, reliability, flexibility/responsiveness, cost, and assets.

Design Material Flow

Chapters 8 to 13 describe the material analysis steps to identify a company's preliminary project list. AS IS analytic techniques include analyzing metric defect; assembling geographic maps and process thread diagrams; conducting a gap assessment using simple brainstorming techniques; using problem-solving tools such as fishbone diagrams, run charts, and affinity grouping; and working with finance to identify both financial and customer service opportunities.

Design Work and Information Flow

Chapters 14 to 18 describe the work and information flow analysis aimed at the effectiveness and efficiency of transactions (purchase orders, work orders, sales orders, forecasts, replenishment orders, and return authorizations). Analytic techniques for this phase include process mapping, transactional data analysis, leading practice assessment, and "staple yourself to an order" interviews. The resulting analysis is additive to material flow and together comprise the final project list.

Implementation Planning and Project Portfolio Development

Chapter 19 discusses the final assembly and sign-off of the project portfolio and introduces an organization and process for effective program management. It also discusses the steps for putting together the implementation plan, including project definition, implementation approach, and Return on Investment.

Value Chain Excellence

Chapter 20 introduces a Value Chain Excellence project roadmap that can be used with any combination of DCOR, CCOR, and/or SCOR process frameworks. Although a project follows the same basic steps as illustrated in Figure 1-5, the deliverables have been expanded to accommodate the broader scope of Value Chain issues, such as product development, sales, post-sale service, or engineering changes and product life cycle management.

The Value of a SCOR Initiative

The Supply Chain Excellence approach is reliable and predictable with respect to project duration, cost, and benefits. Implementation results across the sixty-plus projects for which this approach has been used are consistent:

- ❏ Operating income improvement, from cost reduction and service improvements in the initial SCOR project portfolio, averaging 3 percent of total sales; depending on how your company compares with benchmark data, it could be as high as 4.5 percent or as low as 1.5 percent. Return on investment of two to six times within twelve months—often with cost-neutral quick-hit projects under way on a six-month timeframe.
- ❏ Full leverage of capital investment in systems, improving return on assets for fixed-asset technology investments.
- ❏ Reduced information technology operating expenses through reduced need for customization and improved use of standard system functions.
- ❏ Ongoing profit improvement of 0.5 percent to 1 percent per year, using continuous supply chain improvement.

2

Building Organizational Support for Supply Chain Improvement

Planting the Seeds for Organizational Change: Educate for Support

Brian Dowell called out of the blue after getting my name from a Google search; his keywords included SCOR, Supply Chain, Metrics, and Value Chain. He was looking for some direction for his company, Fowlers Inc., and had enough motivation within the company to justify a visit.

We showed up a week later, and Brian, the company's chief operating officer, gave us a warm greeting. His introductory overview demonstrated Fowlers to be a well-run manufacturing conglomerate with the seeds of a supply chain improvement already in place.

The action plan had been developed at the division level by David Able, vice president of operations in the technology products group—one of the four operating units. He had pieced it together with just a little background in supply chain management and a whole lot of operating pain. His efforts had been encouraged by his boss, the division president, who had brought the strategy to the attention of other executives in the company.

They had become an informal "gang" with a common feeling that, although David's ideas would solve some short-term issues, there had to be a way to solve the company's supply chain problems at a more strategic level. It didn't take much prodding to get this gang to start sharing their thoughts.

"Our products are good for a week, maybe ten days, in the store," said Doris Early, president of the food products group. "We've got to move a lot of product around with a lot of speed. And if regulators were to bring in the label from something we processed six months ago, we need to be able to identify the plant, the line, the day, and the names of everyone on the shift who produced it."

"Our shelf life is short, but not that short," added Martha Tekitch, president of the technology products group. "We also have some other things in common with the food group; we buy a lot of commodities. The prices we pay change day-to-day, but our customers won't let us be quite that flexible. There's some seasonality in our sales, and many new products that are harder to forecast—all of which make it difficult to maintain consistent margins." She added, "Much of the cost of our products is locked in during the product design phase. In hindsight, many times we start out inefficient because the supply chain design evolved as an afterthought." Joe Farelong, president of the durable products group, jumped in: "On a more tactical note, we have tried to tackle the performance issues through our continuous improvement program. Four years ago, we invested in a Lean Six Sigma program that has trained hundreds of black, green, and yellow belts. We have been pretty disciplined as an executive team managing the project list. We started out fast and furious with most projects aimed at our manufacturing plants. In the past year, it seems we started to run out of steam; most of our projects now are aimed at what seem to be smaller and smaller scopes and ultimate pay backs. But we still feel like there are big issues to address. So how do we identify a more strategic list? How do we integrate Supply Chain Operations Reference (SCOR) with Lean Six Sigma?"

Last, Sally Vesting, the Chief Executive Officer, added, "In our strategic planning session last month we—the business presidents and I—theorized which supply chain functions could or should be centralized corporately and the level of benefit that could be achieved. It raised the question: How should we organize ourselves for the future?"

It all came together as they spoke: many products that have short shelf life and short life cycles; disconnected supply chain and product development; price-sensitive customers sold through various and sophisticated channels with volatility on both ends—demand and supply; a continuous improvement program that needs rejuvenating; and an organization that needed the right focus.

The executives described how a chosen leader, David Able, had outlined a strategy and its main components. They then assigned it to their direct reports in other divisions to execute.

Brian wasn't quite ready to admit this at our first meeting, but it was clear what happened: The managers at the next level down thought they'd just been briefed on the latest program-of-the-month and did very little with the strategy. To placate the executives, they did take some small steps: identifying a few projects, assigning some green belts, and improving a metric here or there—generally at the expense of others. But after three months, Brian pushed Joe, Martha, and Doris to join him in looking for an outside perspective. "We can't be the only ones with this dilemma," he said.

Without realizing it, Brian had already taken a few important steps to ensure a successful approach. Selling supply chain management to an organization is tough. It's an educational sell to everyone involved. Not only is the reality of an integrated supply chain complex; everyone has his or her own pre-existing ideas of what supply chains are all about, how they fit in with operational strategy, and what to do to fix them.

SCOR, as an industry standard, makes the sell easier because it has gained credibility from a long list of successful case studies, but the model can't sell itself, and it can't teach people who aren't ready to learn. That's why any SCOR project will depend on four key roles in the education process. These are the evangelist, an active executive sponsor, the core members of an executive steering team, and the analytical design team. Without these, you can't hope for a project's success.

■ The Evangelist

As is the case with any successful SCOR application, the people who brought SCOR to Fowlers started by educating the organization to support the effort. Their first step was to develop an evangelist. This is the person who is best able to learn the SCOR model; who can sell it to upper management; who has the experience to pilot a project and gain early results; and who can become the executive-level project manager for spreading it throughout the business. If nobody steps up to this role, then a SCOR-based project probably cannot succeed.

The evangelist may be self-selected or appointed from above, and his or her first role in this position is typically as project manager of the first SCOR project.

At Fowlers, David Able, vice president of operations in the technology products group, placed himself into the role of evangelist based on his interest in supply chain integration, his diverse background, and his reputation as an effective, influential leader. He was readily confirmed by Brian Dowell, the company's chief operating officer and the man who would quickly assume another important role as the executive sponsor (Figure 2-1).

The Evangelist's Resume

As the appointed evangelist, David Able had a portfolio of experiences that would help create general understanding of the relationship between financial performance and the central factors of organization, process, people, and technology. Over the course of 15 years at the company, he had demonstrated knowledge of "how things work" and built a strong foundation of leadership roles. He had participated on a large-scale re-engineering effort a few years before, so he

Figure 2-1. Fowlers' organizational chart.

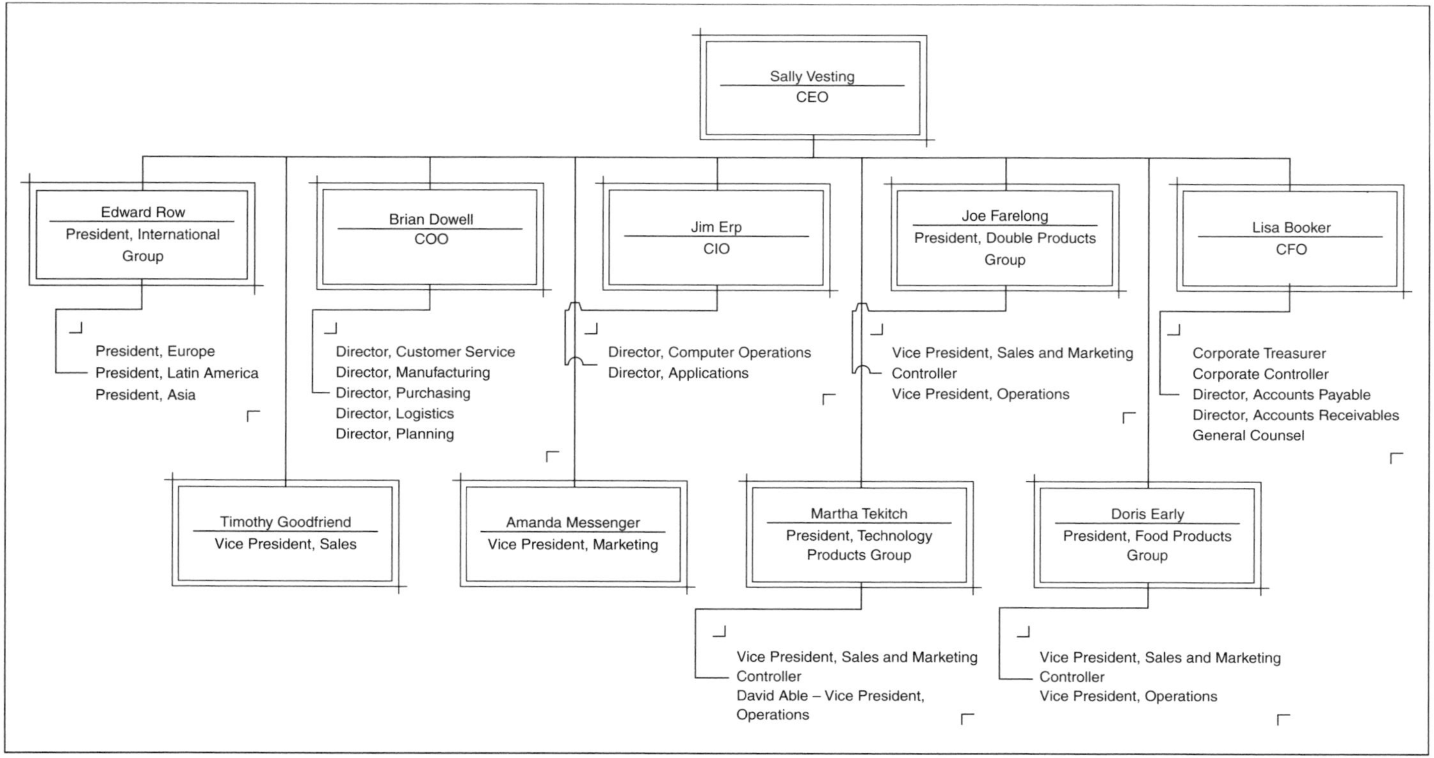

had seen the way an enterprise project works. Those who worked for him also confirmed such important qualities as the ability to teach, communicate, resolve conflict, and add humor at just the right time.

Experience

The right evangelist candidate will have the following experience on his or her resume:

Financial Responsibility and Accountability. The former means understanding the details of how cost, revenue, and assets are assembled on a profit and loss statement and balance sheet—and all the financial impacts in real time. The latter means being able to tell the business story behind the numbers. Accountability also means defending executive critique, explaining bad news with confidence, preparing for operations reviews, and having the ability to focus and effectively motivate an entire organization to "hit" a common set of financial goals and objectives.

Aligning Business Goals with Appropriate Strategy. Cascading goals is the art of organizing objectives in such a way that every employee understands the higher levels of success and how their day-to-day goals support that success.

Setting the Organizational Learning Pace. This means developing an atmosphere that supports team learning and fosters dialogue among individuals, teams, and departments. In managing the performance of individuals and departments, evangelists understand the day-to-day effort that is required to achieve success.

Multiple Worker Roles. The evangelist will have firsthand experience in a variety of business functions that map to the SCOR Level One elements PLAN, SOURCE, MAKE, DELIVER, and RETURN. Leading practices in PLAN—such as sales and operations planning, materials requirements planning, and promotional event forecasting—can come from experiences as a demand planner, forecast analyst, supply planner, and inventory analyst. Leading practices in SOURCE and MAKE—such as Kanban, vendor-managed inventory, rapid replenishment, cellular manufacturing, Six Sigma, total quality management, ISO 9002, to name a few—can come from experiences as a buyer, production superintendent, master production scheduler, and engineer. Leading practices in DELIVER and RE-TURN—such as available-to-promise, Cross-Docking, Cellular Kitting and Packaging, and so on—can come from experiences as a customer service representative, transportation analyst, and supervisor for shipping and receiving.

At Fowlers, as vice president of operations for one of the operating divisions, David Able had experience with a number of the above areas. In addition, his previous participation in a well-run re-engineering effort had exposed him to disciplines in four important areas necessary to a supply chain improvement: process mapping, recommendations, justification, and project management.

Natural Talent. The right evangelist candidate will demonstrate the following five talents in his or her daily work:

1. *A Talent for Teaching.* This is part skill and part art. The skill is showing employees how to perform a task, modeling the appropriate skill, guiding them to understanding, and finally letting them try it on their own. The art is a sixth sense that seems to monitor everyone's level of understanding and automatically adjusts the lesson for each individual. The ability to generate examples or anecdotes in the context of each individual can separate the great teachers from the average ones. Good evangelists are effective storytellers.

2. *A Talent for Listening.* It's important to know when to ask clarifying questions and when not to interrupt, further building an understanding of the speaker's point of view. For a successful evangelist, listening and clarifying are more valuable than preaching.

3. *A Talent for Communicating with Executives and Peers.* There are four prerequisites for effective executive communication. The evangelist must:

    Have earned personal and professional credibility with members of the executive team.

    Be a subject matter expert.

    Be able to assemble effective executive presentations.

    Balance formal group communications (presentations, proposals, meetings) with informal one-on-one communications (lunch, golf, hallway, in private).

4. *A Talent for Using Humor Appropriately.* Every good evangelist has a great sense of humor and can introduce comic relief at just the right moment—whether planned or unplanned. The evangelist doesn't have to be the funniest person in the room; on a team of 15 people, there will be at least two or three others who can be counted on to help at any time.

5. *A Talent for Conflict Management Among Groups and Peers.* The constraint to successful supply chain projects does not always lie in the technical challenges of material flow and application architecture; it's often in the conflicts that occur between people. Successful evangelists can handle large-group conflicts and individual conflicts—not by squashing them, but by constructively helping one side or both to move toward common ground.

■ The Active Executive Sponsor

The active executive represents the leaders in the organization who will sign off on resources needed to make the changes happen. This person has the most to gain or lose based on the success of the project and therefore takes on responsibility to review and approve recommended changes as proposed by the project design team. Behind the scenes, the executive sponsor needs to sell the changes up to the chiefs and down to their managers, eliminate barriers to progress, take ownership of the financial opportunity that comes through improvement, and prepare the organization for implementation.

As with the evangelist, picking the right person is critical. At Fowlers, the obvious choice was Brian Dowell, the chief operating officer and the executive with supervisory responsibility over the directors of planning (PLAN), purchasing (SOURCE), manufacturing (MAKE), logistics (DELIVER and RETURN), and customer service. Organizational role is just one factor.

One gauge of the right executive sponsor uses a scale: "more savings faster" (MF) versus "less savings later" (LL). It sounds intuitive, but there are a lot of LL executives in the world; they behave in a manner that slows the rate of improvement and lengthens timeframes. The nature of a project life cycle demands different behaviors at different times from the active executive sponsor. In all cases, the sponsor will be better served by MF behaviors.

Educate-for-Support Behaviors of the Active Executive Sponsor

At the beginning of a project, the focus is to get things moving effectively through process management in the right direction by understanding the strategic value of supply chain management and with increasing influence by encouraging public learning.

MF executives can look at their organizations from a process perspective as opposed to a collection of individuals grouped by a functional silo. They have experienced the power of process improvement and understand key roles in process management. MF executives have invested personal time learning about the strategic value of supply chain in their respective marketplace. That's why they are comfortable learning new things in a public forum regardless of rank—sometimes setting the capacity for change of the entire organization.

MF executives accelerate the educate-for-support step of a project (from six months to one year) by encouraging the progress of the evangelist as a SCOR subject matter expert and by facilitating core team buy-in.

LL executives, when in public, seem to know everything—whether they do or not. They depend on individual heroics to make things better. Thus, LL executives need to be sold on the merits of supply chain improvement.

Planning and Organizing Behaviors of the Active Executive Sponsor

In this second step of the project life cycle, the focus is on three essential areas: an understanding of how organizational change occurs, a respect for supply chain complexity, and an effective integration of business resources. The critical output of this step is a project charter that defines project scope, objectives, organization, benefits, and approach. MF executives understand their sponsor role and can articulate a burning platform for change. They learn to look at supply chain performance needs from various perspectives such as organization, process, people, technology, and strategy. MF executives can accelerate the discovery stage by effectively involving business leaders and participating directly in early steps of the project design.

LL executives, on the other hand, short-circuit the discovery work by directing efforts to focus on one or two prescribed metrics, rather than actively engaging business teams to define scope and opportunity. LLs delegate learning about SCOR to subordinates rather than understanding the basic steps of the SCOR Project Roadmap and associated deliverables themselves.

Measures and Strategy Behaviors of the Active Executive Sponsor

At this stage of the project life cycle, important behaviors are respect for the schedule and fueling the fire on the platform for change.

MF executives commit themselves, their evangelists, and their design teams to the detailed, 17-week analyze-and-design process. This process involves two days per week for 17 weeks plus homework for design team members and half a day two times per month plus homework for executive members of the steering team. The project manager will work on the effort full time, and the MF executive sponsor will spend part of each week in oversight and review.

MF executives spend time understanding how actual, benchmark, and other comparative data were gathered, and they accept the completed analysis at face value as a defined opportunity. MF executives begin laying the groundwork for organizational change by initiating regular communication regarding the relative opportunity, the expected changes, and the approximate timing of the project.

LLs don't attend design team sessions, miss some executive sponsor reviews, and don't put in any personal time. They discount the validity of the data because they don't understand how they were gathered, and they view the analysis as the end of the project—not the beginning.

Design Solutions Behaviors of the Active Executive Sponsor

At this stage of the project life cycle, the focus is on understanding the integrated nature of material, work, and information flow; sparring with the difficulties of designing improvement; and prioritizing change.

To this end, an MF executive sponsor will spend time each week with the design team learning about the basic steps of producing desired material, work, and information and then leverage this knowledge to educate his or her other C-level peers and prepare them for anticipated supply chain changes.

MF executives constructively challenge the design team on assumptions and results, and invest time to understand the scope and sequence of recommended changes. LL executives are only concerned with the "what," not with how key milestone deliverables were built. LLs use a shotgun approach to savings by initiating all projects at the same time and letting the strong survive.

▨ Establishing Core Team Buy-In

With Brian Dowell established as the active executive sponsor and David Able in the role of evangelist and project manager, the two were solely responsible for picking the right people as the core of the executive steering team.

This group would bear responsibility to review and approve the project as it progressed. The challenge was to build the right mix of leaders who ultimately will determine the supply chain changes that happen.

It's a reality in any corporation that an executive steering team will contain some members who are not going to be helpful and forward thinking. That's why it was so important for Brian and David to hand-select the core of this team—an elite group who would actively power the steering team to provide constructive oversight and help keep the project moving. Leveraging momentum and knowledge gained in David's earlier supply chain strategy discussions, David and Brian picked the core team to include Doris, Martha, and Amanda Messenger, vice president of corporate marketing and a long-time proponent of organizational alignment.

There are four important criteria for the evangelist and executive sponsor to consider as they begin assembling this core group: collective experience, attitude, effective communication skills, and ability to cope well in chaos.

Collective Experience

Experience is measured individually and as a team. In either case, important considerations when forming this group include the following:

Level of Authority. Effective steering teams have members at similar levels of authority within the organization who are willing to assign resources from their own teams to the project design effort and who have earned confidence from the senior executive team.

Cross-Functional Relationships. An effective steering team member has built relationships over time instead of leaving a trail of "my way or the highway" casualties. The best contributors have a sense of how the whole business works and have developed cooperative relationships with other functional leaders.

Knowledge Contribution. Depth of historical perspective is important—not only of the business process evolution but also of the organizational response to change. This perspective can be both good and bad; the right steering team members can balance their addition of knowledge with the occasionally unavoidable attitude of "we've tried that before."

Attitude

Steering team members don't have to go through a battery of psychologic tests to determine whether they have the right attitude, but they should pass three simple ones. First, they should be immune to the "not invented here" syndrome. Second, they should have a controlled and adaptable style of communication. Third, they should be effective learners.

Effective Communication Skills

An effective steering team sets the learning pace of a SCOR project by dictating the effectiveness of the learning environment. It is deliberate about expectations and spells out exactly the type and frequency of feedback it needs to help keep the project moving. The most valued feedback can be categorized as critique, opinion, or clarifying dialogue (team learning). Effective critique assumes that the steering team members understand the material under review, have assembled a list of checking questions for the design team, and are comfortable exploring the logic to check the integrity of the work. Opinion is reserved for forks in the road where decisions must be made to go forward with the project. It's rendered only after dialogue and critique. Clarifying dialogue is as simple as asking questions and discussing work both spontaneously and at planned reviews. The objective is simply to understand the design team's point of view with an open mind.

Ability to Cope Well in Chaos

Many leaders in industry suggest that the closer an organization can get to the edge of chaos without going over, the more it will thrive in today's business environment. Let's not kid ourselves; moving toward the edge of chaos is stressful, so steering team members need an intuitive feel for how close is too close. Process thinking helps set the appropriate distance from the edge. Process thinkers look at performance as the result of the interaction of process steps. They look at an organization from a systems point of view. They can articulate the basic relationships between the supplier inputs (capital, human resources, raw materials), the organization (business processes and functions), the customer (who buys products and services), the competitors (who compete for supplies and customers), and other factors that touch the system. The alternative to a process thinker is a functional thinker who stakes out some territory, builds a big wall, and shuts out the rest of the world. This silo behavior is, at some level, an attempt to avoid chaos, and it is one of the first big changes to be addressed in a SCOR project.

The Fowlers' core team rounded out the short list for an executive steering team to include Lisa Booker, chief financial officer; Tim Goodfriend, vice president of sales; and Jim Erp, chief information officer.

Picking the Project Design Team

With Brian, David, Lisa, Tim, and Jim in place, their first official duty was to pick the right project design team, the group of people who would ultimately spend time analyzing supply chain issues and assembling recommendations for change. Their obvious guideline, like every other significant initiative, was to pick "the best and brightest." Experience has proven four additional factors to equally contribute to the quality of project output: problem-solving experience, personality factors, dedication/discipline to task, and access to data.

Problem-Solving Experience

Design teams who have at least one black or green belt take the analysis deeper and faster at each project phase than those who don't. Real experience (with such Lean Six Sigma disciplines as Value Stream Analysis and Eliminating the Eight Areas of Waste; Kano, Voice of the Customer, and Force Field Analyses; calculating Cost of Poor Quality; putting together data collection plans; calculating process sigma levels; using data analysis tools such as Pareto and run charts, histograms, and scatter plots; process analysis tools such as supplier-input-process-output-custome (SIPOCs), value stream, and cross-functional maps) will help the team pinpoint root causes to problems, identify effective solutions, and more accurately predict the value and confidence with improvement recommendations.

Personality Factors

There seem to be four personality factors to consider when picking individuals for the project design team. The first scale pits FACTS and FEELINGS. The FACTS side of the scale describes people who prefer to look just at the numbers and let the data do the "talking," whereas the FEELINGS side describes people who only look at the human factors of change. The second scale pits DETAILS and VISION. The DETAILS side of the scale describes people who look at situations from the "ground up"; they come to conclusions by putting the pieces together. The VISION people look at the whole, the big picture, and come to their conclusions by looking at the trends. The third scale pits INTROVERT and EXTROVERT. The INTROVERT side of the scale describes people who "think inside" and stereotypically are the quiet ones in groups. The EXTROVERT side of the scale describes people who "think out loud" and, right or wrong, will refine their hypotheses in public and can sway a group through verbal skills. INTROVERTS gain energy with individual down time, whereas EXTROVERTS gain energy in the group. The fourth scale is focused on degree of ORGANIZATION. This scale pits unorganized on the one side with highly organized on the other.

Although these personality factors may seem trivial, considering the right mix of people on the team can help avoid two common pitfalls. The first we'll call "The Loud Lead." Characterized by a majority of FEELINGS, VISION, EXTROVERT, and low ORGANIZATION, this team talks a good game but will likely not have the details to stand up to executive scrutiny at the end. We'll call the second pitfall "Analysis Paralysis." Characterized by a majority of FACTS, DETAILS, INTROVERT, and high ORGANIZATION, this team always needs more data and often freezes when confronted with executive teams who want a recommendation or decision.

Dedication: Discipline to Tasks

There was a sign that hung in a colleague's office that read, "The reward for good work is more work...." As you will come to appreciate, each deliverable in a Supply Chain Excellence project helps make a decision; each decision then becomes a part of the next deliverable and so on until the end. It's like learning algebra (I can hear you groaning): You need to understand multiplying and dividing fractions before you can begin to simplify algebraic expressions; if you don't do your homework, it's difficult to move ahead. Likewise, if the team doesn't complete its project homework, it will be ill prepared to make the next decision.

Access to Data

The last thing to consider in selecting your team is access to data. Although this one is fairly self-descriptive, there are several nuances to consider. The first nuance is in regard to data. During each phase of the project, different "cubes" or "tables" will be queried from your information system in an attempt to extract data. This may be in the form of extracts from the production system, a data warehouse, or standard reports. The second nuance is in regard to access. Team members who have access directly or indirectly to the data versus having to submit a data request generally progress faster and more reliably. The third nuance is in regard to analysis. Team members who have knowledge and skill with MS Excel, Access, Mini-Tab, and so forth, to summarize, segment, and otherwise look at data progress faster and more effectively than team members who don't.

Considering each of the four factors, Fowlers assembled the project Design Team. It consisted of the following:

Director, Logistics
Director, Customer Service
Director, Manufacturing
Director, Purchasing

Director, Planning
Vice President of Sales and Marketing—Food Products Group
Corporate Controller
Director, Applications
David Able—Project Manager
SCOR Coach

3

Week One: Planning and Organizing

Decide What to Work On and How to Get Started

Understanding the business reasons for a project and then properly defining the project's scope are critical steps to a successful launch. There are three primary deliverables for this phase. They are (1) the business context summary, (2) a supply chain definition matrix, and (3) an approved project charter. A fourth deliverable in the first week of active project planning is to assemble a complete presentation of information to be used in the project kickoff meeting.

■ The Business Context Summary

You'll start with a checklist, which outlines information that needs to be reviewed and summarized to gain a full understanding of (and appreciation for) the business context for supply chain improvement. This information eventually helps to set the direction for supply chain focus and project scope.

Just as important, though, are the soft benefits of working through the checklist. By involving the business leaders in this process, they will help set the agenda for the company's supply chain. Getting these important people engaged in the earliest stages of a project has untold value in the change management challenge that all companies face. Understanding their problems, asking for their point of view, and acknowledging their good work goes a long way toward positioning the supply chain as "our thing" versus "a corporate thing."

Assembling the business context summary involves several techniques, including interviewing key stakeholders; scouring the company's Web site and 10K earnings reports; reviewing existing business plans as found in the annual report or any other big-picture document; locating and reviewing competitive analyses that have been conducted internally or by any external entity; and checking out the reviews of financial analysts readily available on such Web sites as hoovers.com, forbes.com, marketguide.com, and reuters.com.

Why all the emphasis on public documents and financial statements? Because the important step you're taking is to create the often-overlooked connection between the company's operations and the real-world business goals as defined by the people who hold the purse strings. There's always a temptation to dismiss investors and bean counters as being out-of-touch and unrealistic in their demands, but by understanding their goals and creating a bridge to operations, you can establish the basis for high performance at all levels over the long term.

There are four categories of information that make up a business context summary: (1) strategic background, (2) financial performance, (3) internal profile, and (4) external profile.

Strategic Background

Strategic background summarizes the business and its status in a competitive environment with respect to meeting customer needs and comparing with competitors.

A business description is the first component of the strategic background. It describes the enterprise, its businesses, and a high-level view of the competitive landscape. It's the kind of information that managers should be able to develop off the top of their heads, or by drawing from the dozens of such descriptions that probably reside in brochures, memos, and written documents throughout the organization.

A strengths/weaknesses/opportunities/threats (SWOT) analysis is another source of information that describes the relationship between the enterprise and its marketplace. First, it outlines where the company surpasses direct competitors and where it falls short. Then it projects ways in which it might grow and ways in which it is most likely to be overtaken by competition. On its surface, the SWOT analysis is a simple, four-point document, but for large or diversified organizations, this can become an intricate document with information on each major product or served market.

Another piece of the strategic background is a value proposition statement, which describes the competitive value of a business from the customer's point of view. Inherent in a good value proposition is an intimate understanding of the business requirements of each major customer or customer segment.

For example, a company such as Procter & Gamble—with a broad range of consumer products sold primarily through large retailers—might view its relationship with Wal-Mart as deserving its own value proposition, owing to Wal-Mart's particular requirements of suppliers. At another level, it might include Wal-Mart in a "large retailer" value proposition while developing a separate value proposition for its network of distributors that serve grocery chains and small retailers.

Common requirements in a value proposition statement are price, product quality, technical innovation, customized packaging, delivery reliability, order lead-time, strategic relationship, and value-added services such as inventory management. Customer value propositions are commonly found directly or indirectly in contracts or Service Level Agreements.

The last important components of the strategic background document are critical success factors and critical business issues.

Critical success factors describe three to five variables most central to an organization's success. (Success is defined as thriving—not merely surviving.)

Supply Chain Operations Reference defines the following as critical success factors in supply chain performance: delivery reliability, flexibility and responsiveness, supply chain cost, and effective asset management.

Critical business issues describe how well an organization stacks up against the competition for each of these factors. In each category, the comparative performance level will be rated as disadvantage, parity, advantage, or superior. Sources for these perspectives are not standardized. Good places to look for ratings include annual business plans, quarterly business reviews, annual reports, analyst web casts, 10K reports, and regular company communications.

Fowlers Inc., Strategic Background

Here are highlights of the strategic background for Fowlers from the business context summary developed by the core team.

Business Description

Fowlers Inc., is a billion-dollar conglomerate with worldwide leadership in three businesses: food processing (food products group), optical technology products (technology products group), and business services (durable products group).

Fowlers' food products group is a leading North American supplier of premium fresh and frozen meat products and management services to the food service, retail, on-line retail, and government sectors. Customers include SuperValu, Wal-Mart, Aramark, Simon Delivers, and thousands of independent grocers and specialty restaurants.

Fowlers' technology products group is one of the world's largest independent suppliers of optical storage products and services such as CD-ROM replication, CD-read and CD-write media, title fulfillment and distribution services, and optical drives. Customers include retail leaders such as Wal-Mart and Target, and category leaders such as Best Buy, Circuit City, Office Depot, and CompUSA. Fowlers is also a major supplier to the North American original equipment manufacturers (OEMs) for the personal computer market. Customers include Compaq, Dell, and Apple Computer.

Fowlers' durable products group was formed by acquiring one of the fastest-growing suppliers of business services, providing personalized apparel, office supplies, and promotional products to more than 14,000 companies and a million individual wearers. By using a dealer franchise as the route delivery mechanism, Fowlers' durable products group has gained a competitive edge by being both knowledgeable and responsive to individual customers in the markets it serves.

SWOT Analysis

Strengths

- ❏ The company has superior product quality in the food products group and technology products group.
- ❏ Low-cost manufacturer status in the technology products group existed before outsourcing several key items in the product line.
- ❏ The durable products group is perceived as the most responsive group in its chosen geographic markets, often delivering products and services on the same day as ordered.
- ❏ The food products group has a reputation of having superior delivery performance, mitigating criticism of its premium prices in a commodity marketplace.
- ❏ The company's growth in durable goods exceeded expectations.

Weaknesses

- ❏ There is a lack of organization-wide assimilation of the new Tier One Enterprise Resource Planning system because of acquisitions and the diversified nature of the company.
- ❏ Delivery performance is inconsistent, especially in the technology products group. Customer complaints in this market are especially high. Because the market visibility is so high, Fowlers is developing a reputation in customers' eyes as being tough to do business with (hard to place an order with, incomplete and incorrect product shipments, inaccurate pricing, poor order status capability, and so on). This is negatively affecting overall satisfaction ratings.
- ❏ Operating income of the food and technical product groups is eroding because of price pressure and too flat of a cost-reduction slope.
- ❏ The company has high indirect purchasing costs, despite lower cost of sales.

❑ The company's rate of cost increase for customer service is significantly higher than the rate of sales growth.

❑ Despite sales growth, Fowlers' stock price has taken a hit because of five quarters of poor profit-after-taxes and a bloating cash-to-cash cycle. Analyst criticism focuses on the inability of Fowlers to effectively manage return on assets and integrate profit potential of the business services acquisition.

Opportunities

❑ Leverage commodity buys across all product groups to improve gross profit.

❑ Improve effectiveness and efficiency of order fulfillment to improve customer satisfaction and reduce rate of spending on indirect goods and services (those that don't add value to the product being produced).

❑ Develop more advanced knowledge management capability to add financial value to customers beyond simple price-cutting.

❑ Accelerate market share in the durable products group by introducing an online catalogue for its end customers.

❑ Leverage cost-to-manufacture leadership in the technology products group to increase profits.

Threats

❑ Key competitors in the food products group are buying their way into the marketplace with a "lowest list price" strategy.

❑ Although the overall market for the technology products group has been in a period of decline, the group's market share is declining even faster; customer satisfaction scores put this group in the lowest quartile of performance.

❑ Price point in the technology products group is getting too low to meet profit targets with the current cost structure.

❑ Established catalogue apparel companies are potential competitors to the online sales channel being introduced this quarter.

Fowlers' Value Proposition

The Fowlers Inc., corporate value proposition is summarized by profitable growth as the preferred supplier of customers in targeted markets, driven by exceeding customer requirements.

Fowlers' Critical Success Factors

❑ Maintaining revenue contribution by increasing the share of the food products group in existing markets.

❑ Driving revenue growth by introducing durable products in the direct-to-consumer market and capturing targeted share.
❑ Achieving overall revenue growth for current year, targeted at 10 percent, and achieving targeted after-tax profit of 7 percent.
❑ Maintaining an image as technical leader in the technology products group and food products group, while improving overall return on assets and aggressively driving costs out of operations.
❑ Improving overall cash-to-cash position.
❑ Optimizing the newly implemented Tier One Enterprise Resource Planning system.
❑ Effectively integrating assets of the new durable products acquisition.

Fowlers' Critical Business Issues

❑ Customer satisfaction from all channels in the technology products group is negatively affecting sales.
❑ Profits are disappearing from the technology and food products groups because of higher direct and indirect costs.
❑ Revenue is targeted to grow to $1.02 billion, but actual projection after nine months is $1 billion.
❑ The durable products group integration of online capability is behind schedule.
❑ Inventory and receivables are expanding, seemingly uncontrollably.
❑ Key customers in the food products group are leaving on the basis of price-only criteria.

Financial Performance

Finding information about a publicly traded company's financial health is as easy as knowing the stock symbol and logging on to hoovers.com. There you can find all the ratio statistics, share price analyses, profit reports, and cash flow data necessary to paint the relative financial picture of a company.

To complete a current-state summary, you'll need information about income and cash position. The income statement contains revenue, cost, and profit data. The balance sheet looks at the right-now cash position by documenting assets and liabilities, including inventory.

In the business context document, profit is considered three ways, and each will eventually have its place in planning a supply chain project. First is gross margin: revenue less the cost of goods sold. This picture of profit is usually stated as a percent of total revenue. The second picture of profit is the operating margin (also referred to as operating income), which is gross margin less the costs of sales and administration. In effect, it's the gross margin with all indirect costs removed. It, too, is usually represented as a percent of total revenue. The third picture of profit is economic profit, which is operating margin less taxes and interest expense. The interest expense is affected by the amount of cash tied up in the business through inventory, receivables, and payables. By using these industry standards for developing your profit picture, you'll gain a better understanding of how your business fits into its competitive environment—an important piece of the business context summary.

In Fowlers' case, the business context summary contains consolidated income (Table 3-1) and balance sheet data (Table 3-2) from the 2006 and 2005 financial reports. In addition, because each operating unit of the company may have its own supply chain requirements, the

Table 3-1. Fowlers' 2006, 2005 consolidated income statement (in millions).

	2006	2005	Change
Revenue	1,000	925	8%
Cost of Revenue (Sales) Expense	860	750	15%
Gross Profit	140	175	−20%
%	14%	19%	
Selling, General, Administrative Expenses	70	65	8%
Research and Development Expense	0	0	0%
Total Operating Expenses	930	815	14%
Operating Income	70	110	−36%
%	7%	12%	
Interest Expense	(10)	(11)	−9%
Income Before Tax	60	99	−39%
%	6%	11%	
Income Tax Expense	23	38	−39%
Income After Tax	37	61	−39%
%	4%	7%	
Extra Item Expense	(2)	(3)	−33%
Net Income	35	58	−40%
%	4	6%	

Table 3-2.   Fowlers' 2006, 2005 consolidated balance sheet (in millions).

	2006	2005	Change
Cash and Short Term Investments	20	15	26%
Total Receivables	371	370	0%
Total Inventory	215	175	19%
Other Current Assets	50	58	−17%
Total Current Assets	656	618	6%
Property/Plant Equipment Gross	269	248	8%
Accumulated Depreciation	(140)	(123)	12%
Goodwill	122	116	5%
Long Term Investments	16	14	15%
Other Long Term Assets	24	25	−4%
Total Net Assets	291	279	4%
Accounts Payables	72	62	14%
Accrued Expenses	31	32	−3%
Short Term Debt	21	26	−24%
Leases	2	2	20%
Other Current Liabilities	62	60	4%
Total Current Liabilities	188	181	4%
Long Term Debt	76	71	6%
Minority Interest	11	13	−14%
Other Liabilities	40	43	−6%
Total Liabilities	127	127	0%

business context summary contains product group revenue and operating income financial reports for 2006 and 2005 (Table 3-3).

This kind of information can be harder to obtain, because not
all companies report division financial reports separate from the parent company.

Internal Profile

The internal profile summarizes the physical aspects of the company
and other performance measures that influence results. The first
physical aspect is the organization chart. In a publicly held company,
you can find this at the top level—usually down to the management
of operating units or divisions—in the executive profile section of a
corporate-reporting Web site such as hoovers.com. Many companies
also share this information, including names, titles, and brief biog-

Table 3-3. Fowlers' product group revenue and operating income performance.

	Food Products			Technology Products			Durable Products		
	2006.00000	2005.00000	Change	2006.00000	2005.00000	Change	2006.00000	2005.00000	Change
Revenue	250	278	-10%	450	463	-3%	300	185	62%
Cost of Revenue (Sales) Expense	215	225	-4%	390	375	4%	255	150	70%
Gross Profit	35	53	-33%	60	88	-31%	45	35	29%
%	14%	19%		13%	19%		10%	8%	
Selling, General, Administrative Expenses	18	20	-10%	36	33	8%	18	13	35%
Research and Development Expense	0	0		0	0		0	0	
Total Operating Expenses	233	245	-5%	425	408	4%	273	163	67%
Operating Income	19	33	-47%	25	55	-55%	28	22	25%
%	7%	12%		6%	12%		6%	6%	

raphies, on their own Web sites. Good starting places for this Web site hunt are the "investor relations" section or "about the company" section of the Web site.

The second physical aspect of the internal profile is identification of all locations where the company has operations, including manufacturing sites, warehouses, call centers, technical service centers, return locations, headquarters, and all contract locations in cases in which these functions are outsourced. This usually takes some work to collect; good sources for this information are the human resources department, the information technology department, the purchasing department, and accounting.

The third physical aspect of the internal business context is a picture of how the organization is set up to plan, manage, and execute key performance measures or indicators. For example, Fowlers' organization chart in Chapter 2 (Figure 2-1) reflects that sales, operations, and finance are controlled at both the corporate level and the business unit level. Note that the chief operating officer is at the same hierarchical level as the product group presidents; corporate directors have potential for conflict with the vice presidents of operations in each product group.

Most companies have such intricacies built into their reporting structures, and it can lead to overly complicated supply chains and delays in making improvements, as politics of control get in the way.

Fowlers' physical locations contain similar quirks. Each product group manages its own manufacturing locations, but the distribution locations are a mix—some are managed by a product group, and others are managed at the corporate level, demonstrating previous efforts to manage efficiency.

A final element of the internal profile is how success is measured. At Fowlers, the project team discovered five key performance indicators that were on the business team's dashboard, which are as follows:

1. Unit Cost
2. Line Item Fill Rate
3. Operating Income
4. Revenue
5. Backorders

External Profile

The external profile lists customers and suppliers in the context of groups that have significant impact on your supply chain. To keep it simple, a customer group is most easily defined by revenue reporting groups. Often these revenue categories are established by business model (i.e., direct-to-consumer, retail, distributor, and OEM).

Likewise, a supplier group is often defined by a major commodity type, such as packaging; tooling; process materials; maintenance, repair, and operations; value-added service; and so on. In both cases, use the 80/20 rule to list the largest customers and suppliers within each group—the 20 percent who get 80 percent of your revenue and material spend.

In Fowlers' case, the customer profile summary yielded seven market/customer channels across all of the product groups:

1. Retail markets, including mass merchant and category killer
2. Distributor/wholesaler markets
3. Direct-to-consumer markets
4. OEM/key account customers
5. The U.S. government

6. Home delivery/route sales markets

7. International markets

Fowlers' key supplier profile included raw material commodity types of resins, packaging, electronic components, live produce, hard goods, and apparel. In addition, the supply base included several contract manufacturers that supply apparel, optical media, pre-cooked food, and computer hardware.

The Supply Chain Definition Matrix

Up to this point in the discovery process, the emphasis has been on gathering background pieces of contextual information. Now is the time when the team needs to develop a consensus on how the company's supply chains are defined—a key to defining the project's scope.

In most cases, a supply chain is defined by a combination of product, customer, and geography. It can also include financial reporting and other factors. To create its definition, the team must take into account all points of view and prioritize the importance of each.

Using a supply chain definition matrix can help. (See Table 3-4 for an example of Fowlers' supply chain definition matrix.) The financial reporting hierarchy can help identify "major" geographies of

Table 3-4.   Fowlers' supply chain definition matrix.

Fowlers		Geography - Customer or Market Channel						
		U.S. Retail Markets	U.S. Distributor Markets	U.S. Direct-to-Consumer Markets	U.S. OEM - Key Accounts	U.S. Government	U.S. Home Delivery	International
Products	Food Products	☑	☑	☑	☐	☑	☐	☑
	Technology Products	☑	☐	☐	☑	☐	☐	☑
	Durable Products	☐	☐	☑	☐	☐	☑	☐

ProcessWizard - Fowlers Supply Chain Analysis (FowlersSupplyChainExcellence061307.bpwp)

File   Reports   Tools   Administration   Help

Supporting Tools

Configure...

Business Context Summary   Supply Chain Definition Matrix   Competitive Requirements Summary   Industry Comparison   Material Flow

15/06/2007 14:47						CAPS OVR NUM

the world. For example, if a company has profit-and-loss reports for Europe, Latin America, the Far East, North America, and Japan, then start with five matrices. To start, choose the geography that either has the most sales or serves as the location of the corporate headquarters.

The columns of each matrix represent demand including markets, customers, and/or channels. To build the columns on your first matrix, look at how sales regions are tracked, market channels are organized, and/or customers are segmented. Adding the revenue in each column should yield total revenue for geography represented in the matrix. The lowest level of detail in a column can be an "invoiceable" customer ship-to address.

The rows in the matrix focus on supply, including business lines or products; indirectly the rows address locations (manufacturing and distribution) and suppliers. To build the rows, start with the highest level of business lines or product families or groups. The lowest level of detail in a row is a Stock Keeping Unit; the rows should total your costs. There may be disconnects between how financial costs are aggregated versus how product families are aggregated. This has been a challenge in nearly every project; the use of more sophisticated data warehouse applications has started to make data more accessible.

Most companies are in the habit of defining their supply chains from a product cost perspective—solely by product and financial definitions, regardless of the customer. They worry about how the product is made, what suppliers are involved, and where the revenues and earnings are credited, but they often don't view a supply chain from the customer point of view. This can potentially derail a project's success. First, customer requirements are key factors that drive supply chain performance; although the gross margin may look good, the net profit might suffer because of high indirect costs to serve. Second, manufacturers are often indiscriminate about what items of the total product line should be available to a particular customer segment. Third, with a product-only view, supply chain costs can evolve to support the delivery requirements of the most aggressive customers—meaning the manufacturer provides superior delivery performance even where it is not needed or valued.

At Fowlers, the number of supply chains could be viewed in more than one way. If defined by product, the company would have three supply chains: food, technology, and durable products. If defined by market or customer channel, there would be seven supply chains: retail/mass merchant, distributor/wholesaler, direct-to-consumer, OEM, U.S. government, home delivery/route sales, and international. Fowlers could also define supply chain by geography, in which case there would be two: international and North America. Last, and the preferred view, Fowlers could say there are ten supply chains as defined by customer and product (count the Xs in Table 3-4).

The next step in the project scoping process is to collect data for each supply chain in an effort to help rank and ultimately prioritize them. A simple priority matrix can help organize the ranking process (Table 3-5). A partial list of Fowlers' supply chains is represented in this example. The matrix is organized by prioritization criteria (columns) and supply chains (rows—combination of product to customer). Each of the columns is weighted against each other. In this example, they all share equal weight. With data, the supply chains are then ranked high to low for each criterion. The total score for a supply chain is calculated using the following equation:

Total Score = [Criteria 1 Weight × Criteria 1 Rank + Criteria 2 Weight × Criteria 2 Rank + ... + Criteria 5 Weight × Criteria 5 Rank] × 100. In this example, the retail supply chains ranked the highest. Other common priority criteria could include gross margin dollars, inventory dollars, or inventory turns.

By using their matrix and some good sparring, the Fowlers' core team narrowed the scope for its supply chain project to six supply chains as defined by the U.S. sales of technology products and food products (Table 3-6).

Now, with the four basic components of a business context summary complete-strategic background, financial performance, in-

Table 3-5. Fowlers' supply chain priority matrix.

Supply Chain Priority Matrix

Supply Chains	Overall Rating	Criteria / Weight	Revenue - Rank 20%		Gross Margin % - Rank 20%		Number of SKUs - Rank 20%		Unit Volume - Rank 20%		Strategic Importance - Opinion 20%	
		Ranking / Weighted Result	Rank	Wtd	Rank	Wtd	Rank	Wtd	Rank	Wtd	Rank	Wtd
Food Products - U.S. Retail Markets	400		4	0.8	2	0.4	3	0.6	5	1	6	1.2
Food Products - U.S. Distributor Markets	360		3	0.6	5	1	4	0.8	4	0.8	2	0.4
Food Products - U.S. Direct-to-Consumer Markets	320		2	0.4	3	0.6	6	1.2	2	0.4	3	0.6
Food Products - U.S. Government	240		1	0.2	4	0.8	5	1	1	0.2	1	0.2
Technology Products - U.S. Retail Markets	400		6	1.2	1	0.2	2	0.4	6	1.2	5	1
Technology Products - U.S. OEM-Key Accounts	380		5	1	6	1.2	1	0.2	3	0.6	4	0.8

Table 3-6.   Fowlers' supply chain project scope.

		Geography - Customer or Market Channel						
Fowlers		U.S. Retail Markets	U.S. Distributor Markets	U.S. Direct-to-Consumer Markets	U.S. OEM - Key Accounts	U.S. Government	U.S. Home Delivery	International
Products	Food Products	☑	☑	☑	☐	☑	☐	☑
	Technology Products	☑	☐	☐	☑	☐	☐	☑
	Durable Products	☐	☐	☑	☐	☐	☑	☐

(ProcessWizard - Fowlers Supply Chain Analysis (FowlersSupplyChainExcellence061307.bpwp) — File, Reports, Tools, Administration, Help — Supporting Tools — Configure... — Business Context Summary Supply Chain Definition Matrix Competitive Requirements Summary Industry Comparison Material Flow — 15/06/2007 14:47)

ternal profile, and external profile-the team was able to move ahead
to the project charter.

▪ The Project Charter

The project charter is created during this phase to establish a complete understanding of the project's scope and objectives. The document helps to align assumptions and expectations among executive sponsors, stakeholders, and team members. The page most
project members jump to first is the schedule. There are two project delivery formats. The first mirrors the organization of this book:
two days of classroom each week focused on specific deliverables to
be completed as "homework" before the next session. The second
format completes the same deliverables in the same elapsed time,
but the classroom sessions are organized by phase, not by week.
Figure 3-1 illustrates an alternative Fowlers' schedule using the "by
phase" approach. This approach uses three days of classroom followed by two weeks of time to complete the deliverables. This approach makes more productive use of teams with members who
must travel as part of the project.

The second page people usually turn to in the charter is the one
defining roles and responsibilities. As illustrated with the Fowlers'
project, there are specific expectations for Fowlers' Steering Team,

Figure 3-1. Alternative schedule by phase.

Phase	Deliverable	Classroom Dates
Phase 0 Building Organizational Support for Supply Chain Improvement	March 1 to April 30, 2007 SCOR Implementation Overview SCOR Framework Workshop SCOR Implementation Workshop Custom Executive Briefing	March 5, 2007 March 19, 2007 April 2, 2007 April 3, 2007
Phase 1 Discover the Opportunity	May 14 to June 8, 2007 Kickoff Workshop Business Context Summary Supply Chain Definition Matrix Supply Chain Priority Matrix Project Charter	May 14, 15, and 16, 2007
Phase 2 Analyze Basis of Competition	Metric Definitions and Data Collection Plan Industry Comparison Competitive Requirements (Chip Exercise) Benchmark Data Preliminary SCORcard SCORcard Gap Analysis	
Phase 3 Design Material Flow	June 11 to July 13, 2007 AS IS Geographic Map Planning Matrix AS IS Thread Matrix Defect Data Collection Plan Defect Analysis The Brainstorm Event and Documentation Disconnect Analysis Preliminary Project Portfolio Opportunity Analysis TO BE Geographic Map TO BE Thread Diagram Quick Hits	June 4, 5, and 6, 2007 June 25, 26, and 27, 2007
Phase 4 Design Work and Information Flow	July 16 to August 31, 2007 Staple Yourself to an Order Interviews AS IS Process Diagram Process Performance Summaries Leading Practice Assessment TO BE Process Blueprint RACI Analysis Level 4 Process Blueprints Project Definitions	July 16, 17, and 18, 2007 August 6, 7, and 8, 2007
Phase 5 Implementation Planning	September 3 to September 14, 2007 Portfolio ROI Implementation Scope and Sequence Implementation Resource Options	August 27, 28, and 29, 2007

Fowlers' Project Sponsor, Fowlers' Project Manager, Fowlers' Design Team, Fowlers' Extended Team, and Coach.

Other components of the project charter include scope, business and project objectives, methodology, deliverables, risks and dependencies, budget, organization chart, stakeholder expectations, benchmarks, benefit analysis, critical success factors, communication plan, and control procedures.

4

Week Two: Project Kickoff and Supply Chain Operations Reference Metrics

Get a Good Start and Begin to Define Supply Chain Metrics

The objectives of this week are to kick off the project effectively and to initiate the design steps for assembling a balanced set of supply chain metrics and associated scorecard. Typically, the project kickoff can be orchestrated in half a day; the remaining day-and-a-half are allocated to identifying and defining supply chain metrics and then initiating homework to collect actual performance data.

■ The Project Kickoff

There are two ingredients necessary for a great kickoff. First, all the right people have to be there. The audience should include all re-

46

sources participating on the project, including the steering team, active executive sponsor, project manager, design team, and extended team. If in doubt about a particular person or group, invite them. Providing the big picture to anyone who might participate in the project makes their support in gathering details more productive.

At Fowlers Inc., executive sponsor Brian Dowell invited the eight-member steering team and ten-member design team as identified on the project charter. He also invited extended team resources from information technology, finance, and site operations from both the technology and food product groups. In all, there were 36 people present.

The second ingredient to a great project kickoff is having the right materials presented by the right people. The most popular and effective agenda organizes the content into three basic chunks: (1) setting the strategic context for supply chain improvement, delivered by the executive sponsor(s); (2) providing a high-level overview of how Supply Chain Operations Reference (SCOR) works, delivered by the coach; and (3) summarizing critical elements of the project charter, delivered by the project manager (Figure 4-1).

To prepare for the kickoff, Brian Dowell, Martha Tekitch, and Doris Early prepared "state of the business" summaries highlighting the issues related to Fowlers' supply chain improvement. Their presentations summarized business plans, strategy, critical success factors, critical business issues, and expectations with regard to supply chain improvement.

The coach prepared the SCOR overview presentation. It provided the big picture of the SCOR framework, highlighted the Supply Chain Excellence project roadmap, and gave examples of the deliverables that individuals across the design and extended teams would be asked to produce in the coming weeks.

Finally, David Able prepared key points from the approved project charter; emphasizing the thing most people were interested in—the schedule. He allowed time for everyone to synchronize their own calendars to the rhythm of the project as outlined in the project charter. In addition to the schedule, the kickoff provided the op-

Figure 4-1. Fowlers' project kickoff agenda.

Supply Chain Project
Project Kickoff Presentation

Kickoff Agenda
- Introductions
- Fowlers' Business Case for Supply Chain Improvement
- Supply Chain FAQs and the SCOR approach
- Lunch
- Fowlers' Project Charter
- Social Event

Fowlers' Business Case
- Technology Products Group Strategy, Critical Success Factors, and Critical Business Issues
- Food Products Group Strategy, Critical Success Factors, and Critical Business Issues
- The case for Supply Chain Improvement

SCOR—FAQs
- What is the Supply-Chain Council?
- What is SCOR?
- How do you use SCOR to achieve supply chain performance improvement?
- How can this apply to my company?
- How can I learn more about SCOR?

Project Charter Review
- Business Objectives
- Project Objectives
- Milestones
- Design Team Schedule
- Steering Team Schedule
- Organization Chart
- Dependencies
- Communication Plan

---

portunity to set remaining stakeholder interviews left over from Week One. These would be incorporated into a revised project charter, in the stakeholder expectations section.

Mixing the three ingredients—the business context for supply chain improvement, the SCOR education, and key points of the project charter—built a powerful shared vision of the pace of the project. It aligned expectations for deliverables and outlined the effort required for the various project roles.

▣ Picking a Balanced Set of Supply Chain Metrics

With the kickoff meeting complete, the real work begins. Typically, the only people in the room at this point are the project manager, coach, and design team. The first order of business is to define the number of scorecards to be assembled. In an ideal world, there would be one scorecard for each supply chain determined to be in scope—as illustrated in the definition matrix (Table 3-4). In reality, the many variables in how financial reports and customer-order data are organized makes it difficult to have all three key metric sets—customer, internal, and shareholder—on every scorecard. For example, a company may report the profitability measures at multiple layers of the organization and the balance sheet only at the corporate level. Or, a company may be able to track revenue by customer channel but costs by product group only. In almost all cases, compromises are necessary between the desire to measure all aspects of every supply chain and the ability to collect that data.

To help the Fowlers' design team figure out what data to put on each scorecard, the coach suggested creating another matrix. This time, the rows would be defined by available customer, internal, and shareholder data. The columns would represent the number of desired scorecards, which in turn was influenced by the scope of the project (Figure 4-2).

Fowlers reported balance sheet data at the corporate level, and profits, customer revenue, and order data were all reported at the business group level. After some discussion, the design team agreed that it needed to build three scorecards: Fowlers' consolidated enterprise, food products group, and technology products group. The consolidated scorecard would include everything. The product group scorecards would omit the return and per-share categories of the shareholder-facing metrics, because such data simply weren't available at the business group level.

The next order of business was to select the appropriate metrics from the SCOR Level One list.

Figure 4-2. Fowlers' scorecard matrix.

Fowlers Scorecard Matrix		Number of Scorecards		
		Fowlers Enterprise	Food Products	Technology Products
Data per Scorecard	External Facing	X	X	X
	Internal Facing	X	X	X
	Shareholder Facing	X	Omit	Omit

The best approach to selecting the right mix of metrics is to educate the team on the pure SCOR definition, calculation, and collection requirements. The team can then contrast the SCOR ideal with their current metrics and ultimately achieve consensus on inclusion, exclusion, or modification. A good general rule is to pick at least one metric from each category. The coach offered Tables 4-1 to 4-9 as guides for the Fowlers' discussion. By day's end, the Fowlers' design team had identified the following metrics for its balanced supply chain scorecard and created a blank scorecard template (Table 4-10):

❑ Line item on time and in full
❑ Perfect order fulfillment
❑ Order fulfillment cycle time
❑ Upside supply chain flexibility
❑ Cost of goods
❑ Total supply chain management cost
❑ Sales, general, and administrative cost
❑ Warranty/returns processing costs
❑ Cash-to-cash cycle time
❑ Inventory days of supply
❑ Asset turns
❑ Gross margin
❑ Operating income
❑ Net income
❑ Return on assets

(text continues on page 60)

Table 4-1.   Perfect line fulfillment. Also called Line Item On Time and In Full.

	Perfect Line Fulfillment			Perfect Line Fulfillment is treated by the Supply Council as a level 3 metric measuring the percentage of lines delivered "on time and in full" to customer commit date AND flawless match of purchase order, invoice, and receipt in your customer's system. SCOR Manual, page 436.
	Measurement Component	**Score**	**Data**	**Calculation Component**	**Query Assumptions**

	Measurement Component	**Score**	**Data**	**Calculation Component**	**Query Assumptions**
Delivery Reliability	Line On Time and In Full to Customer Request	56.8%	10000	Total Number of Customer Lines	Self explanatory. This is the base for Request, Commit, and Perfect Order. In this case the 100 orders averaged 100 line items.
			5899	Total Number of Lines Delivered On Time to Customer Request Date	Request date is the first request date from the customer at the line level. This includes agreed to lead times by SKU that may ultimately be part of the customer's master data settings. This also helps differentiate MTO and MTS items that are on the same order.
			5788	Total Number of Lines Delivered In Full to Customer Request Date	Request quantity is the first request quantity prior to application of Available To Promise (ATP) checks at the line level.
			5680	Total Number of Lines Delivered On Time and In Full to Customer Request Date	Many applications have a difficult time with both on time and in full by order. Each line needs to be evaluated and considered good if quantity and date are met. As with the order, many companies do not store original request data and, hence, do not calculate this component.
	Line On Time and In Full to Customer Commit	72.0%	7456	Total Number of Lines Delivered On Time to Customer Commit Date	Commit date is the original confirmation date first given the customer after the first ATP check at the line level. Ideally this is a committed delivery date to the customer. Many companies are not getting receipt data from their carriers and measure to the committed ship date.
			7209	Total Number of Lines Delivered In Full to Customer Commit Date	Commit quantity is the first confirmation quantity after the application of ATP checks at the line level.
			7199	Total Number of Lines Delivered On Time and In Full to Customer Commit Date	Many applications have a difficult time with both on time and in full even by line. Each line needs to be evaluated against original commit and is considered good of quantity and date are met. Many companies do not store original commit data and, hence, always measure against the latest commit making the metric look like 100%.
	Perfect Line Fulfillment	49.0%	4899	Total Number of Lines On Time and Complete Meeting 3 Way match Criteria	This is the most difficult measure to get. The best method is to evaluate your three way match percentage at the line level via your customers purchasing or payables system. Many companies attempt to measure this metric using the On Time and In Full Commit as a base and then subtract order invoices that have some deduction associated with it.

Table 4-2.   Perfect order fulfillment.

Perfect Order Fulfillment			Perfect Order Fulfillment measures the percentage of orders delivered "on time and in full" to customer commit date AND flaw less match of purchase order, invoice, and receipt in your customer's system. SCOR manual, page 436.	

<table>
<tr><th colspan="2">Measurement Component</th><th>Score</th><th>Data</th><th>Calculation Component</th><th>Query Assumptions</th></tr>
<tr><td rowspan="13">Delivery Reliability</td><td rowspan="5">Order On Time and In Full to Customer Request</td><td rowspan="5">38.0%</td><td>100</td><td>Total Number of Customer Orders</td><td>Self explanatory. This is the base for Request, Commit, and Perfect Order.</td></tr>
<tr><td>47</td><td>Total Number of Orders Delivered On Time to Customer Request Date</td><td>Request date is the first request date from the customer. This includes agreed to lead times by SKU that may ultimately be part of the customer's master data settings.</td></tr>
<tr><td>50</td><td>Total Number of Orders Delivered In Full to Customer Request Date</td><td>Request quantity is the first request quantity prior to application of Available To Promise (ATP) checks.</td></tr>
<tr><td>38</td><td>Total Number of Orders Delivered On Time and In Full to Customer Request Date</td><td>Many applications have a difficult time with both on time and in full by order. Each line needs to be evaluated; if all of the lines are on time and in full to original request then the order is considered good. Many companies do not store original request data and, hence, do not calculate the component.</td></tr>
<tr><td rowspan="3">Order On Time and In Full to Customer Commit</td><td rowspan="3">40.0%</td><td>47</td><td>Total Number of Orders Delivered to Customer Commit Date</td><td>Commit date is the original confirmation date first given the customer after the ATP check. Ideally this is a committed delivery date to the customer. Many companies are not getting receipt data from their carriers and measure to the committed ship date.</td></tr>
<tr><td>50</td><td>Total Number of Orders Delivered in Full to Customer Commit Date</td><td>Commit quantity is the first confirmation quantity after the application of ATP checks.</td></tr>
<tr><td>40</td><td>Total Number of Orders Delivered On Time and In Full to Customer Commit Date</td><td>Many applications have a difficult time with both on time and in full by order. Each line needs to be evaluated; if all of the lines are on time and in full to original commit then the order is considered good. Many companies do not store original commit data and, hence, always measure against the latest commit making the metric look like 100%.</td></tr>
<tr><td>Perfect Order Fulfillment</td><td>24.0%</td><td>24</td><td>Total Number of Orders On Time and Complete Meeting 3 Way match Criteria</td><td>This is the most difficult measure to get. The best method is to evaluate your three way match percentage at the order level via your customers purchasing or payables system. Many companies attempt to measure this metric using the On Time and In Full Commit as a base and then subtract order invoices that have some deduction associated with it.</td></tr>
</table>

Table 4-3.   Order fulfillment cycle time for make-to-stock (MTS).

Order Fulfillment Cycle Time	Simply put, Order Fulfillment Cycle Time measures the number of days from order receipt in customer service to the delivery receipt at the customer's dock. Originally intended only for "Make-to-Order Items," it has been broadened to include stock and engineer-to-order items. SCOR 8.0 Manual, page 445.			
	Score	Data	Calculation Component	Query Assumptions
Responsiveness	12.0	4	Customer Authorization to Order Entry Complete	In practice, this is the time from initial receipt of the customer order Purchase Order (PO) until the order entry is complete. For EDI transmissions, the clock starts with the system receipt day and time.
		5	Order Entry Complete to Order Received at Warehouse	This is normally the time order entry complete until the order delivery is created at the warehouse. This is also where future dated orders sit (dwell time).
		1	Order Received at Warehouse to Order Shipped to Customer	This is the time from delivery creation in the warehouse until the order is shipped to the customer.
		1	Order Shipped to Customer to Customer Receipt of Order	This time bucket is often referred as "in transit" time.
		1	Order Received at Customer to Installation Complete	This category is reserved for those having an installation component and is calculated from receipt of first good until installation complete.

Table 4-4. Order fulfillment cycle for make-to-order and engineer-to-order (MTO and ETO).

Order Fulfillment Cycle Time		Simply put, Order Fulfillment Cycle Time measures the number of days from order receipt in customer service to the delivery receipt at the customer's dock. Originally intended only for "Make-to-Order Items," it has been broadened to include stock and engineer-to-order items. SCOR 8.0 Manual, page 445.		
	Score	**Data**	**Calculation Component**	**Query Assumptions**
Responsiveness	39.0	1	Customer Authorization to Order Entry Complete	In practice, this is the time from initial receipt of the customer order Purchase Order (PO) until the order entry is complete. For EDI transmissions, the clock starts with the system receipt day and time.
		5	Order Entry Complete to Start Manufacture	This is normally the time order entry complete until the production order is created in manufacturing. This is also where future dated orders sit (dwell time).
		21	Start Manufacture to Manufacturing Ship	This is the time from production order create to ship to the warehouse or customer.
		2	Manufacturing Ship to Order Received at Warehouse	This time bucket is often referred as "in transit" time.
		1	Order Received at Warehouse to Order Shipped to Customer	This is the time from delivery creation in the warehouse until the order is shipped to the customer.
		4	Order Shipped to Customer to Customer Receipt of Order	This time bucket is often referred to as "in transit" time.
		5	Order Received at Customer to Installation Complete	This category is reserved for those having an installation component and is calculated from receipt of first good until installation complete.

Table 4-5. Upside supply chain flexibility.

Upside Supply Chain Flexibility	Practically speaking, Upside Supply Chain Flexibility measures the number of days it takes a supply chain to respond to (plan, source, make, and deliver orders) an unplanned significant increase or decrease in demand without penalty. SCOR 8.0 Manual, page 452. In order to make this measure more science and less opinion, SCE has defined this by adding the "Planned Lead Times" found in a SKU's master data.		
	Score	Data	Calculation Component	Query Assumptions

	Score	Data	Calculation Component	Query Assumptions
Flexibility	113.0	305	Re-Plan Planned Lead Time	Often associated with frequency of MRP update
		33	Source Planned Lead Time	This is the longest component planned lead time for a SKUs bill of materials
		45	Make Planned Lead Time	This is frequently associated with SKUs manufacturing scheduling cycle, i.e., weekly, monthly, quarterly, etc., or it ca be part of the "replenishment lead time" found in item setup screens for ATP.
		5	Deliver Planned Lead Time	This is also associated with the "replenishment lead time" and refers to the planned time from order entry to ship.

Table 4-6. Total supply chain management cost.

Total Supply Chain Management Cost					
					This metric was redefined in the 7.0 release. Much of the benchmark data is based on 6.1. This worksheet still uses the 6.1 calculation components. Total Supply Chain Management Cost measures the cost to plan, source, and deliver products and services. Make costs are often captured in COGS while Return costs are calculated in Warranty/Returns Processing Costs. SCOR 8.0 Manual, page 496.
Score	% of Revenue	Raw Data (000s)	Calculation Component	Query Assumptions	
		$1,000,000	Revenue		
	9.8%	$98,011	Order Management Cost		
	3.5%	$35,098	Customer Service Cost	Cost centers that have to do with entering customer orders, reserving inventory, credit check, consolidating orders, processing inquiries and quotes.	
	2.4%	$23,908	Finished Goods Warehouse Cost	Cost centers that have to do with the storage,receiving, picking and shipment of finished goods products.	
21.9%	2.1%	$21,098	Outbound Transportation Cost	Cost centers that have to do with the transportation (all modes, including export) of finished goods products.	
	0.9%	$9,000	Contract and Program Management Cost	Cost centers that have to do with the initiation and ongoing management of customer contracts, including master agreements, compliance to volume-based incentives and other special incentives.	
	0.0%	$0	Installation Planning and Execution Costs	Cost centers that have to do with the planning and execution of product installation at customer-designated locations.	
	0.9%	$8,907	Accounts Receivable Cost	Cost centers that have to do with the processing and closure of customer invoices, including collection.	
	6.2% Cost	$61,638	Material (Product) Acquisition		
	1.9%	$18,997	Purchasing Cost	The cost centers associated with the strategic as well as the tactical parts of the purchasing process.	
	0.6%	$5,987	Raw Material Warehouse cost	The cost centers associated with the receiving, storage and transfer of raw material product.	

Percent	Amount	Cost Center	Description
0.1%	$1,099	Supplier Quality Cost	The cost centers associated with supplier qualification, product verification, and ongoing quality systems for raw materials.
0.3%	$2,987	Component Engineering and Tooling Cost	The cost centers associated with engineering (design and specification) and tooling costs for raw materials, i.e., packaging.
2.5%	$24,678	Inbound Transportation Cost	Cost centers that have to do with the transportation (all modes including import) of raw material and/or purchased finished goods products.
0.8%	$7,890	Accounts Payable Cost	Cost centers that have to do with the processing and closure of supplier invoices, including credit and disputes.
0.8%	$8,092	Planning and Finance Cost	
0.2%	$2,349	Demand Planning Cost	The cost centers allocated to unit forecasting and overall demand management.
0.5%	$4,509	Supply Planning Cost	The cost centers allocated to supply planning, including overall supply planning, distribution requirements planning, master production planning and production scheduling.
0.1%	$1,234	Supply Chain Finance Control Cost	The cost centers in finance allocated to reconcile unit plans with financial plans, account for and control supply chain cost centers, and report financial performance of the supply chain Scorecard.
3.1%	$30,806	**Inventory Carrying Cost**	
2.6%	$25,609	Opportunity Cost	The value of inventory times the cost of money for your company.
0.3%	$3,452	Obsolescence Cost	The additional cost of obsolescence in the form of accruals and/or write-offs.
0.1%	$1,245	Shrinkage Cost	The additional cost of shrinkage in the form of accruals and/or write-offs.
0.1%	$500	Taxes and Insurance Cost	The cost centers allocated to the payment of taxes and insurance for inventory assets.
2.0%	$20,000	IT Cost for Supply Chain	
1.0%	$10,000	Supply Chain Application Cost	The cost centers summarizing the fixed costs associated with supply IT application costs to Plan, Source, Make, Deliver and Return.
1.0%	$10,000	IT Operational Cost for Supply Chain	The cost centers summarizing the ongoing expenses associated with maintenance, upgrade and development of IT costs to support Plan, Source, Make, Deliver and Return.

Table 4-7.   Total returns management – warranty cost.

Total Returns Management-Warranty Costs			This metric was redefined in the 7.0 release. Much of the benchmark data is based on 6.1. This worksheet still uses the 6.1 calculation components. Total Returns Management – Warranty Costs is a discrete measure that attempts to segment the cost centers associated with defective product returns, planned and unplanned returns of maintenance, repair and overhaul products (MRO), and returns associated with excess customer inventory. Total Returns Management – Warranty Cost is additive to Total Supply Chain Management Cost. SCOR 8.0 Manual, page 496.	
Score	% of Revenue	Raw Data (000s)	Calculation Component	Query Assumptions
		$1,000,000	Revenue	
0.4%	0.01%	$134	Returns Authorization Processing Costs	Cost centers that have to do with entering return authorizations, scheduling receipts and processing replacement or credit.
	0.22%	$2,222	Returned Product Warehouse Cost	Cost centers that have to do with labor and space for receipt and storage of return products.
	0.02%	$222	Returned Product Transportation Costs	Cost centers that have to do with the transportation cost of returned products.
	0.10%	$1,000	Warranty Costs	Cost centers that have to do with the material, labor, and problem diagnosis for verification and disposition of returned product.

Table 4-8.   Cost of goods sold.

Cost of Goods			COGS is a common measure that includes the material and labor to manufacture products. This cost includes direct costs (labor, materials) and indirect costs (overhead). This is not intended to be additive to Total Supply Chain Management Cost. SCOR 8.0 Manual, page 502.	
Score	% of Revenue	Raw Data (000s)	Calculation Component	Query Assumptions
		$1,000,000	Revenue	
76%	55.6%	$556,000	Material Cost	Cost centers that include all materials directly incorporated into the cost of the finished good product.
	13.4%	$134,000	Direct Labor	Cost centers that include all labor that directly impacts the manufacturing – assembly of the finished good product.
	7.5%	$75,000	Indirect Labor	Cost centers that include indirect labor and overhead supporting the manufacturing – assembly of the finished good product.

Table 4-9.   Cash-to-cash cycle time.

Cast to Cash Cycle Time		Cash-to-Cash Cycle Time is calculated by adding days of inventory to days sales outstanding subtracting days payables outstanding. It provides a snapshot how many days it takes a company to turn its working capital.	
	Raw Data (000s)	Calculation Component	Query Assumptions
Score	$556,000	Material Cost	
	$765,000	COGS	
	$1,000,000	Revenue	
	95.4	Inventory Days of Supply	Total Inventory $ / (COGS / 365); Inventory Turns is calculated by COGS / Total Inventory $
	$200,000	Total Inventory	As defined on your balance sheet
	$100,000	Finished Goods Inventory	Includes both manufactured and purchased FG.
183.0	$25,000	Work in Process Inventory	
	$75,000	Raw Material Inventory	
	54.8	Days Sales Outstanding	Total Receivables $ / (Revenue / 365)
	$150,000	Total Receivables	As defined on your balance sheet.
	32.8	Days Payables Outstanding	Total Payables $ / (Material Cost / 365)
	$50,000	Total Payables	As defined on your balance sheet.

Building on the momentum of the first day and knowing that relationships were critical to executing the schedule, Brian, Martha, and Doris sponsored a social event to finish up a day that all agreed was one of the best project launches anyone at the company could recall.

Data Collection and Benchmarks

The second working day of Week Two begins the process of filling the blank scorecard with data. The main objective is to assemble a data collection plan, including gathering appropriate benchmark

Table 4-10.   Fowlers' Enterprise scorecard template with selected metrics.

data for review during Week Three (Chapter 5). There are generally five important elements to a data collection plan. First and most important is a definition of the metric; use the SCOR definitions as a baseline.

Second, it's necessary to assemble a segmentation strategy that will allow for aggregation and desegregation. Examples of segmentation options are by location, customer, item, country, forecast planning family, or commodity.

The third requirement is a data extract query (taking into account the segmentation strategy) that includes specific data tables and fields from either the live system or data warehouse.

The fourth consideration is the sample size of the data. Collecting customer order data for perfect order fulfillment and order fulfillment cycle time may use a sample size of the last three months, whereas total supply chain management cost may use a sample size of the last fiscal year.

The fifth element in the data collection plan is to identify a data collection team. This team will follow the collection all the way through defect analysis (Chapter 8).

Before launching an all-out effort to benchmark performance, it's important to consider the level of detail necessary, comfort level of divulging company data, and effort required to get the data back. With this in mind, there are two types of sources for benchmark data. First, there are subscription sources that generally require a fee to access the data. Subscription data are evolving in the level of detail, require no company data, and can be acquired with little or no effort. Second, there are survey sources that require a company to complete a survey of supply chain metrics and submit them as contribution to a larger sample. Although the effort is greater (up to forty hours), these kind of resources provide a higher level of detail. Table 4-11 summarizes some frequently used benchmark sources. In any case, the goal is to get multiple sources of benchmark data for each selected metric.

With the data collection plans in place, the second part of the day focuses on planning how to assemble an industry comparison spreadsheet using hoovers.com. This spreadsheet summarizes actual and benchmark data for the shareholder metrics of profitability, returns, and share performance at the enterprise level (Table 4-12). The industry comparison list should contain at least twenty-five companies for statistical reasons and as many industries as necessary to compare relevant competition at the business group level. Less than twenty-five is considered more a point-to-point comparison.

Table 4-11.   Benchmark data sources.

Source	Link
APQC - Supply Chain Surveys	www.apqc.org
AMR	www.amrresearch.com
CAPS Research	www.capsresearch.com
Hoovers	www.hoovers.com
Manufacturing Performance Institute	www.mpi-group.net
Performance Measurement Group	pmgbenchmarking.com
Supply Chain Council	www.supply-chain.org
eSCM	www.escm.org.sg
Warehouse Education Research Council (WERC)	www.werc.org

(text continues on page 65)

Table 4-12. Sample industry comparison spreadsheet and raw data.

Industry Comparison - Computer Network Industry - Hoovers.com	Revenue	SG&A	Cost of Goods	Cash-to-Cash Cycle Time	Inventory Days of Supply	Asset Turns	Gross Margin	Operating Income	Net Operating Income	Return on Assets
YOUR COMPANY	176.1	41%	47%	159	98	0.66	53%	12%	7%	7.8%
Network Appliance, Inc.	1006.0	29%	40%	58	20	1.58	60%	31%	7%	49.1%
Dassault Systemes S.A.	546.0	57%	14%	91	0	1.17	86%	28%	16%	33.0%
The Titan Corporation	1033.0	25%	73%	105	12	2.23	27%	1%	-2%	3.3%
RadiSys Corporation	340.7	24%	66%	130	87	1.30	34%	10%	10%	12.9%
Convergys Corporation	2320.6	30%	55%	35	0	5.91	45%	16%	9%	70.0%
3COM	2820.9	64%	81%	39	32	1.61	19%	-45%	-34%	-54.9%
Enterasys Networks, Inc	1071.5	66%	52%	106	64	1.08	48%	-18%	-57%	-15.0%
Jack Henry and Associates	345.5	19%	56%	94	0	2.68	44%	25%	16%	49.8%
Novell, Inc.	1040.1	80%	32%	51	1	1.35	68%	-12%	-26%	-11.8%
Reynolds and Reynolds	1004.0	39%	44%	24	9	4.68	56%	17%	10%	60.0%
Cerner Corporation	404.5	71%	22%	149	9	1.87	78%	6%	26%	8.9%
The Black Box Corporation	827.0	26%	60%	79	38	4.13	40%	14%	8%	43.7%
Integraph Corporation	690.5	40%	63%	86	21	2.44	37%	-3%	1%	-6.3%
Entrada Networks, Inc.	25.7	66%	67%	130	98	1.56	33%	-33%	-82%	-38.6%
Inrange Technologies Corporation	233.6	35%	45%	197	102	1.03	55%	20%	6%	15.6%
Computer Networks Industry	100.0	35%	52%	58	20	1.23	48%	13%	2%	12.0%
Networking Solutions Q3	38.9	50%	47%	NA	NA	NA	53%	3%	NA	NA
Storage Solutions Q3	16.5	17%	91%	NA	NA	NA	9%	-8%	NA	NA
Industry Parity - 50th Percentile	759	39%	53%	92	21	1.60	47%	11%	7%	11%
Industry Advantage - 70th Percentile	1165	32%	41%	65	10	2.97	59%	19%	12%	32%
Industry Superior - 90th Percentile	1571	25%	28%	37	0	4.35	72%	26%	16%	54%

(continues)

Table 4-12. (continued)

Raw Data (in millions)	Revenue $	SG&A $	Cost of Goods $	Inventory $	Receivable $	Total Assets $	Gross Margin $	Operating Income $	Net Operating Income $
YOUR COMPANY	176.1	72	83.2	22.4	43.6	268.6	92.9	20.9	12
Network Appliance, Inc.	1006.0	292	402	22.5	187	636	604	312	75
Dassault Systemes S.A.	546.0	313.5	78.3	0	181	467	467.7	154.2	90
The Titan Corporation	1033.0	260.7	757	25.4	347	463.3	276	15.3	-18.7
RadiSys Corporation	340.7	82.9	223.8	53.2	68.2	262.8	116.9	34	32.6
Convergys Corporation	2320.6	685.5	1268.7	0	413	523.1	1051.9	366.4	215.5
3COM	2820.9	1814.6	2287.3	200.1	286.8	2334.8	533.6	-1281	-965.4
Enterasys Networks, Inc	1071.5	711.2	558.4	98.2	210.9	1322.2	513.1	-198.1	-606
Jack Henry and Associates	345.5	65.9	193.9	0	117.1	172.1	151.6	85.7	55.6
Novell, Inc.	1040.1	833	327.9	0.9	227	1027.4	712.2	-120.8	-272.9
Reynolds and Reynolds	1004.0	389.4	442.9	10.8	125	286.2	561.1	171.7	99.6
Cerner Corporation	404.5	288.8	90.1	2.2	188	288.5	314.4	25.6	105.3
The Black Box Corporation	827.0	216.2	493.9	51.1	160.9	267.3	333.1	116.9	64.2
Integraph Corporation	690.5	275.9	438.2	25.3	178.9	377.5	252.3	-23.6	10.1
Entrada Networks, Inc.	25.7	17	17.2	4.6	4.4	22	8.5	-8.5	-21.2
Inrange Technologies Corporation	233.6	81.5	105	29.3	80	301.1	128.6	47.1	14.3
Computer Networks Industry	100.0	35	52	2.8	18.8	108.7	48	13	2.4
Networking Solutions Q3	38.9	19.5	18.3	NA	NA	NA	20.6	1.1	NA
Storage Solutions Q3	16.5	2.8	15	NA	NA	NA	1.5	-1.3	NA

At Fowlers, the corporate controller, director of logistics, and director of customer service divided up the scorecard metrics data because they had the easiest access to the financial and customer order information, and had extended team resources who could help collect the data. The corporate controller, vice president of sales and marketing in the food products group, and—in his capacity as vice president of operations for the technology products group—David Able took responsibility for assembling the industry comparison spreadsheet. Because the team knew that Fowlers' own data were listed in the "conglomerates industry" on hoovers.com, they requested that food and computer industries be added to the list for more specific comparisons with the operating groups. The director of applications planned to assign an extended team resource to help with actual data queries and collection.

The key deliverables that the team set out to produce (which will be needed for review during Week Three) include a completed industry comparison spreadsheet and updated scorecards with actual query results.

5

Week Three: Benchmarks, Competitive Requirements, and Steering Team Review Number One

Start to Put Data to Work

The objectives of the third week are to review the results of the data collected during Week Two, including industry comparisons, metric queries, and other subscription benchmark comparisons (Chapter 4). Also on the schedule is steering team review number one, conducted by the project manager and chosen members of the design team.

▓ Data Review

The first agenda item on Day One is to review the preliminary results of the metric data collection. The owner of each metric should lead the review, including query definition, available segmentation options, adjustments to assumptions, and estimates on the time required to finish collecting data for the scorecards.

The second agenda item is to review the completed benchmark data results assigned during the previous week. For this, the team will use its industry comparison spreadsheet (Table 4-12) and subscription data sources.

When the Fowlers' team reached this point, the corporate controller, the vice president of sales and marketing-food products group, and the vice president of operations-technology products group volunteered to present their findings (Table 5-1).

They had assembled company data and industry summary data for conglomerates, but they also added summary data for the "food/meat products" industry and "media/movie, television, and music production services and products" industries. These provided

Table 5-1.   Fowlers' Industry comparison spreadsheet and raw data.

Fowlers Industry Comparison

Conglomerate Industry	Revenue	SG&A	Cost of Goods	Cash-to-Cash Cycle Time	Inventory Days of Supply	Asset Turns	Gross Margin	Operating Income	Net Operating Income	Return on Assets
Fowlers	1000	7%	86%	197	91	1.52	14%	7%	4%	11%
National Service Industries	963	32%	62%	48	20	0.63	38%	5%	5%	3%
Maxxam Inc	2448	7%	82%	120	82	0.54	18%	11%	1%	6%
US Industries	3088	23%	66%	119	88	1.24	34%	11%	1%	13%
Pacific Dunlop Limited	2120	30%	66%	132	105	1.59	34%	4%	-3%	5%
Sequa Corporation	1773	14%	75%	127	102	1.37	25%	11%	1%	11%
GenCorp Inc	1047	4%	82%	95	76	1.05	18%	15%	12%	11%
Olin Corporation	1549	9%	77%	82	66	1.84	23%	14%	5%	20%
Federal Signal Corporation	1106	20%	67%	103	78	1.49	33%	13%	5%	15%
Kawasaki Heavy Industries Ltd	8395	12%	87%	253	137	1.13	13%	0%	-1%	0%
Valhi Inc	1192	17%	63%	144	118	0.70	37%	20%	6%	10%
Pentair Inc	2748	17%	71%	106	73	1.39	29%	12%	2%	12%
Tomkins PLC	5875	7%	81%	88	52	2.01	19%	12%	2%	17%
ITT Industries Inc	4829	24%	62%	96	65	1.40	38%	14%	5%	9%
Six Continents PLC	5939	27%	49%	39	17	0.69	51%	24%	11%	11%
TRW Inc	17231	9%	80%	42	23	1.40	20%	10%	3%	11%
Textron	13090	11%	73%	231	72	1.07	27%	16%	2%	13%
Johnson Controls Inc	18427	9%	83%	42	14	2.48	17%	8%	3%	15%
Dover Corporation	5401	21%	60%	120	89	1.47	40%	19%	10%	21%
Raytheon Company	16895	10%	76%	123	54	0.84	24%	14%	1%	9%
ABB Ltd	22967	19%	75%	170	68	0.99	25%	6%	6%	4%
RWE AG	48182	27%	68%	95	30	0.87	32%	6%	2%	4%
Emerson Electric	15480	20%	61%	104	74	1.37	46%	19%	7%	20%
Honeywell International	25652	12%	71%	111	75	1.36	29%	17%	6%	18%
United Technologies	26205	17%	69%	108	76	1.38	31%	14%	7%	14%
Koninklijke Philips Electronics NV	36668	17%	70%	105	73	1.31	30%	14%	25%	14%
Minnesota Mining and Manufacturing	16724	30%	46%	142	109	1.54	54%	23%	11%	27%
Vivendi Universal SA	40138	22%	62%	213	45	0.38	36%	16%	5%	5%
Siemens AG	86208	27%	66%	134	85	1.29	34%	7%	2%	7%
Tyco International Ltd	34037	22%	53%	488	102	0.41	47%	25%	12%	8%
General Electric Company	129417	37%	34%	566	65	0.39	66%	29%	10%	9%
Conglomerate Industry	100	30%	54%	291	78	0.67	46%	16%	11%	8%
Food : Meat Products Industry	100	13%	83%	49	52	2.13	17%	4%	3%	7%
Media - Movie, Television, & Music Production Services and Products	100	55%	46%	83	19	0.67	54%	0%	-4%	0%
Diversified Services - Miscellaneous Business Services	100	35%	61%	48	17	1.33	39%	4%	0%	4%
Industry Parity	**8395**	**17%**	**69%**	**119**	**74**	**1.31**	**31%**	**14%**	**5%**	**11%**
Industry Advantage	**4197**	**9%**	**35%**	**60**	**37**	**0.65**	**15%**	**7%**	**3%**	**6%**
Industry Superior - 90th Percentile										

(continues)

Table 5-1   *(continued)*

Fowlers Industry Comparison - Raw Data (in millions)

	Revenue $	SG&A $	Cost of Goods $	Inventory $	Receivable $	Total Assets $	Gross Margin $	Operating Income $	Net Operating Income $
Fowlers	1000.0	70.0	860.0	215.0	371.0	656.0	140.0	70.0	35.0
National Service Industries	563.3	182.0	351.2	19.2	89.0	898.4	212.1	30.1	27.0
Maxxam Inc	2448.0	168.7	1999.3	451.3	453.9	4504.0	448.7	280.0	33.9
US Industries	3088.0	721.0	2040.0	494.0	517.0	2492.0	1048.0	327.0	36.0
Pacific Dunlop Limited	2120.4	629.5	1405.6	405.2	328.4	1773.2	714.8	85.3	-71.1
Sequa Corporation	1773.1	246.6	1334.7	373.7	266.8	1731.1	438.4	191.8	24.0
GenCorp Inc	1047.0	40.0	855.0	182.0	135.0	1324.0	192.0	152.0	129.0
Olin Corporation	1549.0	132.0	1196.0	216.0	197.0	1123.0	353.0	221.0	81.0
Federal Signal Corporation	1106.1	220.7	739.7	157.6	168.0	991.1	366.4	145.7	57.6
Kawasaki Heavy Industries Ltd	8394.8	1040.9	7318.5	2743.4	3371.7	9875.0	1076.3	35.4	-81.7
Valhi Inc	1191.9	201.7	753.3	243.0	183.9	2256.8	438.6	236.9	76.6
Pentair Inc	2748.0	469.7	1952.5	392.5	468.1	2644.0	795.5	325.8	65.9
Tomkins PLC	5875.0	412.4	4780.7	677.6	1060.5	3906.5	1094.3	681.9	95.8
ITT Industries Inc	4829.4	1141.0	2993.5	531.3	814.9	4611.4	1835.9	694.9	264.5
Six Continents PLC	5939.0	1617.0	2895.0	133.0	850.0	13399.0	3044.0	1427.0	676.0
TRW Inc	17231.0	1557.0	13869.0	870.0	2328.0	16467.0	3362.0	1605.0	438.0
Textron	13090.0	1482.0	9534.0	1871.0	6791.0	16370.0	3556.0	2074.0	218.0
Johnson Controls Inc	18427.0	1642.9	15307.3	577.6	2928.3	9911.5	3119.7	1476.8	478.3
Dover Corporation	5400.7	1124.0	3230.1	783.2	903.2	4892.1	2170.6	1046.6	519.6
Raytheon Company	16895.0	1740.0	12836.0	1908.0	4566.0	26777.0	4059.0	2319.0	141.0
ABB Ltd	22967.0	4360.0	17222.0	3192.0	8328.0	30962.0	5745.0	1385.0	1443.0
RWE AG	48181.6	12814.0	32684.0	2721.0	12502.0	74224.7	15497.6	2683.6	1073.1
Emerson Electric	15479.6	3081.9	9410.0	1896.8	2551.2	15046.4	6069.6	2987.7	1031.8
Honeywell International	25652.0	3134.0	18095.0	3734.0	4623.0	25175.0	7557.0	4423.0	1659.0
United Technologies	26206.0	4473.0	18111.0	3756.0	4445.0	25364.0	8095.0	3622.0	1808.0
Koninklijke Philips Electronics NV	35658.0	5894.0	24837.0	4972.0	6122.0	36298.0	10821.0	4927.0	9043.0
Minnesota Mining and Manufacturing	16724.0	5064.0	7762.0	2312.0	2891.0	14522.0	8962.0	3898.0	1782.0
Vivendi Universal SA	40138.4	8935.1	24802.5	3032.1	21802.4	141965.0	15335.9	6400.8	2165.2
Siemens AG	86208.0	23209.0	57107.0	13284.0	18756.0	89298.0	29101.0	5892.0	2069.0
Tyco International Ltd	34036.6	7324.5	18180.0	5101.3	38759.0	111287.3	15856.6	8532.1	3970.6
General Electric Company	129417.0	47437.0	44087.0	7812.0	188317.0	437006.0	85330.0	37893.0	12735.0
Conglomerate Industry	100.0	30.0	64.3	11.6	66.7	200.0	45.7	15.7	11.2
Food - Meat Products Industry	100.0	13.1	82.7	11.8	7.5	62.5	17.3	4.2	2.9
Media - Movie, Television, & Music Production Services and Products	100.0	54.6	45.6	2.4	25.6	200.0	54.4	-0.2	-4.2
Diversified Services - Miscellaneous Business Services	100.0	35.1	61.0	2.8	16.7	100.0	39.0	3.8	-0.4

meaningful comparisons for the company's food and technology product groups, respectively. They used the most recent actual data and didn't bother with current-year data that were reported as preliminary. The team filled out the appropriate sections in the Fowlers' enterprise scorecard but had little time for analysis (Figure 5-1).

Even on the first examination of the data, several things jumped out.

First, the wide range of figures for Cost of Goods and Sales General and Administration costs made it clear that there is no standard for reporting these numbers from one company to another. Operating income seemed to be a good comparison point for expenses. "But there's still no way to compare supply chain costs using the data we have so far," the coach pointed out. "You can't add Cost of Goods and Sales General and Administration and supply chain costs to create a working scorecard metric. Total supply chain management costs are more activity based, and they can borrow from the other two categories, so you'd be double-counting certain costs if you just added them."

Figure 5-1.   Fowlers' enterprise scorecard.

Performance Attribute or Category	Level 1 Performance Metrics	Actual	Parity 50th Percentile	Advantage 70th Percentile	Superior 90th Percentile	Parity Gap	Requirement Gap	Requirement Opportunity
Supply Chain Delivery Reliability	Line Item On Time and In Full							
	Perfect Order Fulfillment							
Supply Chain Responsiveness	Order Fulfillment Cycle Time							
Supply Chain Flexibility	Upside Supply Chain Flexibility							
Supply Chain Cost	Cost of Goods	1%	1%	1%	1%			
	Total Supply Chain Management Cost	15.5%						
	SG&A Cost	0%	0%	0%	0%			
	Warranty / Returns Processing Costs	0.7%						
Supply Chain Asset Management Efficiency	Cash-to-Cash Cycle Time	197	119.0	84.0	48.0			
	Inventory Days of Supply	91	74	48	23			
	Asset Turns	2	1.3	1.5	1.6			
Profitability	Gross Margin	0%	0%	0%	0%			
	Operating Income	0%	0%	0%	0%			
	Net Income	0%	0%	0%	0%			
Effectiveness of Return	Return on Assets	0%	0%	0%	0%			

Second, the metrics of 197 days for the cash-to-cash cycle and 1.5 percent asset turns confirmed what many in the finance community seemed to think about Fowlers: It used physical assets well and cash assets poorly.

Third, the 7 percent operating income in the food products group compared well against the food/meat products industry. It was a similar story for technology products. But sales were declining in each business, and profits were nearly half of what they had been the previous year. The strategy of charging a premium price for a premium product wasn't holding, and in fact was causing some customers to go elsewhere.

As the team looked at the "parity opportunity" portion of the chart, their eyes got wide. As a conglomerate with a $1 billion in revenue, Fowlers' 7 percent operating income ($70 million) was only half the level of the conglomerate industry benchmark. To achieve parity in operating income, they would need to find another $70 million of additional benefit through supply chain performance.

Next, the corporate controller, director of logistics, and director of customer service took their turn. In addition to the review of enterprise supply chain and warranty/returns processing costs, they reviewed some data from their preliminary sample not yet recorded on the scorecard. They learned that combined food and technology products Line Item on Time and in Full performance was 22 percent—meaning that just 22 orders of 100 were delivered on time and complete. Perfect Order Fill Rate was 5 percent, Order Fulfillment Cycle Time was 4.1 days, and Upside Supply Chain Flexibility was 122 days. By the next week, they said they'd be ready to provide data for each product group scorecard and the enterprise scorecard.

By this time, everyone was nearly speechless. Each measure in the customer-facing section was new, and it was the first time that the team had really thought about overall delivery reliability through the customer's eyes.

The ensuing discussion sounded a bit like a classic session with a grief counselor; there was denial, bargaining, anger, and eventually acceptance of the data. Every member of the team wanted to bolt from the room and jump right into fixing the problem—as they had all done so many times before. Fortunately, it was the end of the day. Tomorrow's agenda would focus the team on something else, and a good night's sleep would put this information in perspective: The team had found an opportunity for the kind of improvement it needed to make.

■ Competitive Requirements Analysis

The agenda for Day Two is composed of two tasks: conducting competitive requirements (sometimes known as the chip exercise) and preparing for steering team review number one.

Rules for Prioritization

There are four attributes of supply chain performance:

1. Delivery reliability
2. Flexibility and responsiveness (combined)
3. Supply chain management cost
4. Asset management efficiency

The objective of the competitive requirements exercise is to prioritize these attributes for each customer or market channel, determining whether the company needs to perform each attribute—compared with other providers—at a superior level (90th percentile), at a level of advantage (70th percentile), or at parity (50th percentile).

There is a catch: For each customer or market channel, the team is only allowed to set one performance attribute at the superior level and one at the level of advantage. The other two attributes must be set at parity.

One last note, the requirements are established from the company's point of view as they relate to the competitive landscape of the future. This is not a firefighting exercise for trying to identify where to improve the most; it's a strategic exercise, focused on how to differentiate against stiff competition in the future.

Many companies are using the strategic categories written about in *The Discipline of Market Leaders* (by Michael Treacy and Fred Wiersema) defining operational excellence, customer intimacy, or product innovation as the strategy driver. The results of the competitive requirements exercise should reflect and support the strategy driver. At the end of the exercise, the team must reach consensus on the requirements for each supply chain. Empirically, it might help to assign numeric values to each chip: three for superior, two for advantage, and one for parity.

This exercise needs to be performed three times. It's performed first by the design team. It will be performed almost immediately afterward by the full steering team. The third time it's performed by each relevant business team as the Supply Chain Operations Reference process is spun further out through the enterprise. In each case, the coach should review the metric categories and definitions with the players along with available benchmarks, but actual data should not be revealed. That's because people tend to put the "superior" chip where they see the need for the most improvement, not necessarily where the strategic advantage lies.

At Fowlers, the coach facilitated as the design team went through the exercise (Figure 5-2).

Figure 5-2. Fowlers' competitive requirements summary for five channels.

Competitive Requirements		For each channel, prioritize strategic metric performance using 1 superior, 1 advantage, and 2 parity				
		U.S. Retail Markets	U.S. Distributor Markets	U.S. Direct-to-Consumer Markets	U.S. OEM-Key Accounts	U.S. Government
External	Supply Chain Reliability	Superior	Parity	Parity	Parity	Parity
	Supply Chain Responsiveness	Parity	Parity	Superior	Superior	Parity
	Supply Chain Flexibility					
Internal	Supply Chain Cost	Advantage	Superior	Advantage	Advantage	Superior
	Supply Chain Asset Management Efficiency	Parity	Advantage	Parity	Parity	Advantage

By using the five channels identified as being in scope (Table 3-6) as a baseline, the team determined that there were really only three supply chains with unique requirements. Fowlers' U.S. retail markets had the same overall performance requirements regardless of the product group. Similarly, the U.S. distributor markets and U.S. government had similar requirements independent of product type. Last, the U.S. direct-to-consumer markets and U.S. original equipment manufacturer/key accounts were grouped together with similar delivery, cost, and inventory requirements—again, with little distinction required from one product to another.

The results of the competitive requirements exercise were clear. To differentiate in the U.S. retail channel, Fowlers needed to achieve superior delivery performance, advantage supply chain cost, and parity performance in flexibility and asset efficiency.

To differentiate in the U.S. distributor and government markets, Fowlers needed to achieve superior performance in supply chain cost, advantage performance in asset efficiency, and parity on delivery performance and flexibility and responsiveness.

To differentiate in the demanding direct-to-consumer and original equipment manufacturer/key accounts, Fowlers needed to achieve superior performance in flexibility and responsiveness, advantage performance in supply chain cost, and parity on delivery performance and asset efficiency.

Preparing for Steering Team Review Number One

In advance of the first steering team review, consider the following points:

1. The project manager should be the principle person consolidating and preparing the presentation.
2. The project manager should conduct one-on-one discussions with steering team members who are responsible for key data, because they may be called on to provide explanation or detail.

3. Any rumors, objections, and other cultural issues that need to be addressed during the steering team meeting should be discussed candidly.
4. Speaking roles should be determined for the steering team review. In addition to David, design team members who did a lot of homework should be given a chance for exposure.

Overall, the objectives of steering team review number one are to review supply chain metric definitions and preliminary query data, conduct the competitive requirements exercise with the entire steering team, review preliminary industry comparison sample and benchmark data, and establish expectations for steering team review number two.

The corporate controller, the vice president of sales and marketing-food products group, the director of logistics, and the director of customer service worked with David to prepare the first steering team review. They established the following agenda:

❏ Project roadmap status.
❏ Reminder—communications plan.
❏ Conduct chip exercise with the steering team—review design team results.
❏ Review preliminary supply chain metric data—Fowlers' enterprise scorecard.
❏ Review preliminary benchmark data—Fowlers' industry comparison.
❏ Make decisions required today.
❏ Set expectations for steering team review number two.

6

Week Four: Scorecards

Tackle the Difference Between Competitive Requirements and Actual Performance

After a proper debrief of highlights from the steering team meeting, the design team starts to work on the objectives of Week Four: Review data on all scorecards, and begin the process of calculating and assigning financial value to gaps.

▦ The Scorecard Review

For a scorecard to be complete, it must include actual data for each metric, appropriate industry benchmarks, competitive requirements, and gap calculations. In a perfect world, scorecards would cascade neatly from the enterprise level to each business or from the enterprise level to each market segment. But that rarely happens, as the Fowlers' design team learned on Day One of the fourth week.

As the review process took shape for each of the three scorecards (enterprise, food products, and technology products), the team discovered that courageous conversations were necessary to make sense of the data and focus the design effort. The first day centered on the actual and benchmark columns.

Discussion of the enterprise scorecard (Table 6-1), led by the corporate controller and director of logistics, considered three issues. First, although enterprise-wide customer-facing data indicated "below parity" performance, the aggregate data were not helpful in pinpointing the severity of some of the issues. The team agreed that segmenting the reliability, responsiveness, and flexibility metrics by business group, Stock Keeping Unit (SKU), and/or customer "ship to" was the right direction.

A second compromise had to do with the fact that balance-sheet data were only available at the corporate level; trying to precisely allocate that information back to the product groups would have taken a major balance-sheet restructuring. As a result, the team simply used sales as means to allocate inventory on the product group scorecards.

Table 6-1. Fowlers' Enterprise scorecard.

Fowlers Enterprise SCORcard

Performance Attribute or Category	Level 1 Performance Metrics	Actual	Parity 50th Percentile	Advantage 70th Percentile	Superior 90th Percentile	Parity Gap	Requirement Opportunity (Sums Technology and Food Product Groups)
External — Supply Chain Delivery Reliability	Line Item On Time and In Full	49.2%	74.7%	85.0%	95.0%	-26%	
	Perfect Order Fulfillment	30.2%	74.0%	81.0%	88.0%	-43.8%	
Supply Chain Responsiveness	Order Fulfillment Cycle Time	9 days	10 days	6.5 days	3 days	1 day	Enables Inventory and Delivery Reliability
Supply Chain Flexibility	Upside Supply Chain Flexibility	91.5 days	60 days	45 days	29 days	-31.5 days	
Internal — Supply Chain Cost	Cost of Goods	86%	69%	35%		-17%	
	Total Supply Chain Management Cost	15.5%	9.5%	6.7%	3.9%	-6%	$58600000
	SG&A Cost	7%	17%	9%		10%	
	Warranty / Returns Processing Costs	0.7%	1.5%	1.0%	0.5%	1%	$1250000
Supply Chain Asset Management Efficiency	Cash-to-Cash Cycle Time	197	97.9	63.8	29.7	-99	
	Inventory Days of Supply	91	74	37		-18	$18099583
	Asset Turns	2	2.5	4.7	7.0	-1	
Shareholder — Profitability	Gross Margin	14%	31%	15%		-17%	$77949583
	Operating Income	7%	14%	7%		-7%	
	Net Income	4%	5%	3%		-2%	-
Effectiveness of Return	Return on Assets	11%	11%	6%		0%	-

Publicly available financial data researched by PRAGMATEK at Marketguide and Hoovers.com. Subscription data available through Supply Chain Council and Performance Measurment Group (PMG).

Third, and most important, the scorecards weren't organized in the same way as the supply chain competitive performance requirements generated during Week Three. The scorecards were organized by business—because that's how the data existed. The supply chain requirements were determined by market/customer channel—because that represented the ideal situation the team wanted to create. So translating from the competitive requirements to the scorecard would be a challenge.

For example, the food products group supplied goods to food service, retail, and government channels-each requiring its own priorities (summarized in Figure 5-2). How could these different requirement profiles be aligned on a single scorecard?

"You'll come up against more than one roadblock like this," the coach said. "We're not always going to have complete data or perfect alignment. What is your preference? Go back and do some more homework, or pick a direction to go forward?" The team was impatient, and a few minutes of conversation made it clear that there probably was no perfect solution. So they agreed to apply the priorities of the retail channel because it represented the operating unit's largest share of revenue.

The food products scorecard discussion (Table 6-2), led by the group's vice president of sales and marketing, summarized three learning points and considered two compromises. Here was the first learning point: Although it was perceived internally as superior in delivery performance, the actual food products group performance was below cross-industry average; there was an opportunity to improve its competitive gap by focusing on delivery reliability metrics.

Here was the second learning point: The supply chain cost factors helped the team better understand why they were below parity in operating income. Comparing individual components of these costs with industry benchmarks highlighted new opportunities for cost reduction that would help put the division at a more acceptable level.

The third learning point was that the food products business team, to focus on cash-to-cash efficiency, would first need to create

Table 6-2. Fowlers' food products scorecard with competitive requirements.

	Performance Attribute or Category	Level 1 Performance Metrics	Actual	Parity 50th Percentile	Advantage 70th Percentile	Superior 90th Percentile	Parity Gap	Requirement Gap	Requirement Opportunity
External	Supply Chain Delivery Reliability	Line Item On Time and In Full / Perfect Order Fulfillment	68.4% / 35.0%	74.7% / 74.0%	85.0% / 81.0%	95.0% / 88.0%	-6.3% / -39.0%	-26.6% / -53.0%	$350,000
	Supply Chain Responsiveness	Order Fulfillment Cycle Time	5 days	10 days	6.5 days	3 days	5 days	5 days	Enables Inventory and Delivery Reliability
	Supply Chain Flexibility	Upside Supply Chain Flexibility	90 days	60 days	45 days	29 days	-30 days	-30 days	
Internal	Supply Chain Cost	Cost of Goods / Total Supply Chain Management Cost	86% / 17.0%	69% / 9.5%	61% / 6.7%	53% / 3.9%	-17% / -7.5%	-25% / -10.3%	$25,750,000
		SG&A Cost	7%	17%	12%	7%	10%	5%	
		Warranty/Returns Processing Costs	1.5%	1.5%	1.0%	0.5%	0.0%	-0.5%	$1,250,000
	Supply Chain Asset Management Efficiency	Cash-to-Cash Cycle Time* Enterprise Data* .25	197	97.9	63.8	29.7	-99.1	-99.1	
		Inventory Days of Supply* Enterprise Data* .25	91	74	48	23	-17.4	-17.4	
		Asset Turns* Enterprise Data* .25	1.5	2.5	4.7	7.0	1.0	1.0	$6,464,137
Shareholder	Profitability	Gross Margin / Operating Income	14% / 7%	31% / 14%	39% / 19%	47% / 23%	-17% / -7%	— / —	$33,814,137
		Net Income	NA	—	—	—	—	—	—
	Effectiveness of Return	Return on Assets	NA	—	—	—	—	—	—

new data-extraction tools for analysis and better leverage its new Enterprise Resource Planning (ERP) system; percentage allocation would not get to SKU level data for problem-solving purposes.

In this way, the scorecard exercise helped members of the food products business team to visualize a strategy of supply chain excellence as a means to compete, not on list price of its products but on total landed price (or cost to serve) to customers.

The first necessary compromise focused on how to distribute the market/customer channel competitive requirements—the chip exercise priorities from Week Three—onto the food products scorecard. Although their supply chain definition matrix identified four potential supply chains (Table 3-4) that had three distinct competitive scenarios (Figure 5-2), the food products business team agreed to adopt the retail market's superior/parity/advantage/parity priorities for their scorecard gap baseline. Why? Because it was the largest and most profitable segment. Supply chain cost was a high priority in all segments, and lead time requirements for the direct-to-consumer markets and original equipment manufacturers (OEM)/key accounts could initially be set up on a fee-for-service basis for requirements above parity.

The second compromise was recognized at the enterprise level. The competitive opportunity for asset management efficiency would be defined through the enterprise scorecard until information systems and financial reporting could support truer activity-based definitions. As discussed earlier, to calculate opportunity the team used an allocation rule of 25 percent of enterprise cash-to-cash and inventory numbers.

Discussion about the technology products group (Table 6-3), led by David Able in his capacity as the group's vice president of operations, summarized three unique learning points and considered necessary two compromises.

The first learning point was this: Although the decision to outsource manufacture of several products succeeded at achieving lowest unit cost, it drastically reduced the responsiveness and flexibility metrics—which in turn affected inventory levels. The second learn-

Table 6-3. Fowlers' technology products scorecard with competitive requirements.

	Performance Attribute or Category	Level 1 Performance Metrics	Actual	Parity 50th Percentile	Advantage 70th Percentile	Superior 90th Percentile	Parity Gap	Requirement Gap	Requirement Opportunity
External	Supply Chain Delivery Reliability	Line Item On Time and In Full / Perfect Order Fulfillment	10.0% / 1.0%	74.7% / 74.0%	85.0% / 81.0%	95.0% / 88.0%	-64.7% / -73.0%	-64.7% / -73.0%	$877,500
	Supply Chain Responsiveness	Order Fulfillment Cycle Time	8 days	10 days	6.5 days	3 days	2 days	5 days	Enables Inventory and Delivery Reliability
	Supply Chain Flexibility	Upside Supply Chain Flexibility	110 days	60 days	45 days	29 days	-50 days	-81 days	$32,850,000
Internal	Supply Chain Cost	Cost of Goods / Total Supply Chain Management Cost / SG&A Cost	87% / 14.0% / 7%	69% / 9.5% / 17%	61% / 6.7% / 12%	53% / 3.9% / 7%	-18% / -4.5% / 10.1%	-26% / -7.3% / 5.1%	
		Warranty/Returns Processing Costs	0.7%	1.5%	1.0%	0.5%	0.8%	0.3%	$0
	Supply Chain Asset Management Efficiency	Cash-to-Cash Cycle Time* Enterprise Data* .45	197	97.9	63.8	29.7	-99.1	-99.1	$11,635,446
		Inventory Days of Supply* Enterprise Data* .45	91	74	48	23	-17.4	-17.4	
		Asset Turns* Enterprise Data* .45	1.5	2.5	4.7	7.0	1.0	1.0	
Shareholder	Profitability	Gross Margin / Operating Income	13% / 6%	31% / 14%	39% / 19%	47% / 23%	-18% / -8%	— / —	$45,362,946
		Net Income	NA	—	—	—	—	—	
	Effectiveness of Return	Return on Assets	NA	—	—	—	—	—	—

ing point was that the new metrics on service reliability provided empirical evidence to complaints by customers that the company was "hard to do business with." In the third learning point, by assembling supply chain costs it became clear that material acquisition expenses outpaced all other cost increases. Inbound transportation, normally calculated as a cost of material, was isolated for all to see. The last learning point was similar to one of the lessons for the food products group: There was considerable opportunity to improve operating income by attacking supply chain costs, improving use of working capital, and better leveraging the new Enterprise Resource Planning (ERP) system.

Like the food products group, the technology products group's first necessary compromise focused on how to distribute the market/customer channel performance requirements onto the technology products scorecard. The technology products business team agreed to adopt the direct-to-consumer and original equipment manufacturers/key accounts parity/superior/advantage/parity (PSAP) priorities for their scorecard gap baseline. The second compromise was that competitive opportunity for asset management efficiency would be defined at the enterprise level on the basis of information systems and financial reporting. In the meantime, to calculate the opportunity gap, David used 45 percent of the enterprise cash-to-cash and inventory dollars. That effort completed a full day of work.

◼ The Gap Analysis

The agenda for Day Two is focused on completing the scorecard gap analysis. The first step is to calculate the mathematical opportunity for each metric. This is done by calculating both the parity gap and the competitive requirement gap and then subtracting actual performance for each metric from the benchmark number determined by the competitive requirement for the category.

If the gap analysis results in a negative number, it means actual performance is less than the benchmark (e.g., the gap between an actual delivery performance of 78 percent and competitive require-ments of 92 percent is 14 percent). The next step is to translate each gap number into a profit potential; the most frequently used meas-ure is operating income.

The calculations are straightforward for the internal metrics but can be subjective for customer-facing metrics. The basic calcula-tion that the design team, and ultimately the business team, must agree on is the anticipated effect on operating income of improve-ments in delivery performance, responsiveness, and flexibility. This is often more art than science, but there are some accepted ap-proaches:

The Lost Opportunity Measure. This calculates the revenue lost before order-entry because of lack of availability of a product.

The Canceled Order Measure. This measure calculates revenue lost after order-entry because of canceled orders that result from poor delivery performance.

The Market Share Measure. This measure attempts to project a revenue increase based on achieving competitive advantage in the customer-facing metric categories.

Because any approach will have its tradeoffs, just make sure to document the assumptions and details for the financial analysis and identify some of the steering team or business team members to help validate preliminary numbers.

In Fowlers' case, the design team agreed on the organization of the gap analysis itself, agreeing with the norm that all the opportunity dollars should be calculated using an operating income; this would allow them to add up the numbers in the "opportunity" column of the scorecard. Here are some other decisions made by the team:

❏ Group all delivery reliability metrics, and use "lost opportu-nity" and "canceled order" calculation methods. The de-tailed calculation required an estimated revenue increase multiplied by the gross margin, resulting in an operating in-come opportunity.

❏ Use opportunities in the supply chain responsiveness and flexibility category to improve results in reliability and cash-to-cash. This minimized the risk of double counting.

❏ Group the supply chain cost category, and base the opportunity calculation on the total supply chain cost and warranty/returns processing cost metrics.

❏ Base the supply chain asset management efficiency category on the cash-to-cash metric. Because these data were only available at the enterprise level, the calculation first multiplied the enterprise working capital times the cost of capital and then multiplied it by the percent of total revenue for each product group.

❏ Use the number in the profitability section as the sum total of the operating income improvements on the scorecard.

Here are the assumptions made for the food and technology product group gap analysis (Tables 6-2 and 6-3):

❏ Food products delivery reliability assumed a 1 percent increase in revenue because of availability of product at the point of order using a 14 percent gross margin. The 1 percent was based on analysis of lost and canceled orders, conducted by the customer service department over the course of one week.

❏ By using the same study, the technology products group assumed a 1.5 percent increase in revenue using a 13 percent gross margin.

❏ Total supply chain cost was based on the cost centers allocated to material acquisition, order management, Information Systems cost, planning, finance and administration, and inventory carrying cost. Inventory carrying cost and warranty/returns processing cost were eliminated from the opportunity column to avoid double counting.

❏ Warranty/returns processing cost was based on the cost centers to support return transactions, warehouse storage, and transportation.

With a total enterprise working capital of $514 million and a cost of capital at Fowlers of 10 percent, the economic profit potential for Fowlers is $51.4 million. This number was allocated to food products at 25 percent and technology products at 45 percent representing their share of total Fowlers' revenue.

The team's homework for the next week was to identify steering team and extended team members to validate the calculations and, more important, the detailed assumptions behind the numbers.

7

Week Five: Initiating AS IS Material Flow and Steering Team Review Number Two

Transition from Data Collection to Analysis and Action

Week Five marks the close of the pure information-gathering phase of the Supply Chain Operations Reference (SCOR) project life cycle and bridges to the third phase of supply chain design. Specifically, the design team will launch the AS IS material flow and metric defect analysis. To logistical types this is the most interesting part of the project, with the biggest potential for improvement. The objectives for the week are to finish the scorecard gap analysis, initiate the AS IS material flow, and conduct the second steering team review.

◼ Validating Gap Analysis and Preparing Steering Team Review Number Two

The first agenda item for Day One is for each assigned sub-team to review its validated scorecard gap analysis, including revised assumptions, calculations, and feedback from validation resources. The goal is for the entire design team to achieve consensus for each metric on the total opportunity calculated on the scorecard.

The second agenda item is to identify the design team members who will make presentations in the second steering team review and to prepare and conduct a dry run before the steering team review. Do not underestimate the impact of a crisp, clear, and concise presentation delivered by the people who did the work. This review will be the first one where data will be presented that may be contentious.

The agenda for the steering team review includes the following:

❏ Project roadmap status
❏ Review consolidated competitive requirements by supply chain
❏ Review enterprise and product group scorecards (Tables 6-1 to 6-3)
❏ Gap analysis results
❏ Set expectations for steering team review number three

The validation effort ultimately did not change the numbers or assumptions, but the process did reveal some change-management stages that would have to occur. The careful organization of the sub-teams for each metric and the choice of influential validation resources helped to manage the length of these stages as the wider Fowlers' audience was introduced to "the numbers."

Change Management: Dealing with Denial

In the first stage, reactions are predictable as the design team's work spreads through the organization: The numbers are wrong; we aren't that bad.

The technology and food products business teams, when presented with the scorecard gap analysis, reacted predictably: They challenged the numbers. This happens in almost all projects. That's why it's important to have the right design team members from each of the product groups present to explain the data and have their validation resources sitting right next to them (as opposed to a consultant). For people seeing the data for the first time, this builds confidence that the numbers are, in fact, reliable and quickly puts the focus on the issues.

Change Management: Placing Blame

The second-stage reaction is to allocate blame, which is easier than taking responsibility for the results. Positioning design team members to share their personal perspectives on the gap analysis, and to review competitive performance facts, helps accelerate business unit leaders through this stage and moves them beyond the convenient catch-all phrase: "But we're unique."

Change Management: Book the Numbers

The third reaction is to confuse acceptance of the analysis with actually having solved the problem. Agreeing on the opportunity does not improve anything. At this point, the business team is excited at the value of improving supply chain performance; based on benchmarks and competitive requirements, the numbers can add up fast. But it's too soon to start booking the savings in corporate forecasts and memos to the board. The real value of change will show up as part of the next phase.

In closing out Phase II, the Fowlers' project team learned an important lesson: one that would be repeated again and again. They learned that the main goal of the scorecard analysis and validation effort is to manage change, not just to complete a deliverable. Their ability to quickly learn the Supply Chain Excellence process, understand the main idea of the deliverables, and then carefully transfer that knowledge to the wider Fowlers' audience was critical. With ad-

vanced apologies to Dilbert, they realized the essential change management value of "greasing the skids," "getting others up to speed,"
and "touching base with key leaders."

Launching Phase III: Design Material Flow

The third phase of Supply Chain Excellence focuses on material flow
design-the effort to identify inefficient and ineffective material movements between locations that are ultimately linked to the metric gaps
calculated in the scorecards. The design is completed in three steps.

First, the design team focuses on physical material flow.
Primary deliverables are AS IS geographic maps, a planning process
matrix, and AS IS thread diagram.

Second, the team completes a disconnect and gross opportunity analysis including metric defect analysis, a brainstorm event, a
project portfolio, and an opportunity analysis.

Third, the team identifies a TO BE material flow with deliverables including new SCOR Level Two strategies, TO BE material
geographic maps, and TO BE thread diagrams.

Initiating AS IS Material Flow

Day Two of this week is occupied with learning about SCOR Level
Two processes and creating geographic maps of the material flow.
The design team must address three things: (1) determining the
number maps at the appropriate level of detail; (2) assembling the
geographic maps; and (3) characterizing each physical location using
the SCOR Level Two process types.

About the SCOR Level Two Process Types

The SCOR model version 8.0 decomposes from five Level One
process categories—PLAN, SOURCE, MAKE, DELIVER, and

RETURN—to twelve supply chain execution process types and five planning process types (Figure 7-1).

Level Two elements identify the types of material flow strategy used by item that are used to move material from location to location.

Figure 7-1.   SCOR Level Two process types.

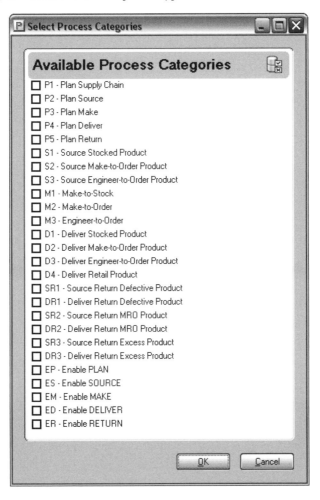

Source

The SOURCE Level Two process types—source stocked product (S1), source make-to-order product (S2), and source engineer-to-order product (S3)—attempt to characterize how a company purchases raw materials and finished goods. The key factors in determining the source process types are the trigger event from PLAN, MAKE, and DELIVER processes, and the state of the material at the supplier when the purchase order is placed.

S1—a make-to-stock environment—is generally triggered by a forecast requirement from PLAN, MAKE, or DELIVER, and the supplier has the item available in a finished-goods inventory before the purchase order; the material movement is a simple pick, pack, and ship. S2—a make-to-order environment—is usually triggered by a specific customer-order requirement from MAKE or DELIVER. The supplier must convert raw materials or semifinished goods in response to a purchase order; manufacturing or assembly lead time is added to transportation. S3—an engineer-to-order environment—is most often triggered by a specific customer order and design specifications from MAKE or DELIVER. A qualified supplier must be identified before a purchase order is issued; the purchase order quantity is dependent on specific customer order quantities and is often executed only once.

Frequently, the supply of a given raw material or finished good evolves through each of these process types over the course of its product life cycle. Just as frequently, a location may use one, two, or all three SOURCE process types. Each purchased component has one of these three strategies.

Make

The MAKE Level Two process types—make-to-stock (M1), make-to-order (M2), and engineer-to-order (M3)—attempt to characterize how your company converts raw materials to work-in-process to finished goods status. The conversion process generally is located in a manufacturing site or sites but can be applied to a warehouse as well. The key factors in determining the make process types are the trigger event from PLAN or DELIVER and the state of the material when the customer order is placed.

M1 is generally triggered by a forecast or replenishment requirement from PLAN; the conversion process is executed before the customer order. The work-order quantity is independent of specific customer order quantities and is often related to a replenishment economic order quantity. M2 is generally triggered by a specific customer order requirement from DELIVER; the conversion of raw materials or semifinished goods is executed in response to a customer order. The work order quantity is equal to customer order quantities. M3 is generally triggered by a specific customer order requirement and design specifications from DELIVER. Manufacturing engineering specifications (product, process, and/or product) must be completed before the issue of a work order. The work order quantity is dependent on specific customer order quantities and is usually executed once.

As with raw materials, work-in-process items can evolve through each process type over the course of the product life cycle, and a location may use one, two, or all three MAKE process types. Each item will have one of these strategies identified in master data.

Deliver

The DELIVER Level Two process types—deliver stocked product (D1), deliver make-to-order product (D2), and deliver engineer-to-order product (D3)—attempt to characterize how a company processes its finished goods in response to customer orders. The delivery process frequently is located in a warehouse site but can be applied to manufacturing or supplier direct ships as well. The key factors in determining the deliver process types are the trigger event from PLAN or the customer, and the state of the material when the customer order is placed.

D1 is generally triggered by a forecast from PLAN that places finished goods in inventory on an available-to-promise basis before the customer order. Inventory levels are independent of specific customer order quantities. D2 is usually triggered by a specific customer order requirement of finished goods that are planned to be converted, assembled, or configured after the receipt of the customer order. The sales order quantity is equal to customer order quantities. D3 is triggered by a specific customer order requirement and design or manufacturing specifications to be completed before the issue of a sales order. The sales order quantity is equal to customer order quantities and is usually executed once. Finished goods items can evolve through each process type over the course of the product life cycle, and a location may use one, two, or all three DELIVER process types.

Return

The RETURN Level Two process types—return defective product (R1), return maintenance, repair, and overhaul product (R2), and return excess product (R3)-attempt to characterize how a company returns its finished goods in response to customer return authorizations. The return process frequently is located in a warehouse site but can be applied to a manufacturer or supplier that directly ships as well.

There are two perspectives built into the return process types: returns from customers (DRx) and returns to suppliers (SRx). Key factors in determining the return process types are the trigger event from the customer of PLAN and the state of the material when the customer order is placed.

R1 is triggered on a small scale by a warranty claim initiated by a customer and on a large scale by a product recall triggered by internal resources executing the process steps in PLAN Return. R2 is triggered by a planned maintenance event initiated by PLAN return, an unplanned maintenance event initiated by engineering, maintenance, or other technical resources. R3 is triggered by planned inventory returns based on contractual agreements with specific customers or unplanned inventory returns based on category management data for retail or distributor shelf space.

Plan

PLAN supply chain (P1) is the process of taking actual demand data and generating a twelve- to eighteen-month supply plan including rough-cut capacity for a given supply chain. The basic steps require the following:

❑ A unit forecast that is adjusted for marketing and sales events.
❑ A supply plan that constrains the forecast based on availability or resources, such as inventory, manufacturing capacity, and transportation.
❑ A balance step where demand/supply exceptions are resolved, financial projections are created, and unit plans are updated on the system.

This planning process type is most closely associated with the leading practice of sales and operations planning.

PLAN source (P2) is the tactical planning process of comparing total material requirements with the P1 constrained forecast generated above, and generating a twelve- to sixteen-week material requirements resource plan based on P3 to satisfy landed cost and inventory goals by commodity type. This translates to a material release schedule that lets the buyer know how much product must be purchased on the basis of current orders, inventory, and future requirements. It is carried out for items on the bill of materials and may be aggregated by supplier or commodity type. This planning process type is most closely associated with the leading practices in material requirements planning.

PLAN make (P3) is the tactical planning process of comparing actual production orders plus replenishment orders coming from P4 against the P1 constrained forecast generated above and then generating a twelve- to sixteen-week master production schedule resource plan to satisfy service, cost, and inventory goals. This translates to material requirements, P2, that tell the purchasing (or commodity)

manager how much product is required by item and a master production schedule that lets the plant scheduler know how much total
product must be made by ship date. It is carried out for each plant
location and may be aggregated to region or another geography type.
This planning process type is most closely associated with the leading practices of master production scheduling.

PLAN deliver (P4) is the tactical planning process of comparing actual committed orders with the P1 constrained forecast generated above and developing a twelve- to sixteen-week distribution resource plan to satisfy service, cost, and inventory goals. The plan
generally translates to replenishment requirements that tell the plant
manager how much product to plan for, P3, and visibility into available-to-promise inventory. P4 is carried out for each warehouse
stocking location and may be aggregated to regional levels or another
geography type. This planning process type is most closely associated
with the leading practices of distribution requirements planning.

PLAN return (P5) is the process of aggregating planned returns
and generating a return resource plan to satisfy service, cost, and inventory goals. The plan generally translates to return requirements
that tell the manufacturing, maintenance, and logistics teams the
type, volume, and schedule of planned and known unplanned returns. P5 is carried out for each warehouse and maintenance return
and may be aggregated to regions or other geography type.

▨ Creating a Geographic Map

The first job in creating a geographic map is to determine the number of maps. On the one extreme is a pure **logical** view where one
map can represent from a macro level how products move using one
supplier, one manufacturer, one warehouse, and one customer to illustrate material flow. On the other extreme is a pure **actual** view
where illustrating product flow for each supply chain checked on the
matrix (Table 3-4) including every supplier, manufacturer, warehouse, shipping, and customer receiving location (very much like a
network study). Which level is the right answer? Unfortunately, it

depends. Experience would suggest to use the highest level that can point to both tactical and strategic inefficiencies in service levels, transportation cost, lead-time (cycle time), and days of inventory. Most teams create an actual geographic map for some of their more complicated supply chains for visual impact and then create one logical geographic map representing all supply chains to make documentation a less complex task.

With the number and level of detail defined, construction of the maps can begin. Physical locations are usually placed on the map first, followed by the product-family routes between the locations. It may be of benefit to focus your transportation design team member on collecting and summarizing the route data using freight bills. Freight bills contain the important details of the item, quantity, sales value, freight expense, and delivery cycle time, point of origin, and destination. Depending on the transportation carriers used, much of these data may be available electronically. In Fowlers' case, the technology products' actual geographic map (Figures 7-2 and 7-3) summarizes the locations and material flow of four product families from supplier location to manufacturing site to warehouse location. It also

Figure 7-2.   Technology products actual geographic map locations.

Figure 7-3.   Technology products actual geographic map with product flow.

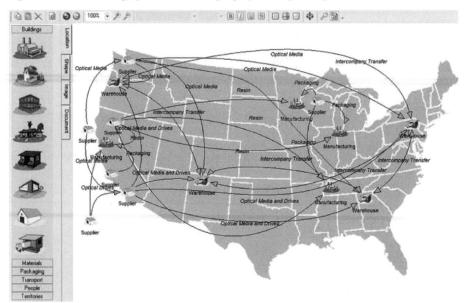

highlights all warehouse-to-warehouse and warehouse-to-manufacturing moves.

The next step is to determine SCOR Level Two process types used by each location on the geographic maps. Start by identifying appropriate process categories specific to the location, that is, SOURCE, MAKE, DELIVER, and/or RETURN. Next, determine the process type-stock-to-order, engineer-to-order, defective, excess inventory, and maintenance, repair, and overhaul. A typical manufacturing location might have a profile defined by S1, S2, M1, and D2.

In this case D2 refers to direct shipments configured in the manufacturing warehouse to customer specs based on the exact customer order. Not all locations have to have all process categories. A warehouse, for example, may have only D1 and D2 profiles because the plan and deliver replenishment orders are driving the supply from manufacturing. The same warehouse that also issues purchase orders to a contract manufacturer for purchased finished goods may have a profile that includes S1, D1, and D2. In Fowlers' case, the

Figure 7-4.   Technology products logical geographic map with SCOR Level Two classifications.

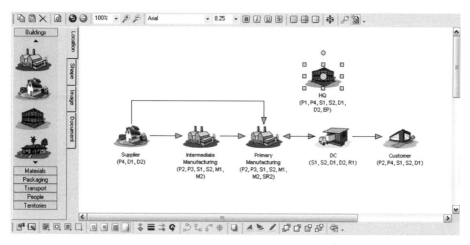

manufacturing locations used all process types for SOURCE, MAKE, and DELIVER and just R1 returns. By using the logical geographic map, they illustrated their primary configuration characterized as S2 for key suppliers of resins and packaging: S1 for contract manufacturers that supplied optical media and optical drives; M2 for CD-ROM replication and M1 for fulfillment and life cycle management; and D2 customer direct parcel ship for CD-ROM replication and D1 for stocking programs for fulfillment and life cycle management. The primary technology products configuration of the Fowlers' corporate distribution locations was characterized as S1, S2, D1, and D2 for optical drives and optical media (Figure 7-4).

With the AS IS geographic maps under construction, the team was ready to move on the planning matrix, thread diagram, and metric defect analysis. The project team agreed that the workload for everyone would be greater in this phase than the scorecard.

8

Week Six: The Planning Process Matrix, Thread Diagram, and Metric Defect Analysis

Build a Deep Understanding of Material Flow

This week, the design team will look at supply chain material flow from two perspectives: process and data. The issue with many supply chains is the way they evolve: one supplier at a time and customer-by-customer. They tend to be less strategic and more events-driven than those that have been engineered. For improvement to occur, process and data are needed to align supply chain strategy with material flow efficiency. Process looks at the macro issues of how supply chain material flows relate to planning, execution, and strategy (i.e., make-to-order vs. make-to-stock). Data look at the micro issues of why the company has failures with respect to supply chain reliability, responsiveness, and flexibility and negative variances in costs for transportation, warehousing, and inventory to meet stated service levels.

The Planning Process Matrix

The planning process matrix is an analytical tool that works to document the horizon, interval for update, and planning level for all the Supply Chain Operations Reference (SCOR) planning and scheduling processes. Horizon is the planning time period (i.e., eighteen months, one year, one quarter). Interval is the time between updates (i.e., a quarter, month, week, daily, real-time). Planning level refers to where the planning data are stored, aggregated, and analyzed (i.e., Profit and Loss business entity, Planning Family, Stock Keeping Unit (SKU), Stock Keeping Unit by Location(SKUL), item). The goal is to identify and document disconnects in planning and scheduling that lead to material flow inefficiency and to illustrate them on the thread diagram. Figure 8-1 illustrates a generic planning process relationship map, and Table 8-1 summarizes the completed Fowlers' planning process matrix.

The design team found three "ahas" in putting the matrix together. First, they were trying to use Sales and Operations Planning to do a little of everything and ended up focusing on orders and short-term revenue; when mixing planning and execution, execution always wins. The consequence was little or no effort in rough-cut capacity beyond six months. This led to demand/supply mismatches that caused either excess inventory or service problems, especially in retail promotional periods. The second "aha" was that the tactical planning processes were absent; enough said. Third, the team found that the scheduling processes were adequate; not surprising because they had perfected the art of fighting fires with pure muscle.

The Thread Diagram

The thread diagram is a process view of the geographic map that illustrates the material flow, material strategy, and planning process relationship map. Figure 8-2 illustrates a Technology Products thread diagram illustrating their "stocking program" customers; these are CD titles that they stock on behalf of their customers and

(text continues on page 102)

Figure 8-1. Planning process relationship map.

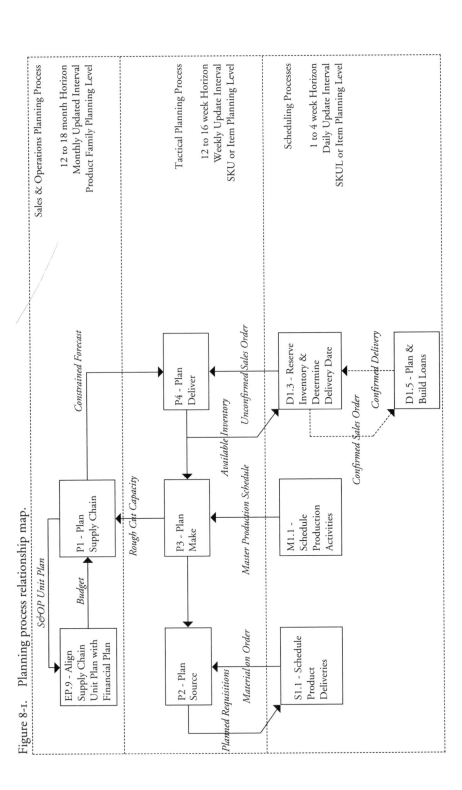

Sales & Operations Planning Process

12 to 18 month Horizon
Monthly Updated Interval
Product Family Planning Level

Tactical Planning Process

12 to 16 week Horizon
Weekly Update Interval
SKU or Item Planning Level

Scheduling Processes

1 to 4 week Horizon
Daily Update Interval
SKUL or Item Planning Level

EP.9 - Align Supply Chain Unit Plan with Financial Plan

P1 - Plan Supply Chain

S&OP Unit Plan

Budget

Constrained Forecast

P4 - Plan Deliver

D1.3 - Reserve Inventory & Determine Delivery Date

Unconfirmed Sales Order

Confirmed Delivery

D1.5 - Plan & Build Loans

Available Inventory

Rough Cut Capacity

P3 - Plan Make

M1.1 - Schedule Production Activities

Master Production Schedule

Confirmed Sales Order

P2 - Plan Source

S1.1 - Schedule Product Deliveries

Planned Requisitions

Material on Order

Table 8-1. Fowlers' planning process matrix.

	Process	Horizon	Update Interval	Level
Budget Business Planning	EP.9 - Align Supply Chain Unit Plan with Financial Plan	Annual budgeting process begins in July to August.	Fowlers formally updates the budget each quarter as part of its SEC reporting requirements.	Budgets are created in using the chart of accounts Profit & Loss (P&L) business groups.
S&OP	P1 - Plan Supply Chain	Fowlers does not have a consolidated S&OP process; the business groups each have their own "forecasting" process and associated horizon. In general, the businesses spend most of their planning time on the current month plus the next two.	All business groups update their "forecasts" once a month; each business is on a different cycle that is dependent on the Presidents management meetings.	All business groups utilize a combination of product family forecast groups and business unit cost centers (driven largely by plants and warehouses).
Tactile Planning	P2 - Plan Source P3 - Plan Make P4 - Plan Deliver	Because the S&OP process focuses so heavily on the near term and the scheduling processes dominate daily and weekly activity, tactical planning processes seem to be absent in all Fowlers business groups.	Not applicable	Not applicable
Scheduling	S1.1 - Schedule Product Deliveries M1.1 - Schedule Production Activities D1.3 - Reserve Inventory & Determine Delivery Date D1. - Plan & Build Loads	The scheduling process horizon ranges from two weeks to four weeks depending on the business group.	Material Requirements Planning (MRP) is run daily and is displayed by day for 7 days, by week for the next 3 weeks, and by month for twelve months. Available-to-Promise (ATP) occurs real time with re-scheduling running each way.	All planning is at the SKUL level.

Figure 8-2.   Technology products AS IS thread diagram for their "stocking
program" customers.

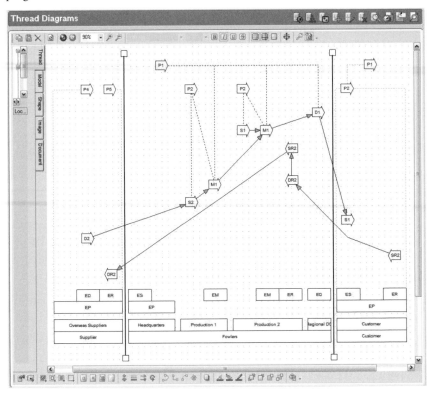

then fulfill according to their customer's customer order. The thread
diagram was generated from their AS IS logical geographic map.

The pieces of a thread diagram include the following:

1. The location labels at the bottom (for Fowlers' Headquarters,
   Production 1, Production 2, and Regional distribution center.
2. The process and material strategy performed in each location (S2, Source Make-to-Order Product, and M1, Make-
   to-Stock in location Production 1).
3. The generic physical process flow as illustrated by the solid
   lines connecting process labels (M1 in Production 1 to M1
   in Production 2). In this case Production 1 is a factory that
   solely makes subcomponents for Production 2.
4. The planning information flows as illustrated by the dotted
   connections (P1, Plan Supply Chain to/from M1 Production
   1). These flows were derived from the planning process matrix.

The Fowlers' design team, after learning how to read the chart, came to several conclusions. First, there was a potential strategy mismatch from D2 Overseas Suppliers to S2 Production 1 to M1 Production 1; poor flexibility and inventory turns seemed to be a result of this issue.

Second, P2 Production 1 and P2 Production 2 were not connected to the forecast; that, in combination with the lack of connection between the Fowlers' P2s and the Overseas Suppliers' P4—Plan Deliver, illustrated how suppliers had limited visibility with respect to longer-term requirements. That, in turn, provided the supplier with poor rough-cut capacity planning data, making it hard to support upside spiked demand.

Second, the M1 to P2 to S2 connection in Production 1 and Production 2 illustrates a Material Requirements Plan (MRP) that is driven off of production schedules, driving lots of purchase order changes. Third, P4—Plan Deliver and P3—Plan Make weren't making the connection between P1 (Sales and Operations Planning), M1, and D1, resulting in less business management and more order management. Fourth, sending the returns back to Production 2 facilities

Figure 8-3.   Food products LOTIF defect analysis. This analysis uses system flags to identify major reasons that a line was not delivered on time and/or complete.

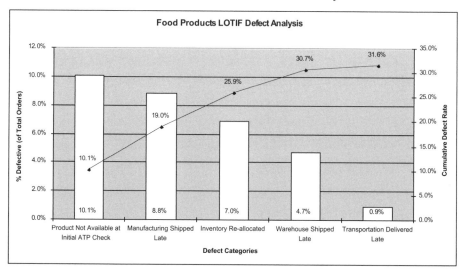

(remember, this is a logical map) versus to a regional distribution center may be inefficient. Finally, there were potentially duplicate enable processes (enable make [EM]) between Production 1 and Production 2.

Although the coach helped with the interpretation at first, the team soon got accustomed to speaking the language of SCOR and was able to begin the process of "thread diagramming" potential future-state scenarios.

Metric Defect Analysis

Metric defect analysis is borrowed from the Six Sigma and Total Quality Management disciplines. The basic idea is that for each metric identified in the scorecard during Phase Two, the team must analyze the failures or defects as they begin to answer the "why" question (Figure 8-3). For example, the food products group line order on time and in full performance is 68.4 percent, meaning 31.6 percent of the lines weren't delivered On-Time and In-Full. The objective of defect analysis is to use simple analytical tools such as Pareto charts, run charts, histograms, control charts, and so forth, to help answer the first "why did this line fail" question. This is the first step in root-cause analysis; an important guideline is to use the technology system to help with the first sort. Many companies resort to manual research right away. Although sometimes unavoidable, manual research right out of the gate generally reduces the frequency of analysis, further reinforces "not using the system," and limits the sample size for analysis.

The Fowlers' design team would need another week to collect the data, but they did identify for each metric a first draft of defect categories.

Perfect Order Fulfillment (and Line Item On Time and In Full)

❑ Product Not Available at Initial Available-to-Promise Check
❑ Manufacturing Shipped Late
❑ Inventory Reallocated
❑ Warehouse Shipped Late
❑ Transportation Delivered Late

Order Fulfillment Cycle Time

❏ Orders that have cycle times exceeding the target in each of the major cycle time segments
❏ Order Receipt to Order Confirmed
❏ Order Confirmed to Shipment Created
❏ Shipment Created to Order Picked
❏ Order Picked to Order Shipped
❏ Order Shipped to Order Delivered
❏ Orders with More than One Category

Upside Supply Chain Flexibility

❏ Part numbers that have planned lead times exceeding the target in each of the major lead time categories
❏ Plan, Source, Make, Deliver
❏ Part Numbers with More than One Category

Cost of Goods, Total Supply Chain Management, and Total Return Management and Warranty Costs

❏ Use Pareto analysis for the level three categories (i.e., material cost, customer service cost, warehouse cost), and then calculate variances for the top 80 percent of the spend

Inventory Days of Supply

❏ For working inventory, conduct Pareto analysis on the inventory days of supply for each Stock Keeping Unit, highest to lowest
❏ For nonworking inventory, Pareto dollars of excess, slow moving, and obsolete

▨ Planning for Next Week: Disconnect Analysis

The data from the metric defect analysis set the stage for the next steps in the process: disconnect and opportunity analysis. The disconnect analysis provides the first opportunity to involve the extended team (and others) in a formal way. The brainstorming event that is central to this step can engage as many as fifty people collecting and sorting up to one thousand anecdotal issues. The metric defect data and the issues list provide the foundation for the first draft of the project portfolio. Figures 8-4 to 8-10 are samples of the work the Fowlers' team would accomplish in the week ahead. Back to the present, the agenda for Day Two focuses on initiating the metric defect data collection, updating the geographic maps and thread diagrams, and figuring out who to invite to the brainstorm event.

Figure 8-4.   Technology products order fulfillment cycle time histogram. This chart portrays the actual order cycle time spread across different time buckets and helps the team define a "defective cycle time" (>7 days).

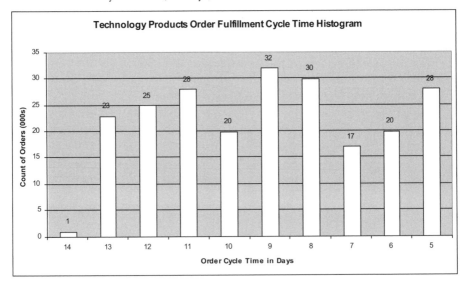

Figure 8-5.   Technology products order fulfillment cycle defect analysis. This analysis attempts to answer the question of which cycle time category contains the most defective orders.

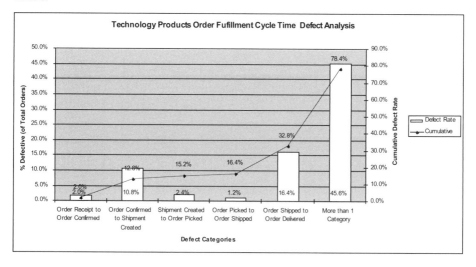

Figure 8-6.   Technology products order fulfillment cycle defect profile. This analysis attempts to aggregate total defective orders by category and gives the team an idea of where the most issues occur.

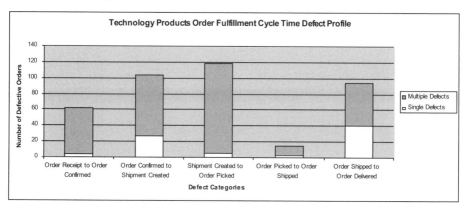

Figure 8-7.   Food products upside supply chain flexibility histogram. This analysis identifies the count of part numbers in different buckets of lead time and helps define "defective" parts for this metric (>60 days).

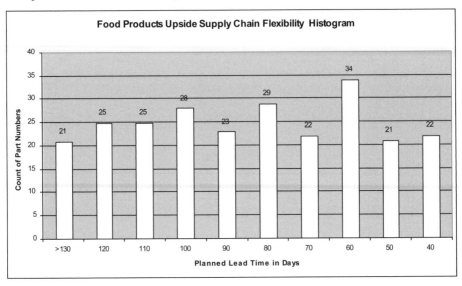

Figure 8-8.   Food products upside supply chain flexibility defect analysis. This analysis
identifies which planned lead time category contributes to the defects. The cumulative
82.8 percent defect rate means that only 17.2 percent of food product part numbers are
better than target.

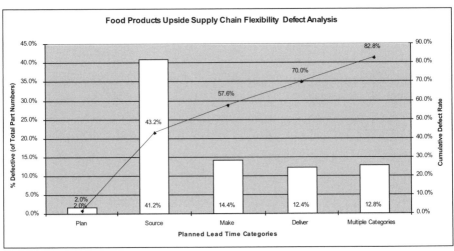

Figure 8-9.   Food products stacked planned lead times sample for multiple categories. This answers two "Why?" questions: which parts are defective and which planned lead time(s) cause the defect.

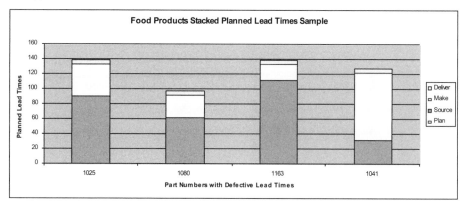

Figure 8-10. Food products total supply chain management cost defect analysis. Defects are defined as "variances" to plan and/or other spending waste.

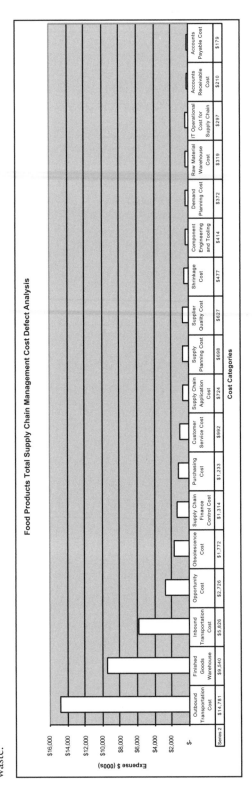

Food Products Total Supply Chain Management Cost Defect Analysis

	Outbound Transportation Cost	Finished Goods Warehouse	Inbound Transportation Cost	Opportunity Cost	Obsolescence Cost	Supply Chain Finance Control Cost	Purchasing Cost	Customer Service Cost	Supply Chain Application Cost	Supply Planning Cost	Supplier Quality Cost	Shrinkage Cost	Component Engineering and Tooling	Demand Planning Cost	Raw Material Warehouse Cost	IT Operational Cost for Supply Chain	Accounts Receivable Cost	Accounts Payable Cost
Series 2	$14,781	$9,540	$5,826	$2,726	$1,772	$1,314	$1,233	$992	$724	$698	$627	$477	$414	$372	$319	$297	$210	$179

Cost Categories

Expense $ (000s)

9

Week Seven: Material Flow Disconnect Analysis and Steering Team Review Number Three

Add Up the Value While Getting the Whole Company Involved

What do the numbers fifty, twenty, one thousand, fifteen, and three have in common? They're the typical results of a successful disconnect analysis, focused on identifying all the issues, inefficiencies, and assorted problems of moving goods from suppliers through the company and on to customers.

Fifty is the typical number of people who participate in a day-long brainstorm event. Twenty is how many disconnects or issues a typical person can come up with in an hour. A thousand is the number of disconnects or issues the whole team can generate in the same amount of time. Fifteen is approximately the number of projects that will be identified to eliminate the issues. Three is the percent of savings (relative to sales) that an average performing company will achieve by implementing these projects. For example, a supply chain supporting $100 million in revenue typically may yield $3 million in gross opportunity savings.

The objectives of the seventh week are to (1) complete the disconnect analysis, which includes conducting the brainstorm event, documenting the brainstorm event output, and assembling the preliminary project portfolio; and to (2) prepare for the third steering team review, providing the first executive look at scorecard gaps.

▪ Planning the Brainstorm Event

A well-planned brainstorm event takes the data and detail collected and analyzed through the metric defect analysis (Figures 8-3 to 8-10) and integrates them with an efficient means of gathering and aggregating employee experiential data. The combination creates a positive feeling of teamwork, shared vision of the real issues, and confidence in the benefit impact. It also provides for greater involvement in the process, giving extended team members a feeling of contribution and, ultimately, ownership of the changes.

There are six ingredients to a good brainstorming event:

1. An appropriate invitee list
2. Effective communication, including advance invitation, project overview, and instructions for event preparation
3. Organized brainstorm categories using the metric defect analysis and scorecard data
4. An appropriate venue
5. Predefined leadership roles for the design team that carry from defect analysis through to opportunity analysis
6. Documentation approach that captures the individual disconnects, problem groups, preliminary projects, and benefits estimate

Invitees

Select people who are close to the day-to-day and week-to-week details of all facets of the movement of materials. Attempt to represent the locations identified in the geographic map as well as expertise from planning, sourcing, manufacturing, marketing and sales, warehouse, transportation, finance, and customer service. For the brainstorm event, the quantity of issues, with examples, is a critical factor. Don't reach too high in the organization; participants at higher levels of management have more trouble generating a detailed list and often cannot point to specific examples. The examples are what help drive the root cause analysis. Invitees are considered part of the extended team listed in the project charter.

Effective Communication

The invitation letter needs to clearly convey the purpose of the event, preparation instructions, and the basics of where, when, and so on. The invitation needs to be in participants' hands one to two weeks in advance; anything less gives the impression that the project is poorly planned and limits the quality of individual preparation. A project overview session conducted before the event provides participants with a wide-angle view of the project, including a status report on the key deliverables of the scorecard gap analysis, AS IS geographic map, and metric defect analysis. Further, it gives them a short tutorial on their homework assignment, including the definition of a "disconnect" (any issue or barrier to achieving a desired level of performance), how to use the Excel template (Figure 9-1), and an expectation of identifying twenty disconnects.

Organized Brainstorm Categories

Setting up brainstorm categories in advance (and incorporating them into the project overview presentation above) helps the participants generate more detail faster. There are three common methods of selecting categories. First, you can use Supply Chain Operations Reference (SCOR) process categories: PLAN, SOURCE, MAKE, DELIVER, RETURN, and ENABLE. Second, you can use physical locations, as illustrated in either the actual or logical geographic maps. Third (and the one Fowlers picked), you can use the Level One SCOR metrics and associated defect analysis. This is a major

Figure 9-1.   Disconnect summary template. Each person participating in the event needs to identify at least twenty issues from their experience; describe the issue, including an item, customer, or supplier example; and include their initials.

Description for Disconnect or Issue - Example	Initials	Disconnect Serial Number
Item master data setup errors cause poor planning data to pass to plants and suppliers resulting in poorer forecasts – item 093232	PB	1
No visibility to customer demand – consumption rate leads to unpredicted spiked demand resulting in customer shortages – order 0930211	PB	2
		3
		4
		5
		6
		7
		8
		9
		10
		11
		12
		13
		14
		15
		16
		17
		18
		19
		20

organizational decision; during the first part of the event, participants will need to place their issues under a metric and appropriate defect category (Figure 9-2).

Other essential data that are helpful include the actual, benchmark, and gaps from the scorecard (Figure 9-3).

The Appropriate Venue

The ideal venue is a large rectangular room with enough theater seating for all attendees. The category titles (typed in large print on 8.5 × 11 paper), defect analysis, and scorecard data are taped on the wall and spaced equally around all four walls of the room (Figure 9-4). Many teams have used "Post-Its," flip chart paper, or "butcher block paper" to capture the individual disconnects. Most of the time will be spent in small groups, frequently standing next to the collected items in a brainstorm category; the activity does not work as well as in a small conference room.

Figure 9-2.   Extended team members during the initial brainstorm part of the agenda perform a three-step task. First, they walk their individual disconnects (recorded on "Post-It" type notes) to the primary metric of impact; second, they decide which defect category is most appropriate; and, third, they "stick" the disconnect on (under) the appropriate defect category.

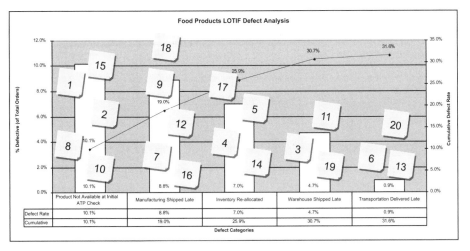

Predefined Leadership Roles

For the brainstorm event, design team members formalize their role in the knowledge-transfer process, transitioning from student to teacher. The project manager (or coach) serves as the master of ceremonies, reviewing the agenda and instructions for each step. He or she also serves as pace keeper, moderator of conflict, and general role model for everyone. Each extended team member is assigned to a brainstorm category; it is important to make the assignment on the basis of each individual's expertise. Each design team member is assigned to lead (co-lead) a brainstorm category and facilitate the disconnect analysis steps. This includes grouping similar issues, defining problem statements, and assembling the preliminary project portfolio. It's a proven strategy for each brainstorm category leader to have also participated in that metric's defect analysis.

Documentation Approach

The preliminary project portfolio worksheet is filled out for each brainstorm category in two steps: assemble problem definition data

Figure 9-3. Posted scorecard data including actual, benchmark, and gaps will help the extended team gain perspective on the overall improvement challenge.

Performance Attribute or Category	Level 1 Performance Metrics	Actual	Parity 50th Percentile	Advantage 70th Percentile	Superior 90th Percentile	Parity Gap	Requirement Gap	Requirement Opportunity
Supply Chain Delivery Reliability	Line Item On Time and In Full	68.4%	74.7%	85.0%	95.0%	−6.3%	−26.6%	$350,000
	Perfect Order Fulfillment	35.0%	74.0%	81.0%	88.0%	−39.0%	−53.0%	
Supply Chain Responsiveness	Order Fulfillment Cycle Time	5 days	10 days	6.5 days	3 days	5 days	5 days	Enables Inventory and Delivery Reliability
Supply Chain Flexibility	Upside Supply Chain Flexibility	89 days	60 days	45 days	29 days	−30 days	−30 days	

External

Figure 9-4.   There are many ways to prepare the room. Listed here is a room scenario.

Line Item On Time and In Full	Order Fulfillment Cycle Time	
Total Supply Chain Management Cost	Brainstorm Room	Upside Supply Chain Flexibility
	Cost of Goods	Inventory Days of Supply	

and then calculate impact (Chapter 10). Figure 9-5 is a screen shot of the whole template, with one worksheet for each brainstorm category.

Figure 9-6 describes how to fill out a worksheet. As illustrated, the team needs to:

❑ Document the brainstorm category.
❑ Give each problem statement a unique number.
❑ Write a detailed description of the problem.
❑ Summarize a problem with a statement phrase.
❑ List the individual disconnect IDs comprising the issue.
❑ List the metric defect category where the issues were grouped.
❑ List the metric defect category rate.
❑ Agree to the weight of this problem relative to the other problems within the defect category.
❑ Calculate the problem impact by multiplying the problem weight by the defect category rate.
❑ And, finally, list the SCOR process where the problem most likely occurs.

▨ Conducting the Brainstorm Session

The Fowlers' brainstorm team included the entire design team; Chief Operating Officer Brian Dowell; product development managers; buyer/planners; customer service representatives; cost accountants; marketing analysts; material planners; focus factory managers; sales managers; product line managers from both the technology and food products groups; functional experts for pur-

(text continues on page 120)

Figure 9-5.   Preliminary project portfolio worksheet.

Brainstorm Category	Problem Statement Number	Problem Statement Phrase	Problem Statement Description	Individual Disconnect IDs	Metric Defect Category	Metric Defect Category Rate	Problem Weight within Defect Category	Problem Impact	SCOR Process
The title of the brainstorm category is listed here. i.e., Line Item On Time and In Full	After the disconnects have been aggregated to problems, a number is assigned, i.e. 1.01, 1.02, etc.	The problem statement phrase briefly describes the problem.	The problem statement description is a sentence or two that describes the problem. It must be relevant to all of the individual disconnects and include an example, i.e. part number, supplier, or customer.	The individual disconnect IDs are recorded here.	This comes directly from the metric defect analysis.	This is the overall defect rate for the category and is taken directly off the defect analysis pareto chart.	This is the weight the team assigns to the problem. For each defect category the weights of all the problems must add to 100%.	This is a calculated field multiplying the METRIC DEFECT CATEGORY RATE times the PROBLEM WEIGHT. This is the estimated impact to the SCOR Level One metric	To the best of their ability, the team attempts to identify the SCOR element where the problem occurs. Some teams use Level Two categories, others use Level Three categories.

Figure 9-6. Preliminary project portfolio worksheet—problem definition.

Brainstorm Category	Problem Statement Number	Problem Statement Phrase	Problem Statement Description	Individual Disconnect IDs	Metric Defect Category	Metric Defect Category Rate	Problem Weight within Defect Category	Problem Impact	SCOR Process
The title of the brainstorm category is listed here (i.e., Line Item On Time and In Full)	After the disconnects have been aggrgated to problems, a number is assigned, i.e., 1.01, 1.02, etc.	The problem statement phrase briefly describes the problem.	The problem statement description is a sentence or two that describes the problem. It must be relevant to all of the individual disconnects and include an example, i.e., part number, supplier, or customer.	The individual disconnect IDs are recorded here.	This comes directly from the metric defect analysis.	This is the overall defect rate for the category and is taken directly off the defect analysis pareto chart.	This is the weight the team assigns to the problem. For each defect category the weights of all the problems must add to 100%.	This is a calculated field multiplying the METRIC DEFECT CATEGORY RATE times the PROBLEM WEIGHT. This is the estimated impact to the SCOR Level One metric.	To the best of their ability, the team attempts to identify the SCOR element where the problem occurs. Some teams use Level Two categories, others use Level Three categories.

chasing, order management, planning, distribution, and manufacturing from the corporate applications group; a transportation manager; an import/export manager; a warehouse manager from corporate logistics; a market research analyst; forecast analysts for each of the product families; and a business development manager from the corporate marketing group. In all, there were forty people on the list. As mentioned earlier, the design team agreed to use their six SCOR Level One metrics as the brainstorm categories. Their rationale was to get the extended team thinking about the relationship of each issue to the defect data and why things failed.

The planning director was assigned to be team leader for the "line on time and in full" category. "Order fulfillment cycle time" was led by the purchasing director; the director of manufacturing oversaw discussion of "upside supply chain flexibility"; "total supply chain management cost" was handled by the director of logistics/customer services; the corporate controller led the "cost of goods" discussion; and the vice president of sales and marketing for the food products group led "inventory days of supply" with help from the director of applications. David Able served as the master of ceremonies, and the coach was used as a floater between teams helping them as needed.

Fowlers' Brainstorm Event

The agenda for the brainstorm event at Fowlers had five line items and looked like this:

1. *Introduction.* David reviews the agenda, room layout, brainstorm categories (line item on time and in full, order fulfillment cycle time, upside supply chain flexibility, and total supply chain management cost, cost of goods, and inventory days of supply), and associated defect analysis, and introduces the category leaders.
2. *Initial Brainstorm: Sixty Minutes.* David facilitates the brainstorming activity, getting all those involved to identify at least twenty individual disconnects. Fowlers opted for the manual version where the Post-It notes were filled out on-site. Participants had one hour to transpose their homework, with one disconnect per note. David reminded those who missed the overview that a good disconnect is one that contains an accurate description of the issue, uses a full sentence, references a real example (e.g., list an item, supplier, customer), provides a frequency estimate (e.g., daily, weekly, monthly), and includes

their initials. They then had to identify the primary metric the issue impacted and stick it under the appropriate defect category (Figure 9-7 for individual disconnect examples under the "Poor Forecast Management—7.18" problem statement).

3. *Affinity Diagrams: 120 Minutes.* By using the predetermined extended team list, David moved people to their appropriate brainstorm categories with their design team leaders. They spent two hours reading through the disconnects and grouping them under each metric defect category. Next they were tasked with completing the problem definition and impact sections of the preliminary project portfolio worksheet.

4. *Question and Answer Review: 60 Minutes.* David then facilitated a public question-and-answer review of each team's problem statements. There was overlap where similar problems oc-

Figure 9-7.   The individual disconnects behind the "Poor Forecast Management—7.18" problem statement, under the "Product not Available at ATP Check" defect category, under the "Line On Time and In Full Metric."

Description for Disconnect or Issue—Example	Initials	Disconnect Serial Number
New product forecasts are inaccurate and result in lost opportunities.	PO	217
Inaccurate forecasting on new products.	LZ	26
Better market information for new product forecast.	CJ	267
Forecast at product family level does not help with individual SKU variance.	SJ	469
Integrate new product growth rates into sales budgets and forecasts.	PA	551
Too heavy a reliance on sales forecasts for new products.	RT	242
Repair parts are not forecasted as separate demand points.	YU	431
Item master data setup errors that cause lack of planning passing to plants or vendors.	JB	181
Lack of accountability between field forecasting, marketing forecasting, and supply chain forecasting.	CB	236
No visibility of sales to end customers and sales to dealers clouded by return.	KB	308

curred in different metrics. This would be rectified during the
project consolidation process (Chapter 10).

    5. *Documentation: 120 Minutes.* The individual disconnect tem-
plate and preliminary project portfolio worksheet are the two
main tools to help document the brainstorm output. Fowlers'
disconnect analysis session yielded 838 individual disconnects
in six brainstorm categories and an initial sixty-two problem
groups with their own statements. For a detailed example, consider the line on time and in full category, which yielded
twenty groups of problems representing 147 individual disconnects (Figure 9-8).

After an exhausting day, the first agenda item for the design
team on Day Two of this week is to prepare for steering team review
number three; below is a tentative agenda. The second item is to
begin to assemble a disconnect analysis summary for each metric.
The coach demonstrated how to build a fishbone diagram using the
brainstorm category as the head of the fish, metric defect categories
as the primary bones, and the problem statements as the secondary
bones (Figure 9-9). He also showed how to build a Pareto diagram
(Figure 9-10) by sorting problem statements from highest to lowest
impact. Although the team grasped the logic, they all agreed that this
task would carry over to homework.

▣ Conducting Steering Team Review Number Three

Prepare and conduct steering team review number three with the
following agenda:

- ❏ Project roadmap status.
- ❏ Education on disconnect process.
- ❏ Introduce team disconnect.
- ❏ Share disconnect statistics.
- ❏ Review group problem statements.
- ❏ Decisions required today.
- ❏ Expectations for steering team review number four.

Figure 9-8. Fowlers preliminary project portfolio worksheet—line item on time and in full problem definitions.

Brainstorm Category	Problem Statement Number	Problem Statement Phrase	Problem Statement Description	Individual Disconnect IDs	Metric Defect Category	Metric Defect Category Rate	Problem Weight within Defect Category	Problem Impact	SCOR Process
Line On Time and In Full	7.06	Poor definition of customer allocation rules	Poor or no customer automated allocation rules and re-confirmation communication plans cause unnecessary and unwanted re-allocation of inventory causing ship date changes and customer frustration over unannounced late orders.	448,453,406, 174,232,40, 146,12,258, 180	Inventory Re-allocated	7.0%	50.0%	3.5%	D1.3, ED
Line On Time and In Full	7.20	Rush Order override FIFO	Special requests to Customer Service to expedite perceived priority accounts from Sales and Marketing causes shipment delays for other equally valuable customers.	319,295,182, 386,385,212, 432,317,493, 383,4,315, 497	Inventory Re-allocated	7.0%	35.0%	2.5%	ED
Line On Time and In Full	7.07	Inventory Transaction Errors—Can't Ship	Per DC tracking data, 5% of the total orders daily cannot ship due to (suddenly) product not being available.	361,375,374, 367,368,145, 184,249,266, 245	Inventory Re-allocated	7.0%	15.0%	1.1%	D1.9
Line On Time and In Full	7.09	Manufacturing Schedule Attainment Rules are not Aligned to Service Requirements	Schedule attainment rules are based on total volume not mix which leads to production order grouping that do not meet product availability objectives.	488,147,461	Manu-facturing shipped late	8.8%	20.0%	1.8%	M1.1

(continues)

Figure 9-8. *(continued)*

Brainstorm Category	Problem Statement Number	Problem Statement Phrase	Problem Statement Description	Individual Disconnect IDs	Metric Defect Category	Metric Defect Category Rate	Problem Weight Within Defect Category	Problem Impact	SCOR Process
Line On Time and In Full	7.08	Manpower Resources	Unplanned absenteeism negatively effects production capacity.	335,333,101, 35,252,37,30, 225,185	Manufacturing shipped late	8.8%	15.0%	1.3%	M1.3, EM
Line On Time and In Full	7.13	Poor Dependent Demand Sharing	A lack of visibility (or sharing) of internal, sister plant demand occurs 95% of the time on 40% of the orders.	443,499,477, 22,497,438, 478	Manufacturing shipped late	8.8%	15.0%	1.3%	EM
Line On Time and In Full	7.14	New Product Component Availability	New product component availability and lack of communication effects ability to manufacture 15% of the time.	167,339,398, 434,202,	Manufacturing shipped late	8.8%	15.0%	1.3%	EM
Line On Time and In Full	7.04	ATP Check Rule Includes Planned Orders	Poor manufacturing schedule attainment causes inaccurate sales order confirmation because the ATP is confirming against planned orders not in physically manufactured product.	198,184,316, 442,191,288, 292,290,170	Manufacturing shipped late	8.8%	10.0%	0.9%	D1.3, ED, EM
Line On Time and In Full	7.10	Internal Quality	Non-conforming parts impact internal manufacturing 10% of the time.	59,430	Manufacturing shipped late	8.8%	10.0%	0.9%	M1.3

Line On Time and In Full	7.17	Stretched Manufacturing Capacity	Lack of equipment resources cause capacity shortages to meet large and impact orders.	161,39	Manu-facturing shipped late	8.8%	10.0%	0.9%	P3
Line On Time and In Full	7.16	Secondary Supplier	According to material data in the SYSTEM, 95% of our supplied components do not have a secondary supplier.	25,317,437	Manu-facturing shipped late	8.8%	5.0%	0.4%	ES
Line On Time and In Full	7.11	External Customer Sales Plan	For 70% of our planning, we have a lack of visibility to the customer's demand or promotions resulting in no forecast and a 36% sales plan error.	321,255,217, 26,267,469, 551,242,431, 181,236,308	Product not available at ATP check	10.1%	37.0%	3.7%	P1.1, EP
Line On Time and In Full	7.18	Poor Forecast Management	SKU level forecasts are inaccurate due minimal analysis, poor input from known sales and marketing input, and a lack of corporate discipline to support one forecast.	217,26,267, 469,551,242, 431,181,236, 308	Product not available at ATP check	10.1%	37.0%	3.7%	P1.1
Line On Time and In Full	7.12	New Product-Manufacturing Lead Time & Planning not Aligned	New Product Development items are not planned and released to production with enough lead-time for production to meet customer orders/demand in units and timetable.	385,142,203, 257,418	Product not available at ATP check	10.1%	26.0%	2.6%	P1, EP
Line On Time and In Full	7.01	Carriers Violate EDI Business Rules	Transportation providers do not adhere to the contractual obligations of EDI transmission requirements on a weekly basis.	1,20,31,232	Trans-portation delivered late	0.9%	33.3%	0.3%	ED6

(continues)

Figure 9-8. (continued)

Brainstorm Category	Problem Statement Number	Problem Statement Phrase	Problem Statement Description	Individual Disconnect IDs	Metric Defect Category	Metric Defect Category Rate	Problem Weight within Defect Category	Problem Impact	SCOR Process
Line On Time and In Full	7.02	Carrier Delivery Performance is Unreliable	Transportation providers are not rigorously scorecarded and performance issues are not systematically dealt with.	384,222,521, 478, 476, 370,227,483, 75,310,372, 475,147,149, 571,109	Transportation delivered late	0.9%	33.3%	0.3%	D1.12, ED6
Line On Time and In Full	7.03	Fowlers Does Not Control Customer Delivery Appointments	Fowlers relies on carrier to make customer delivery appointments.	22,434,268, 557,271,23, 444	Transportation delivered late	0.9%	33.3%	0.3%	D1.2, D1.3, D1.13
Line On Time and In Full	7.15	Poor Supplier Delivery Reliability	Purchased finished goods arrive late from vendors causing missed shipments to customers.	183,351,29, 218,417,209, 353,446,264	Warehouse shipped late	4.7%	50.0%	2.4%	S1, ES
Line On Time and In Full	7.05	Poor Inventory Accuracy at Shipping DC	Location and quantity errors cause allocated orders to ship late.	67,228,144	Warehouse shipped late	4.7%	25.0%	1.2%	D1.8
Line On Time and In Full	7.19	Customer "Order Complete" Requirement	Customer orders are held for 100% quantity fill creating late late shipments	369,318,154, 158,148,72	Ware house shipped late	4.7%	25.0%	1.2%	D1.5, ED

Figure 9-9. Fishbone summary of the Fowlers' line on time and in full disconnect analysis.

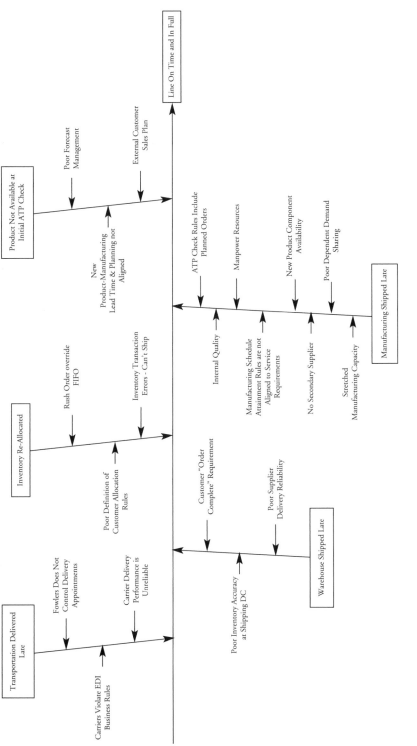

Figure 9-10.   Pareto analysis of the Fowlers' line on time and in full disconnect analysis.
The numbers are slightly different because of rounding errors.

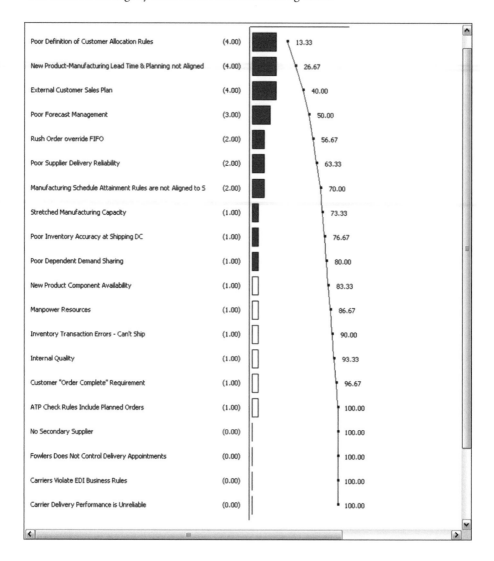

10

Week Eight: The Project Portfolio

How to Take Sixty-Two Issues Down to Fifteen Projects

There is no easy way to take all of the information collected in the brainstorm session and turn it into a working plan of action, but that's the job of the week: consolidating the sixty-two problems across six metrics into a concise set of projects and completing impact-effort assessments for each of them. The tools the team will use are the Supply Chain Operations Reference (SCOR) elements, affinity diagram techniques, and project portfolio worksheet. To reiterate, the objectives of Week Eight are to complete any unfinished documentation, consolidate problems into projects, and complete the impact-effort assessment.

▇ Consolidating Problems to Projects

The four-step process (Figure 10-1) of consolidating problems into projects is an easier task with experience using the Excel spreadsheet functions "filter" and "sort." In preparation for the first day's meeting, the project manager consolidates the problems from each of the

Figure 10-1.   Problem statement to project list consolidation process.

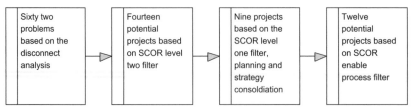

| Sixty two problems based on the disconnect analysis | Fourteen potential projects based on SCOR level two filter | Nine projects based on the SCOR level one filter, planning and strategy consoldiation | Twelve potential projects based on SCOR enable process filter |

metric worksheets onto a single worksheet called something like "All Metrics." With the "AutoFilter" on, the consolidation process begins. There are three levels of filtering that, when applied in the proper order, seem to yield the best results.

Figure 10-2.   Filtering the data field "SCOR Process" using the custom autofilter "contains D1."

A	C	D	E	F	G	H	I	J	K	L
Brainstorm Category	Project Number	Problem Statement Number	Problem Statement Phase	Problem Statement Description	Individual Disconnect IDs	Metric Defect Category	Metric Defect Category	Problem Weight within Defect Category	Problem Impact	SCOR Process
Line On Time and In Full	1	7.06	Poor definition of customer allocation rules	Poor or no customer automated allocation rules and re-confirmation communication plans cause unnecessary and unwanted re-allocation of inventory causing ship date changes and customer frustration over unannounced late orders.	448, 453, 406, 174, 232, 40, 146, 12, 256, 180	Inventory Re-allocated	7.0%	50.0%	3.5%	D1.3, ED
Line On Time and In Full		7.20	Flush Order override FIFO	Special requests to Customer Service to expedite perceived priority accounts from Sales and Marketing causes shipment delays for other equally valuable customers.	319,295,182,386,38 5,212,432,317,492,3 83,4,315,497	Inventory Re-allocated	7.0%	35.0%	2.5%	ED
Line On Time and In Full	1	7.07	Inventory Transaction Errors - Can't Ship	Per DC tracking data, 5% of the total orders daily cannot ship due to (suddenly) product not being available.	361, 375, 374, 367, 368, 266,					
Line On Time and In Full		7.09	Manufacturing Schedule Attainment Rules are not Aligned to Service Requirements	Schedule attainment rules are based on total volume not mix which leads to production order grouping that do not meet product availability objectives.	488,					
Line On Time and In Full		7.06	Manpower Resources	Unplanned absenteeism negatively effects production capacity.	325, 252, 185					
Line On Time and In Full		7.13	Poor Dependent Demand Sharing	A lack of visibility (or sharing) of internal, sister plant demand occurs 95% of the time on 40% of the orders.	443, 497,					
Line On Time and In Full		7.14	New Product Component Availability	New product component availability and lack of communication effects ability to manufacture 95% of the time.	167, 202,					
Line On Time and In Full	1	7.04	ATP Check Rule Includes Planned Orders	Poor manufacturing schedule attainment causes inaccurate sales order confirmation because the ATP is confirming against planned orders not in physically manufactured product.	198, 1 191, 2 170					
Line On Time and In Full		7.10	Internal Quality	Non-conforming parts impact internal manufacturing 90% of the time.	58, 430	Manufacturing shipped late	8.8%	10.0%	0.9%	MI.3
Line On Time and In Full		7.17	Stretched Manufacturing Capacity	Lack of equipment resources cause capacity shortages to meet large and impact orders.	161, 39	Manufacturing shipped late	8.8%	10.0%	0.9%	P3
Line On Time and In Full		7.16	No Secondary Supplier	According to material data in the SYSTEM, 95% of our supplied components do not have a secondary supplier.	26, 357, 437	Manufacturing shipped late	8.8%	5.0%	0.4%	ES
Line On Time and In Full		7.11	External Customer Sales Plan	For 70% of our planning, we have a lack of visibility to the customer's demand or promotions resulting in no forecast and a 26% sales plan error.	321, 295, 217, 26, 267, 469, 551, 242, 431, 181, 236, 308	Product not available at ATP check	10.1%	37.0%	3.7%	P1.1, EP
Line On Time and In Full		7.58	Poor Forecast Management	SKU level forecasts are inaccurate due minimal analysis, poor input from known sales and marketing input, and a lack of corporate discipline to support one forecast.	217, 26, 267, 469, 551, 242, 431, 181, 236, 300	Product not available at ATP check	10.1%	37.0%	3.7%	P1.1
Line On Time and In Full		7.12	New Product-Manufacturing Lead Time & Planning not Aligned	New Product Development items are not planned and released to production with enough lead-time for production to meet customer orders/demand in units and timetable.	385, 142, 203, 257, 419	Product not available at ATP check	10.1%	26.0%	2.6%	P1, EP
Line On Time and In Full		7.01	Carriers Violate EDI Business Rules	Transportation providers do not adhere to the contractual obligations of EDI transmission requirements on a weekly basis.	1, 20, 31, 232	Transportation delivered late	0.9%	33.3%	0.3%	ED6

The first is to filter the heading "SCOR Process" by SCOR level two process. At this point, some problems may have level three IDs, such as P1.1, and some may have level two IDs, such as P1. Use a custom autofilter containing a SCOR level two ID (Figure 10-2) to identify all problems with at least one common process category. This yields fourteen projects: Enable Source, Enable Make, Enable Plan, Enable Deliver, Plan Source, Plan Make, Plan Deliver, Plan Supply Chain, Make-to-Stock, Make-to-Order, Source Stocked Product, Source Make-to-Order Product, Deliver Stocked Product, and Deliver Make-to-Order Product. At this point, the person driving the mouse assigns the same project number to all the problems resulting from each SCOR level two filter; for example, all D1 problems get assigned the project number "1" (Figure 10-3).

After the filtering fourteen times, all problem statements should have a project number.

The next level of filtering, coined "Strategic Similarity," again uses the field "SCOR Process." This time the team uses a custom filter containing a SCOR level one ID (i.e., "S," "M," "P," or "D"). For the source, make, and deliver processes, the team attempts to consolidate projects that can address both "to stock" and "to order" strategies with the same effort and scope. For the plan projects, the team looks for potential consolidation of the planning process projects; for example, a frequent consolidation involves P4, P3, and P2 into a project called "Tactical Planning." Typically, the leader reads each problem phrase and description, the team assesses implementation uniqueness, and then they come to consensus on whether it remains or should be moved to another project. To finish up, the leader changes the project number as appropriate. The Fowlers' team agreed to consolidate all problem statements in the "to order" projects with their "to stock" partners and consolidated P4, P3, and P2 into a project called "Tactical Planning." This level of filtering brings our overall project list to nine.

The last filtering level, called "Enable" again uses the field "SCOR Process," This time the team uses the custom autofilter containing "E." This leaves all problem statements that are connected to

(text continues on page 133)

Brainstorm Category	Project Number	Problem Statement Number	Problem Statement Phrase	Problem Statement Description	Individual Disconnect IDs	Metric Defect Category	Metric Defect Category Rate	Problem Weight within Defect Category	Problem Impact	SCOR Process
Line On Time and In Full	1	7.06	Poor definition of customer allocation rules	Poor or no customer automated allocation rules and re-confirmation communication plans cause unnecessary and unwanted re-allocation of inventory causing ship date changes and customer frustration over unannounced late orders.	448, 453, 406, 174, 232, 40, 146, 12, 258, 180	Inventory Re-allocated	7.0%	50.0%	3.5%	D1.3, ED
Line On Time and In Full	1	7.07	Inventory Transaction Errors - Can't Ship	Per DC tracking data, 5% of the total orders daily cannot ship due to (suddenly) product not being available.	361, 375, 374, 367, 368, 145, 184, 249, 266, 245	Inventory Re-allocated	7.0%	15.0%	1.1%	D1.9
Line On Time and In Full	1	7.04	ATP Check Rule Includes Planned Orders	Poor manufacturing schedule attainment causes inaccurate sales order confirmation because the ATP is confirming against planned orders not in physically manufactured product.	198, 184, 316, 442, 191, 288, 292, 290, 170	Manufacturing shipped late	8.8%	10.0%	0.9%	D1.3, ED, EM
Line On Time and In Full	1	7.02	Carrier Delivery Performance is Unreliable	Transportation providers are not rigorously scorecarded and performance issues are not systematically dealt with.	384, 222, 478, 476, 521, 370, 227, 483, 75, 310, 372, 475, 147, 149, 571, 109	Transportation delivered late	0.9%	33.3%	0.3%	D1.12, ED6
Line On Time and In Full	1	7.03	Fowlers Does Not Control Customer Delivery Appointments	Fowlers relies on carrier to make customer delivery appointments.	22, 434, 268, 557, 271, 23, 444	Transportation delivered late	0.9%	33.3%	0.3%	D1.2, D1.3, D1.13
Line On Time and In Full	1	7.05	Poor Inventory Accuracy at Shipping DC	Location and quantity errors cause allocated orders to ship late.	67, 228, 144	Warehouse shipped late	4.7%	25.0%	1.2%	D1.8
Line On Time and In Full	1	7.19	Customer "Order Complete" Requirement	Customer orders are held for 100% quantity fill creating late late shipments	369, 318, 154,158, 148, 72	Warehouse shipped late	4.7%	25.0%	1.2%	D1.5, ED
Order Fulfillment Cycle Time	1	1.01	Internal pick, pack, ship issues	Internal process problems delay shipments an estimated 10%	263, 251, 265, 261, 553, 51, 143, 282, 199, 554, 386	More than one category	7.0	25%	1.75	D1
Order Fulfillment Cycle Time	1	1.04	Customer service and process problems	Customer service and process problems affect 1% of order allocation.	247, 409, 270, 300, 388, 200, 250, 248, 426, 118, 272	Order confirmed to shipment created	1.5	33%	0.50	D1

some form of enabling process. This last filter drives some consolidations but more frequently separates many enable elements into projects all by themselves, consequently adding to the project total.

As before, the team leader reads each problem phrase and description. Then the team identifies the enable level three identification (i.e., ED1 Customer Business Rules); documents in the "SCOR Process" column; assesses uniqueness against other enable problems; and then comes to consensus on whether to leave it in the current project number, consolidate it with another project, or give it a new project number.

At this stage, Fowlers added three new projects, bringing the overall total to twelve.

The last activity for the day is to write **project** descriptions that include a phrase and a full description (Figure 10-4). This step can use the divide-and-conquer approach within the design team. The big challenge is to describe the project so it represents all its associated problem statements and is written in the positive view. Below are listed phrases and descriptions of the twelve projects the Fowlers' team identified.

1. Improve Demand Management and Forecasting. This project will improve poorly defined practices, underused modeling techniques, and untrained personnel.
2. Optimize Supply Management Practices. This project will focus enabling and execution of tactical processes with targeted suppliers.
3. Improve Information Technology Effectiveness. This project will focus on scaling up more effective and efficient data warehouse capability, and improving the business units' use of the planning-and-forecasting module within the enterprise resource planning package.
4. Improve Data Integrity. This project will define a master data management process and correct errors in supplier, item, and customer master data.
5. Improve Supplier Flexibility. This project will focus on developing vendors' capability to respond to near-term demand fluctuations for source-to-stock and source-to-order items.

(text continues on page 138)

Figure 10-4. Project Benefit Worksheet: food products project phrase, description, and benefit summary.

Project Number	Project Phrase	Project Description	Line On Time and In Full (%)	Order Fulfillment Cycle Time (days)	Upside Supply Chain Flexibility (days)	Total Supply Chain Management Cost ($)	COGS ($)	Inventory ($)
		Baseline	68.4%	5.0	89.0	$42,500,000	$215,000,000	$64,500,000
1	Improve Demand Management and Forecasting	This project will improve poorly defined practices, underutilized modeling techniques, and untrained personnel.	8.4%	2.2				$3,000,000
2	Optimize Supply Chain Management Practices	This project will focus enabling and execution of tactical processes with targeted suppliers.						
3	Improve Information Technology Effectiveness	This project will focus on scaling up more effective and efficient data warehouse capability, and improve the business units' utilization of the planning and forecasting module within the ERP package.				$2,500,000		

#		Description				
4	Improve Data Integrity	This project will define a master data management process and correct errors in supplier, item, and customer master data.	2.0%	7.5		$6,000,000
5	Improve Supplier Flexibility	This project will focus on developing vendors' capability to respond to near-term demand fluctuations for source-to-stock and source-to-order items.		15.0	$2,500,000	
6	Implement Formal Product Life Cycle Management Process	This project will design, develop, and implement an integrated management process for all phases of a product's life cycle, from introduction through commercialization to retirement.		7.5	$2,500,000	

(continues)

Figure 10-4. (*continued*)

Project Number	Project Phrase	Project Description	Line On Time and In Full (%)	Order Fulfillment Cycle Time (days)	Upside Supply Chain Flexibility (days)	Total Supply Chain Management Cost ($)	COGS ($)	Inventory ($)
		Baseline	68.4%	5.0	89.0	$42,500,000	$215,000,000	$64,500,000
7	Engineer an Integrated Tactical Planning Process	This project will design, develop, and implement effective and efficient tactical planning processes to help manage the short term horizon balancing customer orders, stocking levels, replenishment orders to factories and purchase orders to suppliers.	3.5%			$2,500,000	$2,500,000	
8	Implement Sales and Operations Planning	This project will implement a Sales and Operations Planning process integrate demand and supply planning with business plans and reconciliation to financial objectives.	4.0%			$5,000,000	$2,500,000	$6,000,000

#	Project	Description						
9	Improve the Efficiency and Effectiveness of the Physical Supply Chain Network	This project will focus on short and long term physical network strategy improving cycle time, transportation and warehouse spend, and align long term capacity requirements.		−4.0		$10,000,000		$7,500,000
10	Tighten Up Order Management Discipline	This project will cover entry errors, EDI errors, and business rules from inquiry and quote through order entry and inventory allocation. This	6.0%					
11	Establish Formal Return Management	This project will define and implement a reverse logistics processes from goods movement to policy to the authorization process.				$2,500,000		$3,000,000
12	Eliminate Poor Inventory Control Practices	This project will focus on defects that relate to inventory record accuracy, shrinkage, and cycle counting.	2.5%					$3,000,000
		Benefit	26.4%	−1.8	30.0	$25,000,000	$10,000,000	$28,500,000
		Projected Performance Level	94.8%	6.8	59.0	$17,500,000	$205,000,000	$36,000,000

6. Implement Formal Product Life Cycle Management Process. This project will design, develop, and implement an integrated management process for all phases of a product's life cycle, from introduction through commercialization to retirement.

7. Engineer an Integrated Tactical Planning Process. This project will design, develop, and implement effective and efficient tactical planning processes to help manage the short-term horizon balancing customer orders, stocking levels, replenishment orders to factories, and purchase orders to suppliers.

8. Implement Sales and Operations Planning. This project will implement a sales and operations planning process that integrates demand and supply planning with business plans and reconciliation to financial objectives.

9. Improve the Efficiency and Effectiveness of the Physical Supply Chain Network. This project will focus on short- and long-term physical network strategy, thus improving cycle time, transportation, and warehouse spend, and aligning long-term capacity requirements.

10. Tighten Up Order Management Discipline. This project will cover entry errors, electronic data interchange (EDI) errors, and business rules from inquiry and quote through order entry and inventory allocation.

11. Establish Formal Return Management. This project will define and implement reverse logistics processes from goods movement to policy to the authorization process.

12. Eliminate Poor Inventory Control Practices. This project will focus on defects that relate to inventory record accuracy, shrinkage, and cycle counting.

▪ Assessing Impact and Effort

The team is cognitively moving from individual problems to projects. The Impact/Effort Worksheet (Figure 10-5) is used to calculate a project score that will rank the projects using a two-by-two grid (Figure 10-6). The category descriptions for the Impact/Effort Matrix are listed below.

The "total score" field adds the total impact score to the total effort score; the higher the number, the bigger and easier the project. It's the last calculation made in this worksheet.

The "project number" is taken from the "preliminary project portfolio" worksheet (Figure 10-3). The "project phrase" briefly describes the project. The "project description" is a sentence or two that describes the problem; it must be relevant to all of the individual problems. To derive a project's "percent improvement" and/or "dollar savings," use the Project Benefit Worksheet (Figure 10-4) to help assign a 1, 2, or 3 to each metric impacted; second, add the scores together to get the total. For example, the percent improvement and/or dollar savings for project eight is 10:1 for line on time and in full (<10 percent), 3 for total supply chain management cost (>$500K), 3 for cost of goods sold (>$500K), and 3 for Inventory $ (>$500K).

The "time for benefit to book" (measured in months) is an estimate of how long, from the current period until the first benefit begins; this score is based on the criteria in Figure 10-5.

The "customer satisfaction impact" is an estimate and ideally could rely on detailed criteria from an official company survey. "Leverage to other supply chains" is an estimate of the scope of impact to other customers, products, suppliers, locations, and so forth; this is the measure of "Think big, act small, and scale fast."

"Total impact" is a calculated field that adds the impact scores together. "Time to implement" (in months) is an effort factor that measures how long it will take to design, develop, and implement the project solution(s).

On the "effort" side of the worksheet, "Resources required" attempts to characterize the resource requirements to implement the project solution. Within this category, a "project team" refers to a team that is part of a formal project management infrastructure. "FT Job Exclusive" refers to full-time resources (e.g., a black belt or project engineer). "PT Job Inclusive" refers to tasks assigned to individuals as part of their normal job responsibilities.

In the "Complexity" column, "organizational complexity" is low if a single individual or function has control over the outcome;

(text continues on page 142)

Figure 10-5. Preliminary project portfolio Impact/Effort Worksheet.

Impact Worksheet

				1	1	1	1	
Total Score	Project Number	Project Phrase	Project Description	% Improvement and/or $ Savings	Time for Benefit to Book (Months)	Customer Satisfaction Impact	Leveragable to Other Products	Total Impact
				x < 10% or $100K	x > 12	Negative	None	
				2	2	2	2	
				10% or 100K < x < 25% or $500K	3 < x < 12	Neutral	Some to Many	
				3	3	3	3	
				x > 25% or $500K	x < 3	Positive	Most to All	
This adds the impact score to the impact score. The higher	Enter the project number from the "problem definition" worksheet.	The project phrase briefly describes the project.	The project description is a sentence or two that describes the problem. It must be first assign a	To derive a project's % improvement and/or $ savings use the project benefit or	For each project, estimate the number of months from the current period until the first benefit or	Estimate the project's affect on customer satisfaction; ideally the team could use more	Estimate the scope of impact to other customers, products, suppliers, locations, etc. This is	This calculated field adds the impact scores together.

Effort Worksheet

1	1	1	1	
x > 12	Project Team	High	x > $100K	
2	2	2	2	
3 < x < 12	FT Job Exclusive	Medium	$25K < x < $100K	
3	3	3	3	
x < 3	PT Job Inclusive	Low	Minimal	
Time to Implement (Months)	Resources Required	Complexity (Technically/Organizationally)	Project Cost	Total Effort
This effort factor measures the number of months it will take to design, develop, and	This effort factor attempts to characterize the resource requirements necessary to implement the project solution.	Estimate the complexity of the project. Organizational complexity is low if a single individual or function has control over	Estimate the project cost using your company's normal costing methods.	This calculated field adds the effort scores together.

relevant to all of the individual problems.	1, 2, or 3 to each metric impacted; second, add the scores together to get the total.	improvement will begin and then enter the appropriate score based on the above criteria.	detailed criteria found on an offical company survey. Enter the appropriate score based on the above criteria.	the measure of "Think big, act small, and scale fast." Enter the appropriate score based on the above criteria.	implement the project solution(s). Enter the appropriate score based on the above criteria.	Project Team refers to a team that is part of a formal project management infrastructure. FT Job Exclusive refers to full time resources (like a black belt or project engineer). PT Job Inclusive refers to a tasks assigned to individuals as part of their normal job responsibilities.	the outcome. The more functions or departments, the higher the complexity. Involving customers and/or suppliers generally makes the organizational complexity high.	Many companies will include internal and external resource costs plus capital, software, etc. This calculated field adds the effort scores together.
the number, the bigger and easier the project.								

the more functions or departments, the higher the complexity. Involving customers and/or suppliers generally makes the organizational complexity high.

Estimate the "project cost" using your company's normal costing methods. Many companies will include internal and external resource costs plus capital, software, and so forth.

"Total effort" is a calculated field that adds the effort scores together. Figure 10-7 illustrates the Fowlers' Impact/Effort Worksheet for its twelve projects, sorted first by descending total score, then by descending total impact, and then by descending total effort.

Figure 10-8 graphically represents how the projects related to each other.

This day, although extremely rewarding, was mentally exhausting. The team would have agreed to any savings number at this point. With that in mind, the reward was a simple reading assignment as the only homework before the next session. The next topic and design session would focus on detailed opportunity analysis; sometimes it is good to not know what is ahead!

Figure 10-6.   Impact/effort matrix.

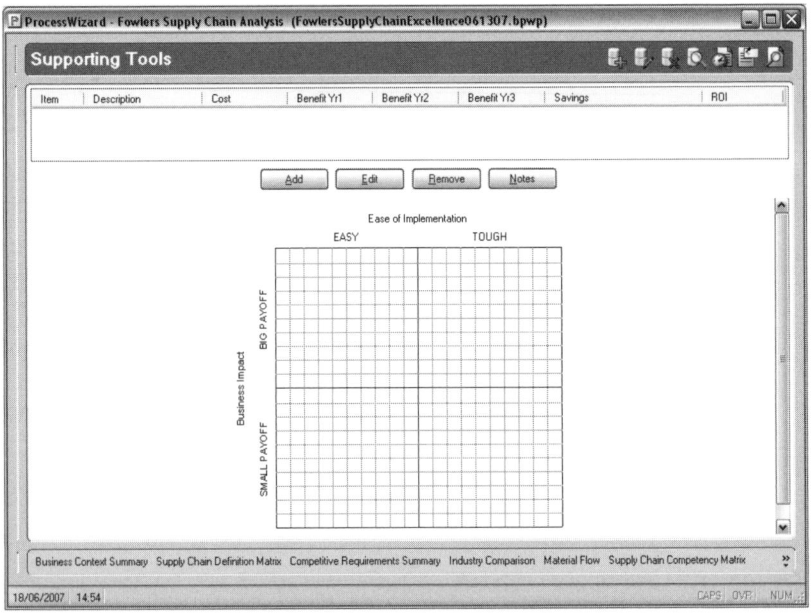

Figure 10-7. Food products Impact/Effort summary.

Scoring criteria

Score	% Improvement and/or $ Savings (All Impacted Metrics)	Time for Benefit to Book (Months)	Customer Satisfaction Impact	Leveragable to Other Products	Time to Implement (Months)	Resources Required	Complexity (Technically/Organizationally)	Project Cost
1	x < 10% or $100K	x > 12	Negative	None	x > 12	Project Team	High	x > $100K
2	10% or 100K < x < 25% or $500K	3 < x < 12	Neutral	Some to Many	3 < x < 12	FT Job Exclusive	Medium	$25K < x < $100K
3	x > 25% or $500K	x < 3	Positive	Most to All	x < 3	PT Job Inclusive	Low	Minimal

Project data

Total Score	Project Number	Project Phrase	Project Description	% Improvement and/or $ Savings (All Impacted Metrics)	Time for Benefit to Book (Months)	Customer Satisfaction Impact	Leveragable to Other Products	Total Impact	Time to Implement (Months)	Resources Required	Complexity (Technically/Organizationally)	Project Cost	Total Effort
25	8	Implement Sales and Operations Planning	This project will implement a Sales and Operations Planning process integrate demand and supply planning with business plans and reconciliation to financial objectives.	10	2	3	3	18	2	1	2	2	7

(continues)

Figure 10-7. (continued)

Total Score	Project Number	Project Phrase	Project Description	% Improvement and/or $ Savings (All Impacted Metrics)	Time for Benefit to Book (Months)	Customer Satisfaction Impact	Leveragable to Other Products	Total Impact	Time to Implement (Months)	Resources Required	Complexity (Technically/ Organizationally)	Project Cost	Total Effort
26	5	Improve Supplier Flexibility	This project will focus on developing vendors' capability to respond to near-term demand fluctuations for source-to-order items.	12	2	2	2	18	2	2	2	2	8
25	7	Engineer an Integrated Tactical Planning Process	This project will design, develop, and implement effective and efficient tactical planning processes to help manage the short term horizon balancing customer orders, stocking levels, replenishment orders to factories and purchase orders to suppliers.	8	3	3	2	16	3	2	2	2	9
24	12	Eliminate Poor Inventory Control Practices	This project will focus on defects that relate to inventory record accuracy, shrinkage, and cycle counting.	3	3	3	3	12	3	3	3	3	12

23	Improve Data Integrity	This project will define a master data management process and correct errors in supplier, item, and customer master data.	4	3	3	2	12	3	3	2	3	11
21	Implement Formal Product Life Cycle Management Process	This project will design, develop, and implement an integrated management process for all phases of a product's life cycle, from introduction through commercialization to retirement.	6	2	3	3	14	2	1	2	2	7
21	Improve Demand Management and Forecasting	This project will improve poorly defined practices, underutilized modeling techniques, and untrained personnel.	4	2	3	3	12	2	3	2	2	9
20	Improve the Efficiency and Effectiveness of the Physical Supply Chain Network	This project will focus on short and long term physical network strategy improving cycle time, transportation and warehouse spend, and align long term capacity requirements.	9	1	3	3	16	1	1	1	1	4

(continues)

Figure 10-7. (continued)

Total Score	Project Number	Project Phrase	Project Description	% Improvement and/or $ Savings (All Impacted Metrics)	Time for Benefit to Book (Months)	Customer Satisfaction Impact	Leveragable to Other Products	Total Impact	Time to Implement (Months)	Resources Required	Complexity (Technically/Organizationally)	Project Cost	Total Effort
20	10	Tighten Up Order Management Discipline	This project will cover entry errors, EDI errors, and business rules from inquiry and quote through order entry and inventory allocation.	2	3	3	2	10	3	3	1	3	10
18	11	Establish Formal Return Management	This project will define and implement a reverse logistics processes from goods movement to policy to the authorization process.	5	2	1	2	10	2	2	1	3	8
15	2	Optimize Supply Management Practices	This project will focus enabling and execution of tactical processes with targeted suppliers.	0	3	2	2	7	2	2	2	2	8

13	3	Improve Information Technology Effective-ness	This project will focus on scaling up more effective and efficient data warehouse capability, and improve the business units' utilization of the planning and forecasting module within the ERP package.	3	1	2	3	9	1	1	1	4

Figure 10-8.   Fowlers' impact/effort Matrix.

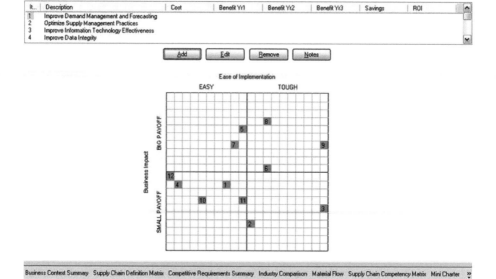

11

Week Nine: Opportunity Analysis and Steering Team Review Number Four

Due Diligence for the Project List

Three percent profit improvement to the sales value of the supply chain: As described earlier, that's the rule-of-thumb opportunity before the data are prepared (read: sanitized) for presentation to executives and the board. For every $100 million in revenue, that means an opportunity for an extra $3 million dollars in earnings. This gem is worth repeating.

Where any company comes in against this rule, however, depends on its distance from parity on four key metrics: perfect order fulfillment, order fulfillment cycle time, upside supply chain flexibility, and total supply chain management cost. The more of these metrics to which a company performs at or better than parity, the more likely it is that the discovery and analysis process will yield opportunity of approximately 1.5 percent. Companies that perform below parity with respect to these metrics typically will find opportunities in excess of that amount—up to 4.5 percent.

Depending on how experienced design team members are at the budgeting process, the opportunity assessment will range from simple to mind-bending. The objectives of Week Nine are to create, refine, and prioritize the project opportunity analyses and prepare for the fourth steering team review.

■ The Opportunity Analysis

The objective for this design session is to educate the team about the process of quantifying the project benefits identified the previous week, document important assumptions, and begin identifying key TO BE material flow design drivers and assumptions.

The quantification process follows five principles.

- ❑ *Principle One.* At a minimum, the sub-teams must revisit the defect analysis with the objective of validating the size of the benefit.
- ❑ *Principle Two.* Factor out the effect of forecasted growth by assuming constant revenue for the financial period; usually savings are annualized. If the sponsor is willing, it's acceptable to include the profit improvement from revenue growth.
- ❑ *Principle Three.* Be realistic in the savings estimates; the steering team and ultimately the executive team should add the appropriate safety buffer to the numbers, observing the doctrine of "under-promise and over-deliver." Conservative realism is normal; gross sandbagging is not helpful at this point.
- ❑ *Principle Four.* Document all assumptions behind the savings estimates. This is the most important principle; any pushback by the steering team typically has more to do with the assumptions than the numbers.
- ❑ *Principle Five.* Identify validation resources (finance!) that can objectively test or spar with the numbers and assumptions—before the estimates are shared with the steering

team. There are two kinds of value that result from this effort: change management and content. The validation resources accomplishes both, giving others the opportunity to participate and feel ownership while making the content more accurate.

Documenting the opportunity analysis varies from using sophisticated supply chain modeling and simulation software tools to simple spreadsheets. In all cases, the true challenge is to represent the value of implementing the project in the context of the profit-and-loss statement and balance sheet. This part of the process makes many people uncomfortable. Engineers and other detail-minded folks on the project team may have a difficult time getting comfortable with estimating opportunity. Even with sophisticated modeling tools, acronyms such as WAG (wild-ass guess) and SWAG (super wild-ass guess) frequently show up at this phase of the analysis, but there should be some comfort in the fact that you'll round to the nearest $100,000 or $50,000.

The Project Opportunity Worksheet

Each project will require an opportunity spreadsheet (Table 11-1). The spreadsheet is organized using information that has been gathered over the past six weeks. The first section—project phrase, number, and description—is taken from the preliminary project portfolio. The first two columns are taken from the 2006 actual performance in the cost of goods sold and total supply chain management cost metrics. The columns under 2007, 2008, 2009, 2010, and 2011 are where the team needs to enter estimated savings recorded as a negative number for costs and a positive number for revenue. The bottom line—Operating Income/Economic Value Added Impact—simply adds the absolute value of Total Cost of Sales benefits to Total Supply Chain Management Cost benefits. The most frequent question from design teams at this point is how to portray project savings over multiple years. There is only one an-

Table 11-1.   The Opportunity analysis worksheet.

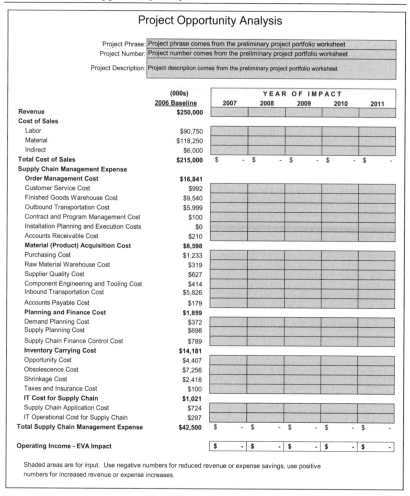

swer to this: It depends! The finance and executive leadership teams will have the answer. Some will require only new savings to be recorded in each year; some would like to see cumulative savings recorded in each year; some may use a formula yet to be discovered. To illustrate the difference, let's use transportation cost savings over three years. Year one nets one million dollars in savings in the western region, year two nets another million in savings in the central region, and year two nets another million in savings in the eastern region. By using the "new savings" guideline, the three-year total is three million dollars. By using the "cumulative savings" guideline, the three-year total is six million dollars (one plus two plus three).

The assumptions are the most important part of this chart. There's no magic in assembling a good one; it's a matter of format. Each metric that shows benefit gets its own statement of assumption. It could include an item number or numbers by type (i.e., raw material, work in progress, finished goods, or returns); estimated volume, calculated using such data as market share, geographic segment, unit volume, or unit forecast; cost or revenue impact, calculated by cost per unit or margin per unit; and/or delivery reliability, lead time, and necessary business conditions. There are different kinds of assumptions. One kind describes the impact of cost reduction or productivity improvement in direct or indirect categories. Another describes the revenue impact of delivery reliability through fewer lost opportunities or pure growth. Yet another type of assumption describes the working-capital impact of lead time and delivery performance, as measured in inventory, payables, and/or receivables.

As an example, the Fowlers' team identified five major profit opportunities that would result from project eight (Figure 11-1). They aligned these opportunity assumptions with the numbers in the last column as summarized below:

1. Reduce lost opportunity orders, calculated as 1 percent of total orders, or 26,532 orders missed on account of no immediate material availability. At $339.20 average value per order with a 50 percent gross margin, the profit opportunity calculates to $4,500,000.
2. Achieve a 1 percent decrease in price per part for the ability to provide accurate forecast data to all suppliers. At $118,250,000 material cost, that equates to a $1,182,500 annualized cost decrease.
3. Have inventory immediately available. This will reduce 10 percent of the amount of time spent per order picking multiple times, expediting inventory transfer orders, and providing phone status to customer service representatives. At $4.40 warehouse cost per order with 1,326,632 orders per year, this equates to $583,718.

Figure 11-1.   Fowlers' "Project No. Eight" opportunity analysis worksheet for the first-year benefit.

Project Opportunity Analysis

Project Phrase: Implement Sales and Operations Planning
Project Number: 8
Project Description: This project will implement a Sales and Operations Planning process integrate demand and supply planning with business plans and reconciliation to financial objectives.

	(000s) 2006 Baseline	YEAR OF IMPACT				
		2007	2008	2009	2010	2011
Revenue	$250,000	$4,500				
Cost of Sales						
Labor	$90,750					
Material	$118,250	−$1,182				
Indirect	$6,000					
Total Cost of Sales	$215,000	$ (1,182)	$ –	$ –	$ –	$ –
Supply Chain Management Expense						
Order Management Cost	$16,841					
Customer Service Cost	$992					
Finished Goods Warehouse Cost	$9,540	−$584				
Outbound Transportation Cost	$5,999					
Contract and Program Management Cost	$100					
Installation Planning and Execution Costs	$0					
Accounts Receivable Cost	$210					
Material (Product) Acquisition Cost	$8,598					
Purchasing Cost	$1,283					
Raw Material Warehouse Cost	$319					
Supplier Quality Cost	$627					
Component Engineering and Tooling Cost	$414					
Inbound Transportation Cost	$5,826	−$2,039				
Accounts Payable Cost	$179					
Planning and Finance Cost	$1,859					
Demand Planning Cost	$372					
Supply Planning Cost	$698					
Supply Chain Finance Control Cost	$789					
Inventory Carrying Cost	$14,181					
Opportunity Cost	$4,407					
Obsolescence Cost	$7,256	−$3,628				
Shrinkage Cost	$2,418					
Taxes and Insurance Cost	$100					
IT Cost for Supply Chain	$1,021					
Supply Chain Application Cost	$724					
IT Operational Cost for Supply Chain	$297					
Total Supply Chain Management Expense	$42,500	$ (6,251)	$ –	$ –	$ –	$ –
Operating Income - EVA Impact		$ 11,303	$ –	$ –	$ –	$ –

Shaded areas are for input. Use negative numbers for reduced revenue or expense savings, use positive numbers for increased revenue or expense increases.

4. Reduce unplanned changes to purchase orders, decreasing the number of instances of expedited transportation within lead time. Sixty-five percent of purchase orders are currently expedited, incurring 35 percent higher inbound transportation costs than necessary. Inbound transportation totals $5.8 million; improvement would reduce cost by $2.0 million.

5. Reduce nonworking inventory by 50 percent—from 18 percent of overall inventory value to 12.5 percent of overall inventory value, equivalent to $3,628,000. Accrual is already in place for the 25 percent level.

Identify Further Validation Resources

As the team tweaks the assumptions, they also review the list of names of people involved in building them and considers additional validation resources.

There are two reasons to add more names. First, it may be necessary to add more content expertise about details to further refine assumptions. For example, one might include a marketing research analyst to help refine market share and volume numbers or a cost accountant to calculate the impact of accruals or balance sheet changes. Second, adding these topical experts gives them extra time to digest the information before deciding to stand behind the numbers and therefore widen support for the project. It is normal for the numbers from the preliminary project portfolio to change (reflected in project eight from Figure 10-4 and Figure 11-1); as the team digs deeper into the numbers and assumptions behind them, confidence will grow. Now is the time when documentation discipline will start to pay off. The opportunity spreadsheets and the project metric summary are two of the most important items to keep accurate. For example, teams often need to add "Revenue Impact" to the project metric summary and adjust the benefit dollars as they are refined (Figure 11-2). The next week will be spent refining dollars and assumptions and increasing the level of support for the change. With the path to the next week clear, the team turns toward preparing for steering team review four.

Figure 11-2. Fowlers' "Project No. Eight" updates for the project benefit summary.

Project Number	Project Phrase	Project Description	Line On Time and In Full (%)	Order Fulfillment Cycle Time (days)	Upside Supply Chain Flexibility (days)	Total Supply Chain Management Cost ($)	COGS ($)	Inventory ($)	Revenue ($)
		Baseline	68.4%	5.0	89.0	$42,500,000	$215,000,000	$64,500,000	$250,000,000
8	Implement Sales and Operations Planning	This project will implement a Sales and Operations Planning process integrate demand and supply planning with business plans and reconciliation to financial objectives.	4.0%			$2,623,000	$1,182,000	$3,628,000	$4,500,000
		Projected Performance Level	94.8%	6.8	59.0	$19,877,000	$206,318,000	$38,372,000	$245,500,000

Conducting Steering Team Review Number Four

Prepare and conduct steering team review number four with the following agenda items:

- ❏ Project roadmap status.
- ❏ Review disconnect analysis.
- ❏ Review project metric impact summary.
- ❏ Review the preliminary project portfolio and impact-effort grid.
- ❏ Decisions required today.
- ❏ Expectations for steering team review number five.

12

Week Ten: TO BE
Material Flow
Identify the Drivers for Change

The first two days that the team spends identifying TO BE material flow changes often seem anticlimactic. From the first day of the first week, people had ideas on how to fix things. By this point in the analysis, it's usually already clear what changes are needed to improve profits and customer satisfaction. Sometimes, identifying the details of TO BE change is as simple as adding the phrase "thou shalt not" to the problem statements imbedded in the projects. However, you can't count on it being that easy. So the objectives of Week Ten are to identify the change drivers to implement the projects.

▓ Identifying the Drivers of Change

So far, analysis of AS IS material flow has been conducted by sub-teams. For some reason, TO BE solutions are best developed by the entire group. It may be more time-consuming, but in a discipline that can be as much art as science, it just seems to work better. Figure

12-1 is another matrix to help put more science to the TO BE development process. The diagram "TO BE change drivers" (also known as implementation scope factors) lists fifteen unique factors to consider as the team finalizes its TO BE plans for each project. The matrix is organized in rows listing five levels of change to potentially include as part of a project's implementation scope and organize assumptions. For each level, there are potentially three factors to include: goals, design, and measurement. For each project, the team must estimate the scope of change by identifying the unique level and factor. A large scope would include TO BE changes in all cells of the matrix; a small scope would include just one cell.

The trading partner level includes changes involving customers and suppliers, and could contain factors that affect their cost versus

Figure 12-1.   TO BE project implementation factors (assumptions).

		Factors of Change		
TO BE Change Drivers also known as Implementation Scope Factors		**Goals—Strategy**	**Design**	**Measurement— Management**
Levels of Change	**Trading Partner**	Cost & Service Priority	Replenishment & Purchasing Relationship	Service Level Agreement
	Organization	Competitive Requirements, i.e., SAPP	Organizational Structure	Scorecard
	Process	Customer Responsive More Efficient	TO BE Geographic MapLevel 2, 3, and 4 TO BE Processes Leading Practices	Defect Analysis
	People—Jobs	Annual Performance Goals	Job Scope and Responsibilities	Performance Appraisal
	Technology	Technology Strategy	Screenshot Storyline Detailed Solution Design Configuration	Uptime Response Time

service priorities; replenishment and purchasing personnel relationships; and/or service level agreements (contracts).

The organization level calls for structural changes to the company, including prioritization of competitive requirements organization chart (including headcount adds and subtracts) and/or metrics associated with a level one scorecard.

The process level involves setting goals for process performance, balancing efficiency and customer responsiveness; TO BE process definition including geographic maps, Supply Chain Operations Reference (SCOR) level two, three, and four blue prints, and leading practices; or process continuous improvement using regular defect analysis.

The people-jobs level involves changes to individual goals and objectives (often an annual process); job scope, description, and responsibilities; and/or the performance appraisal process.

The technology level includes changes to technology strategy, often including macro-level architecture and platforms (i.e., demand planning functionality will be based on SAP APO); detailed solution design and configuration (functionality often illustrated using a screenshot storyline); and/or system uptime and response time measures.

Thoughts on Leading Practices

The TO BE material flow design is the first time when the team can consider incorporating leading practices into solutions; the SCOR blueprint is the second (Chapter 17). When incorporating leading practices as a process design change factor at this stage, it is better to pick a few and implement well, as opposed to a shotgun approach where you initiate as many as possible and hope some of them stick.

There are some logical steps that will help the design team focus their efforts on the important few. The first is to develop a short list of leading practices appropriate for your company and industry that will help drive material flow efficiency and effectiveness. Sources for this list include the SCOR dictionary; experience and education of design team members; professional and industry associations; and disciplines learned from such initiatives as business process reengineering, quality function deployment, Six Sigma continuous improvement, efficient consumer response, total quality management, theory of constraints, lean manufacturing, and so on.

The second step—and it takes some research—is to find a good case study for each of the leading practices on the short list; "good" in this case is measured by at least three criteria:

1. The case study should describe detailed characteristics of the desired state. These include strategy, design, and management factors for the organization, processes, job tasks, and technology.
2. The case study should describe the transition from current practices to the end state, including lessons learned.
3. The case study should have relevance by industry, by the role in a supply chain, or, preferably, both.

With the case studies in hand, assemble a business use scenario that illustrates the before-and-after using the geographic material flow and/or thread diagram.

TO BE Material Flow Design at Fowlers

As part of project seven, "Engineer an integrated tactical planning process," the Fowlers' team identified a short list of four leading practices: distribution requirements planning; master production scheduling; material requirements planning; and collaborative planning, forecasting, and replenishment (CPFR). Although there were remnants of distribution requirements planning, master production scheduling, and material requirements planning in the thread diagram, CPFR was well beyond Fowlers' current practices; forecast and replenishment variability from large retail customers was creating financial chaos in returns, inbound and outbound transportation cost, poor inventory positions, and inconsistent delivery reliability. CPFR was identified as a proven practice that would help get a handle on near-term demand variability.

Leading retailers have been practicing CPFR for years with their largest suppliers. As technology solutions helped bring down the cost of communication infrastructure and forecast analytics, the number of suppliers investing in CPFR competency was growing. So the team had little trouble finding good information.

The Voluntary Interindustry Commerce Standards organization proved a rich source of research data through its *Collaborative Planning, Forecasting and Replenishment Voluntary Guidelines,* published in 1998. Its 1999 *Roadmap to CPFR* provided case studies. The Fowlers' team used the Voluntary Interindustry Commerce Standards web site (www.vics.org) to locate a case history that addressed these critical issues: Why CPFR? What are the steps to CPFR? How is CPFR aligned with SCOR? What are some step-by step guidelines? Where can further references be found?

The team's Implementation Scope Factors matrix summarizes, at a high level, the drivers of change and their assumptions (Figure 12-2).

▓ Refining TO BE Models and Initiating Quick-Hit Plans

The second day will be spent refining the implementation scope factors including assumptions, high-level scenarios, risk assessment, and other pertinent detail. Particularly helpful at this point are the before-and-after material flow illustrations that add visual detail and clarity; the ones that take a spaghetti diagram and make it look simple. In next week's steering team review, the executives are anticipating seeing the first clear map of the company's future, and the solutions need to be delivered simply enough for fast and easy understanding—yet with enough detail for full appreciation of their impact.

For Fowlers, the visual detail (the "process"—"design" cell of the matrix) for CPFR involved four key changes. First would be more direct ships from suppliers to targeted retail warehouses; this changed connector lines on the geographic map. Before, material flowed from supplier to Fowlers' warehouse to Fowlers' warehouse to customer retail location. In the TO BE map, material would flow from supplier to customer regional warehouse.

In the second key change, consigned inventory would be consolidated to fewer locations closer to the customer point of sale. Before, a specific inventory item was stored in all Fowlers' ware-

Figure 12-2. Fowlers' "Project No. Seven" implementation scope factors worksheet.

Project 7 Engineer an Integrated Tactical Planning Process / Implementation Scope Factors	Factors of Change		
	Goals—Strategy	Design	Measurement—Management
Trading Partner	Must include customer gross margin return on investment, service, and inventory goals	Must define transactional and leadership relationships with replenishment managers and buyers	Service level agreements will need revision for CPFR customers
Organization	Align competitive requirements for retail to CPFR service level agreements	Establish a key account team organization structure to support CPFR customers; complete RACI analysis for demand, supply, and factory planning roles.	Need to update scorecard to include CPFR key performance indicators
Process	Must establish material flow goals for cycle time and reliability	Complete TO BE geographic maps for each CPFR customer; process blueprints for P4, P3, P2, P1.1, D1.2, and D1.3; leading practice white papers for DRP, MPS, MRP, and CPFR.	Establish defect analysis for tactial process performance measures
People—Jobs	Establish annual performance goals for all tactial planning roles	Write job description CPFR planner; align roles and responsibilities for demand, supply, and factory planners	
Technology	Assume functionality of next Advanced Planning release	Complete detailed process design and screen shot storyline; set configuration, test, and go live requirements	Define uptime and response time requirements

Levels of Change

houses. In the TO BE, the item would be stored in a single Fowlers' warehouse and in designated customer regional warehouses.

In the third key change, lead-time expectations were eased because of improved inventory handling; the result would be improved delivery reliability and reduced transportation costs.

The fourth change optimized the flow of returned goods. Before, returns moved from customer locations to the closest Fowlers' warehouse. In the TO BE, returns were consolidated at the customer regional warehouse and shipped to a single Fowlers' warehouse designated to accept all returns.

The other expectation at this stage of the project is that the team needs to identify and initiate quick-hit plans—one or two projects that will deliver fast return on investment with a minimum of cultural change. There are two guidelines for this activity. First, the quick-hit scope needs to be small enough so that the change can be designed, developed, implemented (to some scale), and reported on by the last steering team review. The quick hit is intended as a confidence builder both for the design team and the steering team—a "slam dunk," as one team member put it.

The second guideline for initiating quick-hit plans is to effectively move ownership of quick-hit implementations to extended team members and others in the organization by developing a mini-charter. It's like the original project charter, but specific to the quick hits. Elements of the mini-charter include a summary of the issue and root cause analyses; recommended changes; action plans, responsibility, and timing; benefits as calculated in the opportunity spreadsheets; an implementation leader (extended team or other resources); implementation resources (including capital, expense, and people); and an implementation sponsor (steering team).

In Fowlers' case, the quick-hit plan involved supplier shipments from the Pacific Rim (Figure 12-3).

Figure 12-3.   Fowlers' Asia Pacific transportation consolidation—quick-hit mini-charter

ISSUE & ROOT CAUSE ANALYSIS	
Inbound shipments from Asia are consolidated by each supplier in quantities large enough to support full container shipments. While each shipment has low transportation cost, inventory value is high while flexibility and responsiveness are low.	
RECOMMENDATION Setup a regional consolidation for all suppliers in the region.	
ACTION PLAN 1. Identify suppliers 2. Identify service provider 3. Define and pilot process 4. Roll out changes	**RESPONSIBILITIES/TIMING** 1. Sort supplier list and validate with business team—2 weeks—Buyer/Planner Analyst 2. Define 3rd party logistics requirements and issue request for proposal—4 weeks—Transportation Analyst 3. Develop and pilot changes—2 weeks—Joint 4. Plan and roll out consolidation—4 weeks—Joint
PAY-OFFS Quantify in terms of cost, cycle time, quality, and/or customer service 1. $1,750,000 annualized transportation cost reduction 2. 6 weeks lead time improvement 3. 35% improvement in delivery reliability by purchase order	**IMPLEMENTATION RESOURCES** Full Time Equivalent (FTE) Personnel, Capital, and Expensed Items 1. 2 FTEs as identified for the duration defined in the responsibilities/timing section including a Buyer/Planner and Transportation Analyst
IMPLEMENTATION LEADER 1. Buyer/Planner	**IMPLEMENTATION SPONSOR(S)** 1. Directors of Purchasing and Logistics
CHARTER STATUS 1. Approved as of Steering Team Review 5	

13

Week Eleven: Quick-Hit Plans, Steering Team Review Number Five, and Initiating the Work and Information Flow Analysis

Dig into Work and Information Flow

There are several points during a Supply Chain Operations Reference (SCOR) project that seem to draw people into reflecting on the significance of their work relative to the potential opportunity for their company—as opposed to thinking about next week's homework. The scorecard gap analysis during Steering Team Review Number Two (Chapter 7) is often such an occasion. This is another.

At this point, members of the design team have reason to feel like they've produced something of great value to their company—measured in millions of dollars of potential profit improvement and customer satisfaction. Better still is the feeling that they've created a detailed understanding of the improvements—projects that will deliver the results. If this swagger shows up among presenters at the steering team review, the steering team gets excited too.

By this time, project momentum has reached something close to full speed, and other people throughout the organization are looking for ways to participate, saying things such as, "This is one of the most committed things our company has ever done."

A careful mix of common sense, analysis, and measurable results has moved the project to the executive team's center of attention. The organization stands poised for a transition to something big and new. So does the design team. After six weeks of work on metrics and material flow, everyone will be eager to put the geographic maps behind and move on to work and information flow.

With these thoughts as background, the objectives for Week Eleven are to review and refine quick-hit mini-charters, prepare for and conduct steering team review number five, and, finally, to initiate analysis of work and information flow.

Reviewing and Refining Quick-Hit Mini-Charters

Day One begins by focusing on the people who will take on the quick-hit projects, including the implementation leaders and sponsors. To identify these people, the project manager and sponsor must complete four tasks:

1. Identify and rank a short list of potential implementation leaders—ideally from the group of people who have already participated as members of the extended project team. The short-list candidates also should report up through one of the departments represented on the steering team.
2. Discuss the list with the steering team and gain consensus on the leading candidate for the quick-hit project or projects

(no more than one or two). This is followed by a phone call from a steering team member to each candidate's boss to endorse the recommendation and discuss time commitments.

3. Meet individually with each leading candidate's boss to describe the contents of the mini-charter and seek commitment to support the time allocation.
4. Meet individually with the candidates to discuss the mini-charter and any changes or suggestions brought out through this process.

This commonsense but time-consuming activity is an important piece of the change-management work that must accompany a supply chain improvement. Ultimately, the implementation leader—after dealing with the stress of suddenly having so much more to worry about—will start to show ownership by tweaking the mini-charter action steps, timing, and responsibilities given his or her own personal expertise and style. This leader's role in establishing early success is critical; the candidates should understand that fact and be recognized for taking on the responsibility.

As part of the knowledge-transfer process, the project manager acts as the personal coach for the quick-hit implementation leader—providing background on the issue and benefit analysis and the incorporation of the changes into the greater SCOR design process.

In Fowlers' case, David Able and Brian Dowell identified two short-list candidates: a buyer/planner for the largest commodity purchases in Asia and a logistics engineer specializing in import/export. Both candidates, they reasoned, had knowledge of logistics solutions and relationships with suppliers in a region at the center of the quick-hit project. Further, they both had participated in the material flow disconnect brainstorm session and reported through the directors of purchasing or logistics.

With both candidates being highly considered, specific supplier relationships became the tiebreaker and the buyer/planner got the nod. After meeting with the commodity manager in charge, David and Brian shared the good news.

▧ Initiating AS IS Work and Information Flow

The primary agenda for Day Two is to plan and initiate the transactional analysis; the activity itself is similar to the brainstorming event that launched the material flow-disconnect analysis. There are three initiating tasks to complete: Brush up on the SCOR Level Three process elements; identify the transaction analysis teams; and plan the "staple yourself to an order" kickoff event.

Using SCOR Level Three elements is like speaking a foreign language; if you don't use it, you lose it. At the end of this phase of the project, the whole design team will be fluent in SCOR. To accelerate fluency, it's helpful to have a quick-reference resource and dictionary. *The SCOR Quick Reference Guide* provides a summary of just the elements. *The SCOR Dictionary* provides individual definitions for each element, along with suggested metrics, leading practices, inputs and outputs, and supporting technical features (Figure 13-1).

(For members of the Supply-Chain Council, the SCOR Model can be downloaded from the council web site, supply-chain.org.)

The brush-up involves brief discussion on each element in the quick reference guide, with reference to the dictionary for official definitions and an example of the process steps in action. As with any language, there is room for interpretation. For example, it is not black and white where M1.3 Produce and Test ends and where M1.4 Package begins. Many companies have developed rules of thumb where M1.3 stops at primary package and finished goods test and use M1.4 to describe the "storage" pack that prepares the products for work in process storage, staging, transportation, and so on; palletizing would be a good example. This is the moment to achieve consensus on the elements that cause contention.

Identifying the transaction analysis team—"team staple" if you will—is not trivial. The objective, like the brainstorm activity, is to assign members of the design team to lead sub-teams focused on each of the six SCOR Level Three transaction types. These transactions are

Figure 13-1.   SCOR level three dictionary sample.

S1 Source Stocked Product
S1.2 Detail

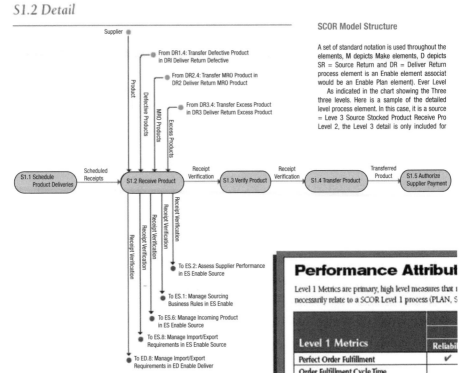

aligned with the SCOR processes. They are purchase order—SOURCE; work order—MAKE; sales order—DELIVER; return authorization—RETURN; forecasts—PLAN; and replenishment orders—PLAN. The ENABLE elements will follow the appropriate process, that is, ENABLE PLAN belongs to the PLAN sub-team, and so forth.

The design team leader(s) uses the staple yourself interview planning worksheet (Figure 13-2) to help identify a group of individuals, by location, who know the details of each step. For example, in SOURCE, the purchase order co-leaders need to assemble interviews in the sites that can provide a detailed hands-on tour of how purchase orders move through:

S1.1—schedule product deliveries
S1.2—receive product

Figure 13-2. "Staple yourself" interview planning matrix.

SCOR Process	Design Team									Locations			
	Source Team Co-Leader	Name	Name	Name	Source Team Co-Leader	Name	Name	Name	Name	Site 1	Site 2	Site 3	Site 4
S2.1 Schedule Product Deliveries										Interview List		Interview List	
S2.2 Receive Product										Interview List		Interview List	
S2.3 Verify Product										Interview List		Interview List	
S2.4 Transfer Product										Interview List		Interview List	
S2.5 Authorize Supplier Payment										Interview List		Interview List	

S1.3—verify product
S1.4—transfer product
S1.5—authorize supplier payment

This SOURCE team might be one person or five persons, depending on the expertise and the uniqueness at each location. The notion of a guided tour is discussed in the classic *Harvard Business Review* article, "Staple Yourself to an Order" (July 1, 1992; Benson P. Shapiro, V. Kasteri Rangan, John J. Sviokla).

Planning the Staple Yourself Interviews

The objective of the "staple yourself" interviews is to collect AS IS data for each relevant SCOR Level Three element by physically following it from the moment it's opened until the moment it's closed. The AS IS data categories include steps to complete the process; input trigger events and key process outputs; enabling technology (including system modules); manual steps right down to the level of Post-It notes; business rules—both formal and informal; and disconnects or issues that cause cycle-time delays and rework of the transaction.

Staple yourself interview preparation has three components similar to the brainstorm event. First, a pre-meeting is planned with targeted extended team members. Second, a proper invitation for the event is sent to the participating extended team members along with the *Harvard Business Review* article as pre-read material. Third, the pre-meeting is held focusing on providing the interviewees necessary background about the project, a brief primer on SCOR using the Quick Reference Guide, and a highlight of the kind of data that will be gathered as part of the interview.

Fowlers' Staple Yourself Structure

At Fowlers, the teams were organized in the following manner:

PLAN (ENABLE PLAN). The director of planning (team leader) focused on the aggregate unit forecast and replenishment plans with extended team members from corporate supply planning; forecast analysts from each of the business groups; and the president, controller, and vice president of operations for the technology products group.

SOURCE (ENABLE SOURCE). The director of purchasing (team leader) focused on the entire acquisition process with extended team members from corporate accounts payable; requisition agents from both Food and Technology Products; a warehouse supervisor to support receipts; and a buyer/planner from the technology products group (not the same individual who was chosen to lead the quick-hit projects).

MAKE (ENABLE MAKE). The director of manufacturing (team leader) focused on scheduling, staging, and releasing work orders with team members from plant scheduling, materials control, and manufacturing.

DELIVER (ENABLE DELIVER). The director of customer service (team leader) focused on quotation to order promise, credit check, inventory allocation, and the warehouse processes from order consolidation through shipment and receipt at the customer's site. Enlisted to help were customer service managers from both food and technology products; a manager from corporate credit and accounts receivable; and warehouse managers from two of the Fowlers' warehouses.

RETURN (ENABLE RETURN). The vice president of sales and marketing/food products group (team leader) focused on return authorization and goods movement with team members from corporate customer service; a warehouse supervisor from the largest returns site; corporate credit; and corporate quality assurance.

▦ Conducting Steering Team Review Number Five

Prepare and conduct the next steering team review meeting with the following agenda items:

- ❑ Project roadmap status.
- ❑ Review TO BE geographic maps.
- ❑ Review quick-hit plans.
- ❑ Work and information flow overview with introduction of the staple yourself interviews.
- ❑ Decisions required today.
- ❑ Expectations for steering team review Number Six.

14

Week Twelve: The Staple Yourself Interview
Follow the Information Step by Step

This week marks the second time during the project that a large group of people from across the organization are polled about issues and opportunities in their piece of the company's supply chain. The first time—the material flow—disconnect analysis-the extended resources came to the design team. This time, the design team will travel to them.

The "staple yourself interview" is fieldwork that attempts to learn how key transactions flow from supplier to customer and back. Guided by the interview plan (Figure 13-2), members of the design team travel to the site where their assigned transaction is created and then follow it to its closure—literally cradle to grave. For example, a sales order field trip may start at a salesperson's home office, where the quote is generated; then move back to headquarters to see how the order is received, validated, and entered; then go to the warehouse to watch how the inventory is allocated to the order, so the customer service representative can communicate a delivery date to the customer; and ultimately end in accounts receivables where reconciled invoices are archived. The design team covers just fifteen of potentially 130 planning and execution processes. To dedicate a full week to gathering and summarizing this critical information is frequently not enough. The objective for Week Twelve is to conduct the staple yourself interviews and document the findings.

Preparing for the Staple Yourself Interview

The interview process is composed of three basic steps.

First, the design team leader—on arriving at the site—provides a quick briefing to the interviewees regarding the Supply Chain Operations Reference (SCOR) Level Three processes under investigation. This can be done in a small conference room with a dry-erase board, by sketching out the flows (Figure 14-1) and labeling the connections with primary inputs and outputs. The interviewees can then help determine the best locations and strategies for conducting the interviews.

Second, the leader should review a sample staple yourself interview worksheet (Figure 14-2),making sure the team understands the type of information, form samples, and screen shots that will be helpful.

Third, the design sub-team and interviewees should proceed to the planned locations and complete the interviews. A location could be a desk, work station, production line, warehouse location, and so forth. If the processes are completed primarily on the computer system, then physically the interview may be accomplished at the desk; the real tour will be through the computer system screens. In other cases, the design team may perform the main interview in a conference room with a live computer log-on, and then walk the path adding the finishing details.

Figure 14-1.   Sample process flow for MI Make-to-Stock.

Process Element Diagram

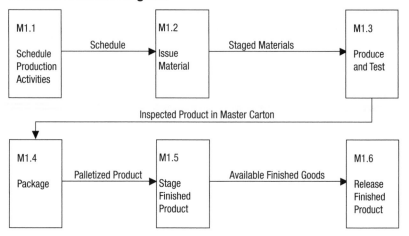

Understanding the Staple Yourself Interview Worksheet

On the worksheet (Figure 14-2), *process* refers to the SCOR Level Three process summarizing the element under analysis, including both abbreviation and words. In many cases, the system completes multiple SCOR processes in a single keystroke, batch run, or algorithm. In those cases, teams often gang processes together. A common gang example is entering and running available-to-promise checks for "to stock" and "to order" sales orders; the individual worksheet would group D1.2, D2.2, D1.3, and D2.3 together. Sometimes teams will use the notation DX! where the "X" is a wild card that applies to all types of orders. In the sample case in Figure 14-3, the process-M1.2 issue material-refers to the pull and staging of component material in advance of a manufacturing run of make-to-stock product.

Primary Input(s) and Output(s) refers to the primary trigger(s) to start the process and primary output(s) of the process. In the sample case, production schedule and pull instructions are triggers to the warehouse operator issuing material to the production line; staged material is the primary output as a result of four processing steps.

(text continues on page 181)

Figure 14-2. Staple Yourself Interview Worksheet.

Interviewees	Enter the interviewees from the interview planning worksheet		
Accountable Function	Enter the title of the ultimate role accountable to the performance of this SCOR Level Three process		
Primary Input(s)	**SCOR Element**		**Primary Output(s)**
Enter the primary transactional input(s) to this process	Enter the SCOR Level Three Process element ID and description, i.e., M1.1 Schedule Production Activities		Enter the primary transactional output(s) to this process
	Step	**Description**	**Responsible**	**Event Time**
	1	Enter the description of each of the process steps; often referred to as level four process steps	Enter the title(s) of those doing the work	This is an effort of the amount of time (often calculated in minutes) and is normalized to one of four transactions, i.e., purchase order, work order, sales order, return authorization, or forecast
Process Steps (>4 and <11)	2			
	3			
	4			
	5			

(continues)

Figure 14-2. (*continued*)

	Total Event Time for Process Steps		0
Technology Used	Enter the relevant technology utilized in this SCOR Level Three process including appropriate system screens or transaction IDs		
Business Rules	Enter the business rules both formal and informal that directly or indirectly influence process performance		
	Disconnect Description	**Initials**	**Relative Weight**	**Project Number**
Disconnect Description, Initials, Relative Weight, and Project Number	Describe major disconnects that cause process steps to be reworked and/or add to process wait time (delay)	Interviewee's Initial	This compares the relative impact disconnects in the list	This designates the project that will eliminate this disconnect

Figure 14-3. Staple yourself interview worksheet for M1.2 Issue Product.

Interviewees	Joe Buick, Lisa Sent		
Accountable Function	Warehouse Manager		
Primary Input(s)	**SCOR Element**		**Primary Output(s)**
Production Schedule Kan Ban Signal	M1.2 Issue Product		Staged Components
	Step	**Description**	**Responsible**	**Event Time (minutes)**
	1	Receive Kan Ban signal	Warehouse Operator	5
	2	Locate components	Warehouse Operator	25
Process Steps (>4 and <11)	3	Wand components out of the warehouse	Warehouse Operator	5
	4	Move components to manufacturing process staging area	Warehouse Operator	5
	5	Sequence components based on the schedule	Warehouse Operator	15

(continues)

Figure 14-3. (*continued*)

	Total Event Time for Process Steps			55
Technology Used	Kan Ban Board, RF Terminal and handheld, Excel, Manufacturing Execution System, and Warehouse Management System			
Business Rules	Don't let the production line stop—informal			
Disconnect Description, Initials, Relative Weight, and Project Number	Disconnect Description	Initials	Relative Weight (Total 100)	Project Number
	Sometimes if receiving is behind, we will pull materials from the receiving area before official receipt in the system; we do the paperwork later	JB	75	12
	Production schedule changes multiple times per day causing a resequencing of components	LS	25	75

Process steps refers to a maximum of ten tasks to complete the SCOR Level Three process element. Why ten? Some teams need more processes to describe how they do their work; the important idea is to use the same maximum number of process steps for each SCOR element to help normalize the level of detail. In the sample case, the warehouse operator completed five tasks: receiving the Kan Ban signal, locating, transferring, physically moving, and sequencing the components to be staged.

Technology used refers to the information tools used to complete the tasks identified in the previous step. The tools can range from an Enterprise Resource Planning module or Internet signal to a fax, phone call, or simple Post-It note. In the sample case, the warehouse operator used Kan Ban Board, Radiofrequency Terminal and Handheld, Excel, Manufacturing Execution System, and Warehouse Management System.

Event Time is the time spent from start to finish on the tasks, assuming no lag time; the team tries to normalize this to time-per-transaction. In this sample case, it would normalize to the event time per production work order. Event time is in contrast with *elapsed time*—the actual time that passes from start to finish, including wait time for steps such as "get approval" (see Chapter 15).

Yield is another topic that will be covered in more detail in Chapter 15; for now, it's enough to say that it represents the number of transactions requiring no rework, measured as a percentage of the total.

Business rules are policies and informal guidelines that govern decisions and behavior. Processing all orders by 3:00 P.M. may be a policy, but onsite supervisors might enforce an unwritten practice of accepting an order an hour later—with the same delivery expectations—as part of a customer-focused culture. Both are business rules. In the sample case, the most significant business rule supporting the warehouse operator's decision and behavior is informal; don't let the production line stop.

Disconnects are issues that result in gaps between elapsed time and event time—too much waiting—and bring yield below 100 percent-reworking orders unnecessarily. In the sample case, the warehouse operator would often respond to the informal business rule to keep the production line moving by pulling material from receiving. This reduced transaction yield, because it created discrepancies in documentation of where materials were located.

Fowlers' Staple Yourself Analysis

In Fowlers' case, the first draft of the consolidated transaction analysis for D1.2 reserve inventory and determine delivery date and D2.2 receive, configure, enter, and validate order transaction analysis is summarized in Figure 14-4.

The tour stop for this process element included customer service representatives in each of the business groups, corporate credit, and corporate customer service. It's noted in the interviewee summary at the beginning of the document that six people were interviewed in this staple yourself exercise. The team agreed that the analysis could group sales orders of stock items (D1) as well as configure-to-order items (D2). Types of inputs are summarized including customer call, fax, or e-mail; web order; field sales call-in; and customer master setup. The output was appropriately called an entered order.

The design sub-team finished its staple yourself tours for the duration of Week Twelve, documenting all fifteen DELIVER elements. The other sub-teams gathered the rest of the forty-five other processes spanning PLAN, SOURCE, MAKE, and RETURN.

The goal for homework is to complete the staple yourself interview worksheets for distribution on Day One of Week Thirteen. This data packet will be the source for building the AS IS process flow and the process performance summary. Extra time may be needed, and more resources should be brought in to complete this step promptly to keep up the project momentum.

Figure 14-4. Fowlers' "staple yourself" interview worksheet for D1.2 Reserve Inventory and Determine Delivery Date and D2.2 Receive, Configure, Enter, and Validate Order.

Interviewees	Susan, Terri, Julie, Jane, Dan, and Mike			
Accountable Function	Customer Service Director			
Primary Input(s)	SCOR Element			Primary Output(s)
Customer call, fax, or e-mail Web order Field sales contact Customer profile	D1.2 Receive, Enter, and Validate the Order D2.2 Receive, Configure, Enter, and Validate the Order			Entered sales order
	Step	Description	Responsible	Event Time
	1	Retrieve or enter new customer master record	Customer Service Representative	1
	2	Verify ship to/bill to addresses	Customer Service Representative	1
Process Steps (>4 and <11)	3	Review customer special notes	Customer Service Representative	5
	4	Enter customer contact, payment terms, ship method and P.O. number	Customer Service Representative	1
	5	Sequence components based on the schedule Enter requested ship date	Customer Service Representative	1

(continues)

Figure 14-4. (continued)

	Step	Description	Responsible	Event Time
Process Steps (*Con't*)	6	Enter part number and quantity	Customer Service Representative	1
	7	Review part description and modify as necessary	Customer Service Representative	1
	8	Input default price and unit of measure	Customer Service Representative	1
	9	Update or save order record	Customer Service Representative	1
	10	Call back customer when inventory allocation fails and re-date the order	Customer Service Representative	2
		Total Event Time for Process Steps		15
Technology Used		MS Word, Access, and Excel; Legacy Mainframe; Fax; E-mail; Fowlers Website		
Business Rules		Formal—orders can be held waiting for payment for a maximum of 30 days after stock is committed.		
		Formal—Credit reviews holds once daily.		
		Informal—once an order is entered, each order line is manually reviewed for correct quantity, part number and price.		
		Informal—If the ship-to address or bill-to address is modified or a new address is added, the order will go on a sales hold. Customer Service must review and approve the address change/addition before it becomes a permanent change/addition.		

	Disconnect Description	Initials	Relative Weight (Total 100)	Project Number
Disconnect Description, Initials, Relative Weight, and Project Number	System pricing does not match spreadsheet version of the customer price	JH	40	4
	Manual entry to add new customer ship-to addresses for drop shipments from suppliers	ST	20	10
	Customer requests different terms than contract	MJ	17	10
	Customer order incorrect increments, i.e., unit of measure and order minimums	DS	10	10
	Customer part number cross reference is not correct	JK	7	4
	New items aren't setup	JH	2	6
	For EDI orders, the item is not available at default source of supply	TY	2	4
	Missing instructions on customer special instruction orders	ST	2	4

15

Week Thirteen: The AS IS Process, Understanding Functional Responsibility, and Steering Team Review Number Six

Learn About Who Really Does What and When

Coming off an intense week of travel, the design team is armed with a packet of interview summaries covering more than forty Supply Chain Operations Reference (SCOR) Level Three process elements. Members have discovered unwritten rules, policy shortcuts, work-arounds, and a real-time validation of how silo mentality is destroying productivity. Now they're ready to start assembling the picture of how their supply chain processes function (or not) in the current state. The main objective of Week Thirteen is to assemble the AS IS Process, Functional, and Responsibility Diagrams using the data summarized in the Staple Yourself interview worksheets.

▪ Assembling the Preliminary AS IS Process Diagram

Process mapping is not a new technique for analyzing operational efficiency. Its effectiveness rests in the ability to pictorially portray how seemingly disparate processes are connected; to illustrate the essential information needed to drive the work; and to ultimately illustrate how process flow relates to organizational roles and responsibilities. The last topic will be discussed in the next section.

The SCOR approach to process mapping considers the Level Three elements as "the work" in "work and information flow." The input–output is "the information" or transaction (Figure 15-1). In the sample case, the system's material requirements planning (P2.1 and P2.2) generated planned requisitions for a planner to (1) balance, (2) convert (P2.3) to firm requisitions, and (3) release to the buyer (P2.4). The released requisitions are converted to purchase orders (S1.1) by a buyer; the purchase order record on the system and the physical delivery of the material and packing slip trigger receipt

Figure 15-1.   Source stocked product process diagram.

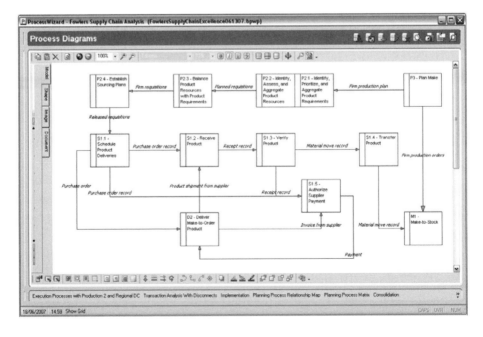

of the product (S1.2). The initial receipt record then triggers appropriate quality checks (S1.3); then a material move record assigns the material to a warehouse location (S1.4). The purchase order record, receipt record, and invoice from the supplier (D2) trigger accounts payable to issue payment (S1.5). Meanwhile planning is transmitting the next firm production plan (P3), which triggers the manufacturing team to send a signal to issue stored raw material (M1) to a production line. The firm production plan also then begins the next cycle of material requirements planning (P3 to P2.1).

(If your work involves flying, you might try to create SCOR process diagrams of your own processes while waiting for the announcement giving permission to turn on electronic devices.)

Assembling the Functional Areas and Responsibilities Diagrams

The functional areas diagram (Figure 15-2) illustrates for each location (in this case, Production 2) the functions that participate in the performance of each SCOR process. The responsibilities diagram adds a slight twist; it illustrates the role each function plays in each SCOR process (Figure 15-3).

In the example, a basic RACI set of categories are used. "R" stands for those *responsible* to actively participate in the activity and contribute to the best of their abilities—to do the work. "A" stands for the person or function ultimately *accountable* for the results. "C" stands for *consult*: those who either have a particular expertise they can contribute to specific decisions (i.e., their advice will be sought) or who must be consulted for some other reason before a final decision is made (e.g., finance is often in a consulting role for projects). "I" is for *informed*: those affected by the activity/decision and therefore need to be kept informed, but do not participate in the effort; they are notified after the final decisions are made.

In Fowlers' case, here are the thoughts that team members discussed about the process, functional areas, and responsibility diagrams for P1—Plan Supply Chain (Figures 15-4, 15-5, and 15-6).

Figure 15-2. Functional areas diagram.

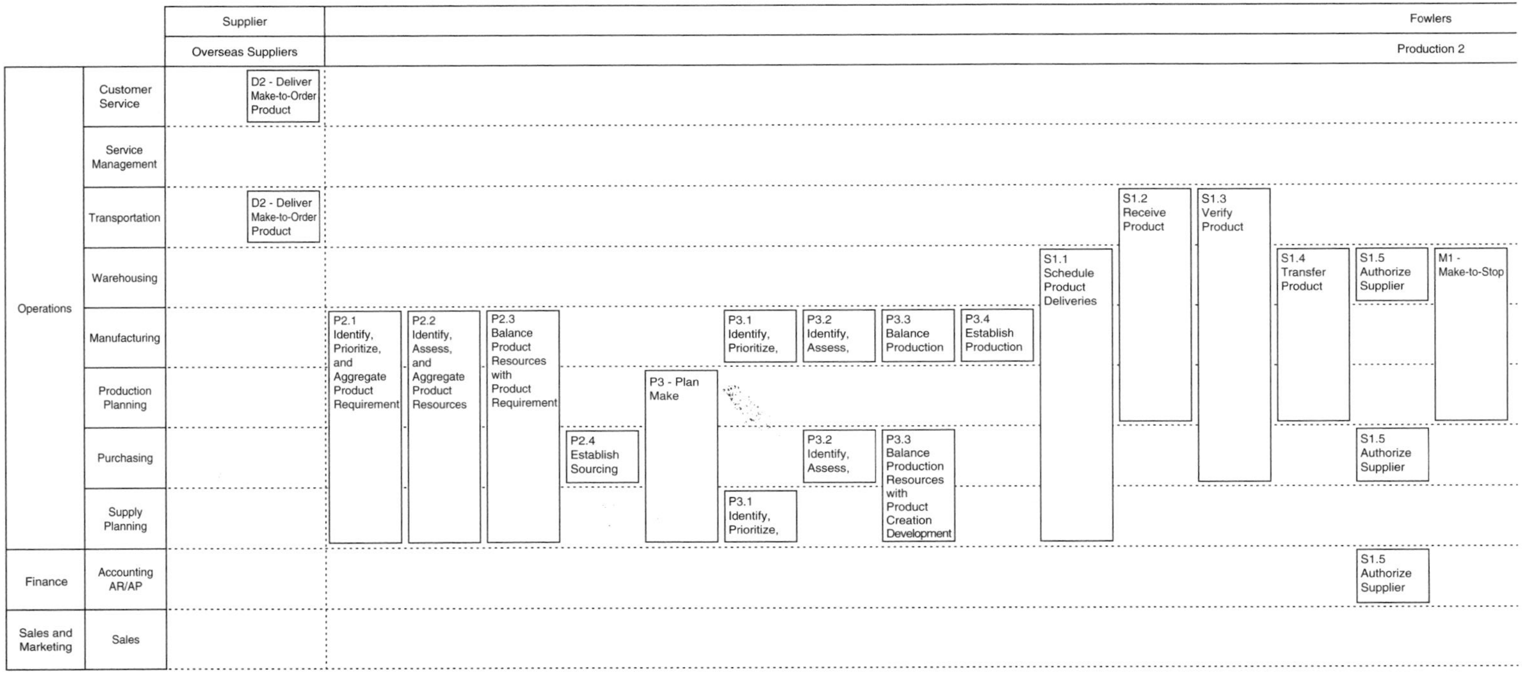

		Supplier														Fowlers		
		Overseas Suppliers														Production 2		
Operations	Customer Service	D2 - Deliver Make-to-Order Product																
	Service Management																	
	Transportation	D2 - Deliver Make-to-Order Product											S1.2 Receive Product	S1.3 Verify Product				
	Warehousing										S1.1 Schedule Product Deliveries				S1.4 Transfer Product	S1.5 Authorize Supplier	M1 - Make-to-Stop
	Manufacturing		P2.1 Identify, Prioritize, and Aggregate Product Requirement	P2.2 Identify, Assess, and Aggregate Product Resources	P2.3 Balance Product Resources with Product Requirement			P3.1 Identify, Prioritize,	P3.2 Identify, Assess,	P3.3 Balance Production	P3.4 Establish Production						
	Production Planning					P2.4 Establish Sourcing	P3 - Plan Make										
	Purchasing								P3.2 Identify, Assess,	P3.3 Balance Production Resources with Product Creation Development						S1.5 Authorize Supplier	
	Supply Planning						P3.1 Identify, Prioritize,										
Finance	Accounting AR/AP															S1.5 Authorize Supplier	
Sales and Marketing	Sales																

Figure 15-3.   Responsibilities diagram.

	Customer Service	Transportation	Warehousing	Manufacturing	Production Planning	Purchasing	Supply Planning	Accounting AR/AP	Sales
P4 - Plan Deliver									
D2 - Deliver Make-to-Order Product									
P2.1 - Identify, Prioritize, and Appreciate									
P2.2 - Identify, Assess, and Appreciate				C	R		C		
P2.3 - Balance Product Resources						R, A			
P2.4 - Establish Sourcing Plans									
P3 - Plan Make					C	I	R, A		
S1.1 - Schedule Product Deliveries				C	R, A	C	I		
S1.2 - Receive Product		R	R, A	I					
S1.3 - Verify Product		C	C	R, A	I	I			
S1.4 - Transfer Product			R, A	C					
S1.5 - Authorize Supplier Payment						R, A		R	
M1 - Make-to-Stock		C		R, A	C				

P1.1: Identify, Prioritize, and Aggregate Supply Chain Requirements (Demand Planning)

Who is involved in the process steps to complete the work? During the staple yourself interviews it was discovered that five functions compile a forecast—each somewhat independently of the others

Figure 15-4.   Fowlers' P1 level three process diagram.

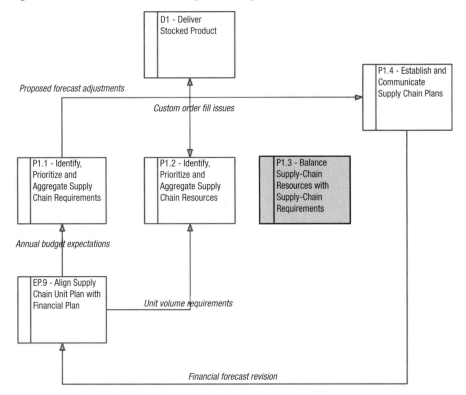

and with different objectives in mind. Marketing develops a net revenue forecast in dollars, based on assumptions for product mix and average selling price. Sales develop a gross revenue forecast as the largest factor in personal compensation plans, independently of product mix and discounts. Sales and marketing fight to gain consensus, with issues of control involving pricing approval and promotional programs. Manufacturing develops a history-based unit forecast to support volume and unit-cost goals in the budgeting process. Marketing relies on manufacturing to guess at the right product mix. Meanwhile, the planning department assembles a forecast to estimate inventory needed to support forecasted revenue; planning doesn't trust marketing's product mix forecast, and it doesn't trust the manufacturing unit plan. Finally, the finance department assembles annual budget data for all of the above, runs a

Figure 15-5.   Fowlers' P1 functional areas diagram.

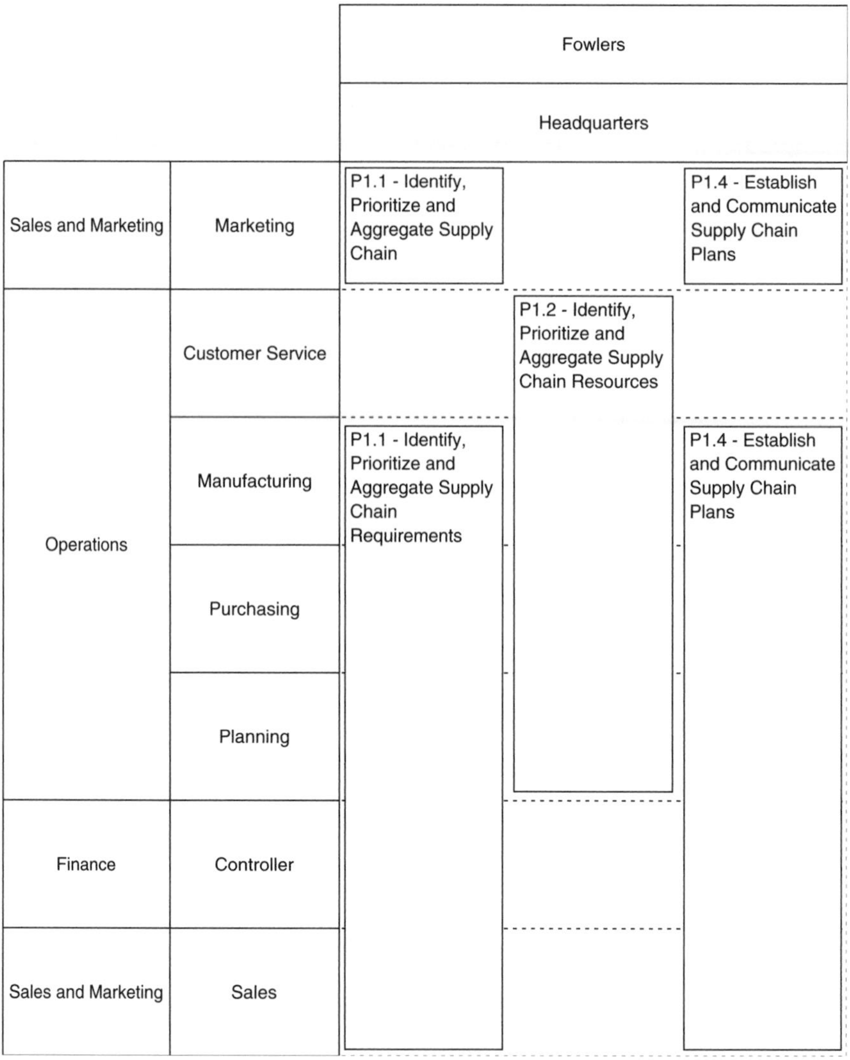

| | | Fowlers | | |
		Headquarters		
Sales and Marketing	Marketing	P1.1 - Identify, Prioritize and Aggregate Supply Chain		P1.4 - Establish and Communicate Supply Chain Plans
Operations	Customer Service		P1.2 - Identify, Prioritize and Aggregate Supply Chain Resources	
	Manufacturing	P1.1 - Identify, Prioritize and Aggregate Supply Chain Requirements		P1.4 - Establish and Communicate Supply Chain Plans
	Purchasing			
	Planning			
Finance	Controller			
Sales and Marketing	Sales			

pro forma profit-and-loss statement, and then usually sends the numbers back for each function to rework because the profit picture isn't ideal. The responsibility diagram sheds the most light; everyone does work, no one is consulted or informed, and no one accepts accountability.

So what is really the primary piece of information that triggers work to begin?

Figure 15-6. Fowlers' P1 responsibilities diagram.

	Marketing	Customer Service	Manufacturing	Purchasing	Planning	Controller	Sales
P1.1 - Identify, Prioritize and Aggregate Supply Chain Requirements	R					R	R
P1.2 - Identify, Prioritize and Aggregate Supply Chain Resources		R	R	R	R		
P1.4 - Establish and Communicate Supply Chain Plans	R					R	R

The team identified three things to produce a forecast. First is the annual budget cycle, which starts in July and is supposed to wrap up in November, but usually extends into January. Second is the event of a missed quarterly profit plan, where some line on the income statement or balance sheet (whether it's revenue, cost, or inventory) is off. Third is acquisitions and divestitures.

They decided to aggregate them into one input called "annual budget expectations."

What is the primary information output from this work that triggers the next process? The only consistent information output is a revised financial forecast in dollars, which is notorious across Fowlers for having almost nothing to do with actual production of units. The disconnects on this transaction analysis summary were staggering.

P1.2: Identify, Assess, and Aggregate Supply Chain Resources (Supply Planning)

Who is involved in the process steps to complete this work? Three functions: manufacturing, planning, and purchasing. Manufacturing responds to volume fluctuations; demand is created and pushed to the warehouses based on unit-cost goals. Planning responds to short-term order-fill issues by moving inventory from warehouse to warehouse and expediting factory replenishment orders. Purchasing wags the tail of the plan by expediting and de-expediting supplier purchase orders in response to actions taken by manufacturing and planning. Once again, all parties feel responsible for doing the work that serves their own respective interests, with no designated process accountability role, zero functions consulted before action, and zero functions informed after action.

What is the primary information trigger to begin the work? Sadly, it's not the sales forecast generated in P1.1 above. Order-fill problems result from a chronically poor inventory position. And it is unit volume expectations from finance. The only output for supply planning was back to customer service with an expedited supply plan to support individual order fill issues.

P1.3: Balance Supply Chain Resources with Supply Chain Requirements (Reconciliation)

Who is involved in the process steps to complete the work? There are no functions formally involved in a balancing process; the means to address delivery issues is an 8 A.M. meeting that lasts three hours—led by manufacturing, with support from planning and purchasing. What is the primary information trigger to begin the work? The agenda for the 8 A.M. meeting is set by a daily backorder reporting showing the status and age of everything in the backorder pool.

P1.4: Establish and Communicate Supply Chain Plans (Senior Leadership Review)

Who is involved in the process steps to complete the work? The budget update is driven by the president of each business group, but the process that they use is to "beat up" each individual function for their piece of the pie. Marketing is in trouble for average selling price declines, sales takes it on the chin for revenue decline, manufacturing gets tagged for unit cost, purchasing is blamed for purchase price variance, planning is blamed for inventory increases, and the controller is in trouble for simply being the messenger. As in the previous processes, everyone is responsible for their own interests, no one is ultimately accountable, and information isn't shared before or after decisions. What is the primary information trigger to begin the work? It's the forecast adjustment generated in P1.1. What is the primary information output that triggers the next process? A revised budget and review for the executive team and board of directors.

As the team completed the assembly of the picture of their supply chain processes, they were already thinking about assembling process performance summaries that would include transaction data for process cycle efficiency, rework, and leading practice maturity. They were reminded about the steering team review that afternoon.

■ Steering Team Review No. 6

Prepare and conduct Steering Team Review No. 6 with the following agenda:

- ❑ Project roadmap status.
- ❑ Anecdotal remarks from the "staple yourself" activity with sample productivities, including the tour maps, interviews, and so forth.
- ❑ Preview of transactional productivity data.
- ❑ Quick lesson on swim diagrams and the business blueprint.
- ❑ Expectations for Steering Team Review No. 7.

16

Week Fourteen: The Process Performance Summary

The Numbers Behind the Pictures

The objective of this week is to summarize overall process performance—volume, cycle time, leading practice maturity, and yield—from the sixty or so Staple Yourself interviews, some form of leading practice assessment, and some creative data collection. The summary takes the form of six spreadsheets—one for each purchase order, work order, sales order, return authorization, forecast, and replenishment order.

The second objective is to introduce the Supply Chain Operations Reference (SCOR) process blueprint, which starts the design team thinking about how transactions flow *should* work.

▪ Assembling the Process Performance Summary

The activity for Day One, assembling process performance summaries (Figure 16-1), involves five steps: First, prepare the templates. For each major transaction listed above, the coach needs to work with some of the system-savvy design team members to identify and label minor transactions that have date and time stamps attached to them

Second is to group the minor transactions to the appropriate SCOR level three elements; it is usually easiest to group multiple SCOR elements to one minor transaction. Third, collect and average the minor transaction's time stamp data (including the volume) and then estimate the frequency that the minor transaction needed to be "reopened" to be reworked (called "yield" in the template). The yield data collection is the most fun; ideally this would be purely data driven but frequently must incorporate some educated guesswork.

Fourth, assess and enter appropriate leading practices maturity scores. Fifth, calculate a process performance grade that can be used to visually rate the performance of the process on the AS IS process diagram.

Leading Practice Assessment

A typical leading practice assessment involves four steps. First, the team needs to pick an assessment tool that will adequately balance good content with an easy to answer approach. Frequently used tools include the following:

- ❏ The Supply Chain Management Process Standards established by the Council of Supply Chain Management Professionals
- ❏ The Supply-Chain Council's SCOR model
- ❏ The Oliver Wight ABCD Checklist for Operational Excellence
- ❏ *Sales & Operations Planning: The How-to Handbook, 2nd Edition*

Figure 16-1. Process performance summary template.

From SYSTEM	From Coach	From SYSTEM	Calculation	From SYSTEM	From Leading Practice Assessment Tool	From SYSTEM	From Staple Yourself Interviews	From SYSTEM
SYSTEM Status Event	SCOR Element	Time Stamps	Process Efficiency	Yield	Leading Practice	Volume	Event Time Minutes	Average Elapsed Time Minutes
Order Created	The coach and team achieve consensus on how the minor transactions map to the SCOR elements	This section lists the "from" and "to" time stamps; the difference is defined as the elapsed time for the minor transaction.	This is calculated by dividing event time by elapsed time.	The yield is an estimate of the number of minor transcations that require NO rework; rework refers to having to reopen and modify, adjust, and/or change.	The leading practice score is derived from a leading practices assessment that has been normalized to the SCOR elements.	Volume is the number minor transactions in the data sample.	The event time total comes from the staple yourself interview worksheet; this needs to be normalized to the elapsed time to calculate process efficiency.	This is the average of the data sample and is driven by the time stamps recorded in the SYSTEM.
Order Booked	D1.2 to D1.3	Order Create Date (Time) to Order Release Date (Time)	4.17%	60%	66%	100,000	15	360

❏ APQC's Open Standards Benchmarking Collaborative[SM] (OSBC)
❏ The Efficient Consumer Response (ECR) Scorecard
❏ For those who have completed previous SCOR projects, your own company's SCOR Level Four processes

Second, the team with coaching support needs to group the assessment questions by appropriate SCOR element(s) similar to the minor transactions above.

Third, the team needs to complete the assessment, making sure to record the results numerically. Last, the team needs to calculate the score by dividing the number of points awarded by the total points possible. This percentage is then transferred to the process performance summary.

This percentage score helps to color-code the SCOR Level Three process elements on the process diagrams: red means broken or missing; yellow indicates need for repair; and green means acceptable. A fully colored AS IS process diagram sends an excellent visual message on the state of your supply chain's process performance. Calculating a "final grade" for each SCOR process has been an evolution. The most frequently used grading scale evaluates process efficiency, yield, and leading practice scores independently and then uses a consensus process for the final color code.

For example, process efficiency Red is less than 10 percent, Yellow is between 10 percent and 20 percent, and Green is greater than 20 percent.

Leading practice R is less than 50 percent, Y is between 50 percent and 80 percent, and G is greater than 80 percent.

Yield R is less than 75 percent, Y is between 75 percent and 95 percent, and G is greater than 95 percent.

To achieve consensus on the final color, many teams have adopted the following logic. To be considered a G, process efficiency, yield, and leading practice scores must be G; to be considered an R, two of the three scores must be R. All other combinations will be considered Y.

In Fowlers' case, Figure 16-2 summarizes the Deliver process performance focused on the sales order transaction. Five minor transactions were identified that had relevant and accurate time-and-date stamps, including order created, delivery created, shipment created, order "goods issued," and customer receipt. In each case, the minor transaction grouped one or more SCOR elements together. This helped the team identify the right worksheets to add together for the event time column. As Fowlers had customers either involved in vendor managed inventory programs or wanting to be involved, the team agreed that The ECR Scorecard would be the appropriate tool for the job. The team graded itself using the efficient replenishment section including the categories of strategy and planning, order management, electronic data interchange, efficient delivery, efficient receiving, and payment. For each category, the tool listed multiple indicators each with descriptions of four levels of maturity.

For each indicator, the team simply had to read the statements and achieve consensus, applying a score of zero through four. The category score simply dividing the points awarded by the points possible. The coach then helped map the categories to the appropriate SCOR elements and finally transferred the percentages accordingly. The Council of Supply Chain Management Professionals' Supply Chain Management Process Standards was used for SOURCE and RETURN. The Oliver Wight ABCD Checklist for Operational Excellence was used for MAKE. *Sales & Operations Planning: The How-to Handbook, 2nd Edition* was used for PLAN.

The final process performance grades reflected in the process color, using the logic above, are illustrated in Figure 16-3. D1.2 to D1.3 scored R for process efficiency, R for yield, Y for leading practice, and R overall; both D1.2 and D1.3 are colored R. D1.4 scored G for process efficiency, R for yield, Y for leading practice, and Y overall. D1.5 to D1.7 scored R for process efficiency, R for yield, Y for leading practice, and R overall.

Initiating TO BE Work and Information Flow

Like the TO BE material flow process, the TO BE work and information flow process seeks to improve transactional productivity by lever-

Figure 16-2. Fowlers' process performance summary for the delivery processes/sales order major transaction.

From SYSTEM	From Coach	From SYSTEM	Calculation	From SYSTEM	From Leading Practice Assessment Tool	From SYSTEM	From Staple Yourself Interviews	From SYSTEM
SYSTEM Status Event	SCOR Element	Time Stamps	Process Efficiency	Yield	Leading Practice	Volume	Event Time Minutes	Average Elapsed Time Minutes
Order Created	D1.2 to D1.3	Order Create Date (Time) to Order Release Date (Time)	4.2%	60%	66%	100,000	15	360
Delivery Created	D1.4	Order Release date to Delivery Create Date	26%	50%			10	39
Shipment Created	D1.5 to D1.7	Delivery Create date to Shipment Create Date	1%		70%	832	19	1560
Order "Goods Issued"	D1.9 to D1.11	Shipment Create Date to Goods Issue Date (Time)	1%	75%			38	3859
Customer Receipt	D1.12 to D1.13	Goods Issue Date (Time) to CL Code	2%	90%	33%	671	120	5947

Figure 16-3.   Fowlers' process performance scores for D1.2 to D1.3, D1.4, and D1.5 to D1.7 (red is represented by the dark gray boxes while yellow is represented by the light gray box).

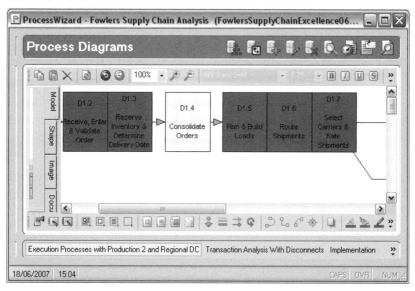

aging appropriate leading practices and eliminating disconnects. Disconnects in this case were generated more narrowly during the interviews with two questions. Why is the yield low for this process (meaning frequent rework)? Why is process efficiency low (meaning a big difference between event and elapsed time)? Unlike material flow, the end is already in mind—it starts with a blueprint. The SCOR process blueprint shows the integrated processes for five leading practices: sales and operations planning, distribution requirements planning, master production scheduling, material requirements planning, and available to promise. The blueprint also incorporates closed-loop execution processes for all SCOR Level Three SOURCE, MAKE, DELIVER, and RETURN process elements (Figure 16-4). This template is the starting point for the TO BE work and information flow. In this specific example, RETURN was not modeled.

The Blueprint Education

At first glance, the blueprint does not appear to be a simple document. Its purpose is to picture a more effective way to work than the tangle of evolutionary procedures that holds most businesses together (or tears them apart). Predictably, after the team (including executives) spends some time going through the detail, the blueprint is perceived to be a very simple diagram of their supply chain complexity.

So the main objective for Day Two is to educate the design team on how integrated supply chain processes should work together. Some people find this to be an energizing part of the project. Executive reaction to the blueprint is—to use G-rated language— arm's length. And design teams, after coming this far, don't usually stop at G-rated language.

That was the case for the Fowlers' design team. It was the coach who kept Day Two focused and effective. He did so by first explaining the strategic intent of the process and then tracing the flow on the blueprint diagram. It was conducted like a tour. The whole process took about three hours, and with team members contributing true examples of poor practices at Fowlers, the group's humor quickly improved.

The tour took the team from PLAN P1 to P4 to P3 to P2 to the SOURCE execution processes S1.1 to S1.5. Then it went on to the MAKE execution process M1.1 to M1.6 and finally to DELIVER execution processes D1.1 to D1.13. Finally, the tour ended with the RETURN execution processes DR1.1 to SR1.6 and DR3.1 to SR3.7. The epilogue covered one of the most frequently asked SCOR questions: "What do the enable processes do?"

The Fowlers' SCOR Blueprint Tour

The following elements comprised the tour:

❑ *PLAN Supply Chain—P1.* This is the process of taking actual demand data and generating a supply plan for a given supply chain (defined in this case by customer, market channel, product, geography, or business entity). This process step is most closely associated with the discipline of sales and operations planning. The basic steps require a unit forecast that's adjusted for marketing and sales events; a supply plan that constrains the forecast based on resource availability (resources could be inventory, manufacturing capacity, or transportation); and a balance step where demand/supply exceptions are resolved and updated

Figure 16-4. The SCOR process blueprint.

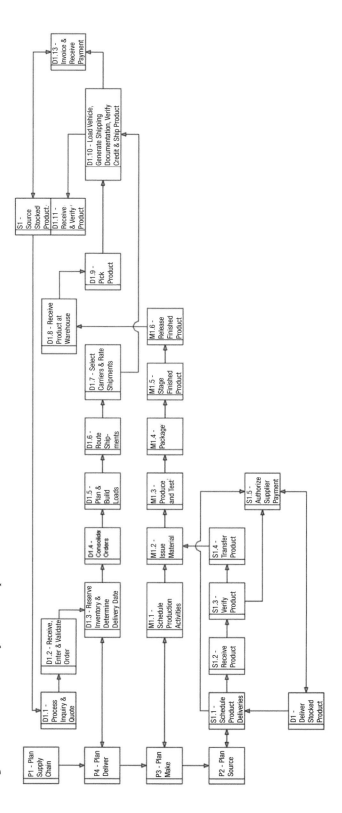

on the system. The output between this process step and the next—PLAN DELIVER (P4)—is a "constrained unit plan."

❏ *PLAN DELIVER—P4.* This is the process of comparing actual committed orders with the constrained forecast generated above and generating a distribution resource plan to satisfy service, cost, and inventory goals. It is carried out for each warehouse stocking location and may be aggregated to region or another geography type. This process step is most closely associated with the discipline of distribution requirements planning. The relationship between this process step and PLAN MAKE (P3) are "replenishment requirements," which tell the plant manager how much product to plan for. Reserve inventory and promise date (D1.3) is a "distribution requirements plan," which lets customer service know how much inventory will be available to promise.

❏ *PLAN MAKE—P3.* This is the process of comparing actual production orders plus replenishment orders with the constrained forecast generated above and then generating a master production schedule resource plan to satisfy service, cost, and inventory goals. It is carried out for each plant location and may be aggregated to region or another geography type. This process step is most closely associated with the discipline of master production scheduling. The relationship between this process step and PLAN SOURCE (P2) are "replenishment requirements," which tell the purchasing manager how much product to plan for. It's all rolled up into schedule manufacturing activities (M1.1), which is the master production schedule that lets the plant scheduler know how much total product must be made by the ship date.

❏ *PLAN SOURCE—P2.* This is the process of comparing total material requirements with the constrained forecast generated above and generating a material requirements resource plan to satisfy landed cost and inventory goals by commodity type. It is carried out for items on the bill of materials and may be aggregated by supplier or commodity type. This process step is most closely associated with the discipline of material requirements planning. The relationship between this process step and schedule product deliveries is the "material requirements plan," which lets the buyer know how much product must be purchased on the basis of current orders, inventory, and future requirements.

❏ *SOURCE—S1.* This set of execution processes involves the material acquisition process—initiating and scheduling the purchase order, receiving and verifying product, transferring the product to available raw material, and authorizing supplier payment through. In the case of sourcing engineer-to-order products, there are accommodations to identify and select appropriate suppliers.

❏ *MAKE—M1.* This set of execution processes encompasses the conversion process of raw materials to finished goods—scheduling production activities, issuing and staging the product, producing and testing, packaging, and release of finished goods to customers or warehouses. In the case of making engineer-to-order products, there are accommodations to finalize engineering specifications before initiating a manufacturing work order.

❏ *DELIVER—D1.* This set of execution processes involves the order fulfillment process—processing inquiries and quotes, entering orders, promising inventory, consolidating orders, planning and building loads, routing shipments, selecting carriers and rating shipments, receiving, picking, shipping, customer receipt, necessary installation, and final invoicing. In the case of delivering engineer-to-order products, there are accommodations to include the request for proposal or quote and negotiating contracts before order entry.

❏ *RETURN—R1 and R3.* This set of execution processes involves the return authorization process, return shipment and receipt, verification and disposition of product, and replacement or credit process for defective and excess inventory. In the case of R2, more detailed scheduling, determination of product condition, and transfer of maintenance, repair, and overhaul items are modeled.

❏ *ENABLE Processes.* Enable processes prepare, maintain, and manage information or relationships on which planning and execution processes rely. There is no decomposition of enable elements. Think of them as necessary processes. There are eight management categories of enable that are applied appropriately to PLAN, SOURCE, MAKE, DELIVER, and RETURN. They are business rules, performance improvement, data collection, inventory, capital assets, transportation, physical network configuration, and regulatory compliance. Another enable process, unique to PLAN, manages alignment of the financial and unit plans; another enable process—this one unique to SOURCE—manages supplier agreements. Supply chains can have well-integrated planning and execution processes and still underperform if enable processes are poorly managed. For example, a good sales and operations planning process cannot overcome a poor EP.9—align unit and financial plans.

With this education, the design team was ready to begin building their own blueprint for Fowlers' work and information flow.

17

Week Fifteen: The TO BE Work and Information Flow Blueprint and Steering Team Review Number Seven

Define How the Business Should Work

The goal of many design efforts is to "think outside the box." There was some kind of brain research from a college psychology class that indicated children who haven't yet started school will score an average of 95 percent on a creativity test, whereas third-graders score 30 percent on the same test—and adults in the workplace score 5 percent. So much for "outside the box."

Blend brain research with the fact that the relationships between supply chain processes are integrated and complex, and it's too much to ask for a design team to start building TO BE processes from scratch. So the objective for this week is not fluid creativity. Rather, it's to help define how the business should work. As previewed toward the end of the last session, the tool for this is the Supply Chain Operations Reference (SCOR) blueprint (Figure 16-4).

Configuring the Blueprint

The agenda for Day One is to configure the SCOR blueprint to how the company *should* operate its supply chain. There are six basic configuration guidelines that facilitate the process:

Guideline One suggests that all SCOR Level Three elements remain on the diagram unless there is consensus that the process is not applicable (i.e., omitting D1.14 Install Product because that is not part of your company's business model).

Guideline Two requires all inputs and outputs to be translated into the language of your company's information system(s); that is to say, SAP and Oracle, as examples, have different transactional titles for intercompany "orders."

Guideline Three requires the team to identify at least the TO BE RACI accountable and responsible roles. The next section in this chapter on organizational considerations will provide guidelines as to overall functional additions and/or subtractions.

Guideline Four requires the team to use the process performance grading criteria to estimate the color of the process based on the successful implementation of the project portfolio (i.e., an AS IS red P1 Plan Supply Chain may turn yellow or green in the TO BE blueprint).

Guideline Five requires the process diagram to illustrate additional leading practices that are a part of the project portfolio, such as make-to-make blueprint scenario for subcomponents using Kan Ban signals (Figure 17-1).

Guideline Six suggests that the team keep a running list of assumptions regarding business rules, setup requirements, policies, and so forth that will enable the TO BE process to perform effectively. The change driver matrix, Figure 12-1, is a helpful assumption organizer.

Figure 17-1.   Make-to-make blueprint for subcomponents using Kan Ban signal.

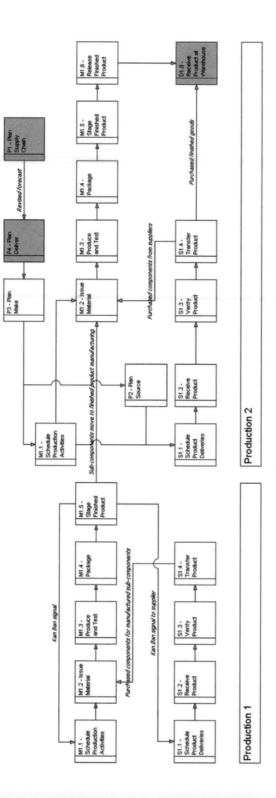

Fowlers' P1 Plan Supply Chain Configuration

The P1 Plan Supply Chain changes identified in the Fowlers' case (Figure 17-2) included the use of all six guidelines. With respect to Guideline One, the team used all the P1 process elements (remember that in the AS IS, P1.3 was not attached) and included other SCOR elements to illustrate how (1) distribution resource planning (P4) acts as an interface between the revised forecast and the execution of the order fulfillment processes (D1); (2) the enable process for planning data management (EP.3) provides input to initiate the demand planning process (P1.1); and (3) the budget and financial project process (EP.9) is incorporated into the process.

Under Guideline Two, the team detailed inputs and outputs. The following is part of a definitions page of their white paper. "Triggers for a new unit forecast (P1.1) include sales history (with promotions); revised item master data; and annual unit and financial budget. Sales history in this case refers to the month-end update of the planning software, based on actual demand. Promotion refers to the revised promotional calendar for specific customer or item events, as well as the general marketing campaigns. Revised item master refers to changes in item data that would change the method of forecast, for example, corporate marketing needs to release new products and a list of rationalized items to be retired. The annual unit and financial budget is the month's previous agreed-to plan—the most recent sales and operations plan compared to the annual budget that was shared with the street. The consensus unconstrained forecast triggers a new supply plan (P1.2) with the output defined as a constrained supply plan."

In this case, Fowlers is assuming that the rough-cut capacity assumptions, inventory stocking strategies, and other essential supply planning setups are completed as part of the actual P1.2 work. The constrained supply plan triggers the balance activity between requirements and resources, which resolves unit demand and supply mismatches (often called exceptions) and then converts the numbers to a financial projection that can be compared with the budget. Financial gaps to budget are calculated, and the business team put action plans in place to resolve them. In supply planning terms, the exception list is defined by item and location where there is real potential to miss designated customer service levels. Exceptions also point out where there is too much inventory. The revised financial project with gap actions triggers a forecast and financial projection update process, with the output forecast feeding the distribution resource planning process and the approved rolling eighteen-month unit plan and financial projection feeding the corporate budget process.

Figure 17-2.   Fowlers' TO BE P1 plan supply chain level three process blueprint.

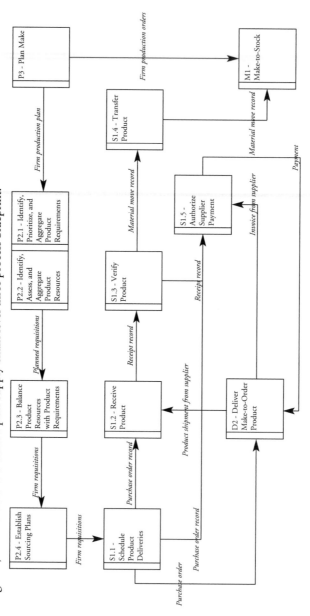

Under Guideline Three, the roles and responsibilities were detailed and attached (as addressed below under "Organizational Considerations for the TO BE blueprint").

For Guideline Four, the team color-coded the P1 process performance summary as yellow for the first six months after implementation, with a one-year goal of achieving green. Their conclusion was that while the "learn by doing" approach they selected would take longer, the ultimate process would be installed for the long term.

Under Guideline Five, they chose the *Sales & Operations Planning: The How-to Handbook, 2nd Edition*, by Thomas Wallace to guide their leading practice checklist. Figure 17-2 illustrates the high-level design. Chapter 18 illustrates how that book helped them to detail the necessary Level Four processes that will guide implementation.

For Guideline Six, the team compiled many assumptions and grouped them into five major categories. Organization design changes would be needed to support resource requirements; although the process could operate without a perfect information system, more robust demand planning and supply network (rough-cut capacity planning) tools would be necessary; the finance organization would need to incorporate Sales and Operations Planning (S&OP) output with their budget project process.

Organizational Considerations for the TO BE Blueprint

In preparing to address Guideline Three—roles and responsibilities—it is helpful to give the team a crash course in formal organization design. Usually one of the first questions executives have before the project even starts is around "How should we reorganize?" There are no fewer than fifty Dilbert comic strips dealing with that topic! The truthful answer—which doesn't appear in any of those cartoons—is "I'm not sure yet."

Organization design can be viewed as the process of grouping functions together and defining formal and informal reporting relationships. Leading practice methods to define effective organization structure have five rules and two corollaries in common.

Rule One: Three prerequisites must be in place: (1) effective strategy, (2) efficient and effective TO BE process flows, and (3) a balanced scorecard that measures organization, customer, and process performance.

Rule Two: Departmental groupings are based on TO BE processes with boundaries that maximize scorecard performance, that is, customer reliability, flexibility, and responsiveness, as well as company internal efficiency.

Rule Three: Establish structural goals that minimize handoffs, move the organization closer to customers or suppliers, optimize span of control balancing that with effective employee development, minimize layers of management, and drastically reduce or eliminate gray areas.

Rule Four: Formal organization structure needs to account for enabling processes, that is, managing business rules, data, performance, and so forth that make planning and execution more effective.

Rule Five: The bottom layers of the organization are the most important; RACI roles for the primary planning, execution, and enabling processes must be clear, effective, and efficient; and job level performance expectations, tasks, and feedback must be in place. Corollary One: The degree of centralization is neither good nor bad, but it is dependent on the structural goals defined in Rule Three. Corollary Two: Simply choosing to organize by process versus by function is not inherently better or worse; there are successes and failures in both cases. The challenge is to balance process performance against functional or business needs as defined in Rule Two.

Fowlers' Organizational Changes Around P1 Plan Supply Chain

The team agreed that the requisites of Rule One were satisfied with the competitive requirements, TO BE SCOR blueprint, and scorecard deliverables. The team recommended three changes to satisfy Rule Two relative to P1. First, two additional functions were added to the list: logistics and the business team (Figure 17-3). The absence of those two roles in the AS IS caused much pain and rework. Second, planning was divided in half, based on tasks and proximity to the customer. Demand planning aligned to the forecast and was to develop intelligence around demand including sales, marketing, and customer behavior. Supply planning, on the other hand, aligned to manufacturing, logistics, purchasing—the supply resources. Third, the team recommended that all the functional and business leaders incorporate the scorecard metrics as a significant part of their annual incentive program; the thought was that this would drive more collaborative behavior. The team satisfied some of the requirements of Rule Three by reordering the line of site from customer to supplier. The list included sales, marketing, demand planning, customer service, logistics, production, purchasing, supply planning, controller, and business team. The team, to address Rule Four, identified one enabling process (EP.9) as critical to the performance of the Plan Supply Chain and included it in RACI analysis. The results of Rule Five are illustrated in Figure 17-4. In summary, the team was able to gain consensus agreement on changing the "everyone owns everything and trusts no one" illustrated in the AS IS version (Figure 15-6) to a process with more mature cross-functional teamwork.

Process Maturity and Executive Change: Thinking Ahead

In thinking about the steering team review, the coach suggested adding a topic covering the topic of process maturity. He described that about six months after TO BE processes have been successfully implemented, an interesting dynamic starts to occur at the executive, process owner, and/or sponsor levels. As disconnects that once occupied such a large part of their time (and job expectations) go away and the lower layers of the organization manage processes and performance more effectively, a feeling of "What do I do now?" can set in.

As part of the TO BE blueprint, the coach and sponsor need to help the steering team and other leaders plan for addressing this question proactively.

The checklist below is helpful in gauging process maturity; to arrive at a maturity score, give yourself a 2 for yes, 1 for partial, and 0 for no. Divide your total by twenty-four to arrive at a percentage; 90 percent is an A, 80 percent is a B, and so forth.

Maturity Checklist

Organizational

- ❏ Your competitive requirements are aligned to your customers' cost-service strategies.
- ❏ Your organizational design is effective and efficient, with clear roles and responsibilities, and decisions being made at the appropriate level.
- ❏ Your performance measurement system (scorecard) is aligned to the customer and is being managed monthly.

Process

- ❏ Process goals have been established in alignment to competitive requirements.
- ❏ Processes are defined to Level Four—RACI roles are clear.
- ❏ Processes are being performed—process measures (per Thomas Wallace) are being managed.

Figure 17-3. Fowlers' TO BE P1 Plan Supply Chain functional areas diagram.

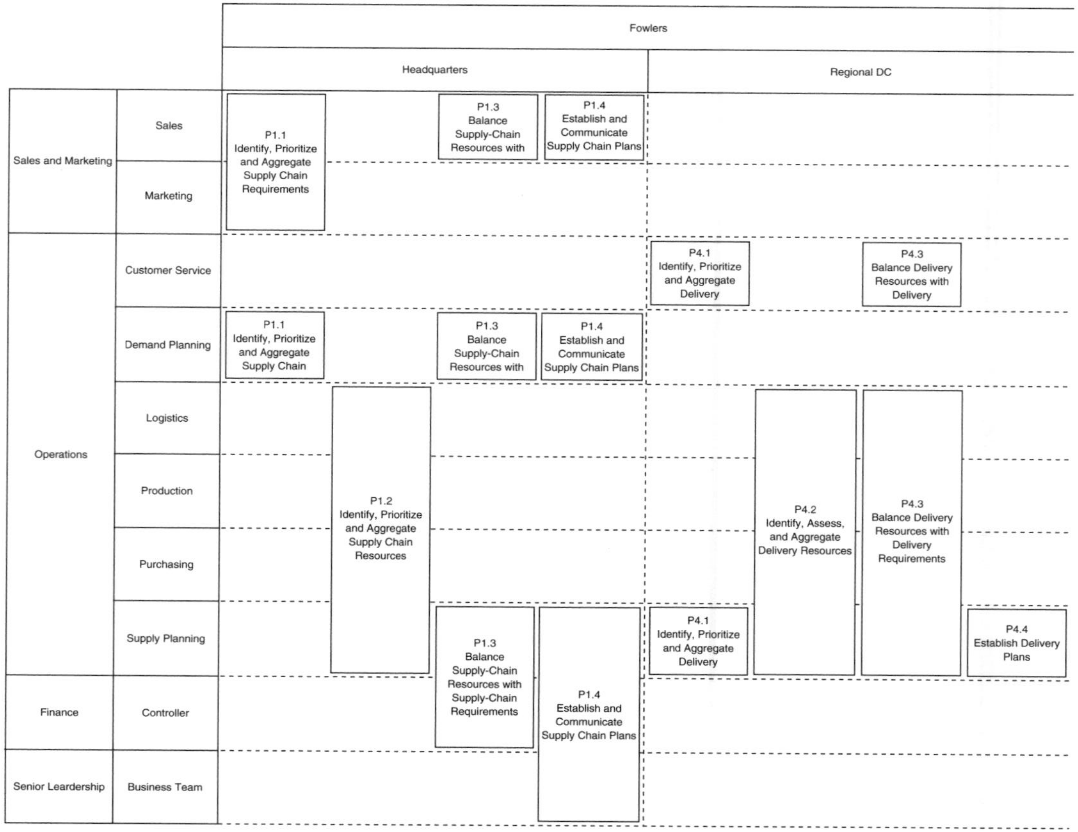

Fowlers

Headquarters | Regional DC

Sales and Marketing
- Sales
- Marketing

Customer Service

Operations
- Demand Planning
- Logistics
- Production
- Purchasing
- Supply Planning

Finance
- Controller

Senior Leadership
- Business Team

Sales:
- P1.1 Identify, Prioritize and Aggregate Supply Chain Requirements
- P1.3 Balance Supply-Chain Resources with
- P1.4 Establish and Communicate Supply Chain Plans
- P4.1 Identify, Prioritize and Aggregate Delivery
- P4.3 Balance Delivery Resources with Delivery
- P4.4 Establish Delivery Plans

Demand Planning:
- P1.1 Identify, Prioritize and Aggregate Supply Chain
- P1.3 Balance Supply-Chain Resources with
- P1.4 Establish and Communicate Supply Chain Plans
- P1.2 Identify, Prioritize and Aggregate Supply Chain Resources

Supply Planning:
- P1.3 Balance Supply-Chain Resources with Supply-Chain Requirements
- P1.4 Establish and Communicate Supply Chain Plans
- P4.1 Identify, Prioritize and Aggregate Delivery
- P4.2 Identify, Assess, and Aggregate Delivery Resources
- P4.3 Balance Delivery Resources with Delivery Requirements
- P4.4 Establish Delivery Plans

Figure 17-4. Fowlers' TO BE P1 Plan Supply Chain responsibilities diagram. R, responsible; A, accountable; C, consult; I, inform.

	Sales	Marketing	Customer Service	Demand Planning	Logistics	Production	Purchasing	Supply Planning	Controller	Business Team
P1.1 - Identify, Prioritize and Aggregate Supply Chain Requirements	A	A		R						
P1.2 - Identify, Prioritize and Aggregate Supply Chain Resources					C	C	C	R, A		
P1.3 - Balance Supply-Chain Resources with Supply-Chain Requirements	C			C				R, C	R, A	
P1.4 - Establish and Communicate Supply-Chain Plans								C	R	A
P4.1 - Identify, Prioritize and Aggregate Delivery Requirements			A					R		
P4.2 - Identify, Assess, and Aggregate Delivery Resources					C	A	I			
P4.4 - Establish Delivery Plans										

Job performer

❏ Annual job performance goals are aligned to the organization.
❏ Job descriptions are complete and support RACI process roles.
❏ Job performance is being managed with development opportunities being identified as needed.

Technical

❏ Technical platform is aligned to process requirements.
❏ Detailed solution design is derived from process requirements.
❏ Technical performance (uptime and response time) is managed.

Typical Impact of Increasing S&OP Maturity on the Executive

Here's a list of typical changes through successful implementation of S&OP that can lead an executive to wondering what to do next.

❏ Daily, weekly, and monthly tasks shift from "managing orders" to "managing strategic growth," that is, new products, new customers, new markets, and so forth.
❏ Awareness grows of how a decrease in "fire fighting" has translated into more value-added time with the customer.
❏ Management needs evolve from people and event issues to metric and process issues.
❏ Issues that belong on an executive's plate become easier to separate from those that can be delegated.
❏ It becomes possible to focus more on the profit and loss and potential gaps.
❏ Data are used more often, and the words "I think" less often in supporting arguments and decisions.

Conducting Steering Team Review Number Seven

Prepare and conduct Steering Team Review Number Seven with the following agenda items:

❑ Project roadmap status
❑ Process performance summary by transaction type
❑ TO BE Blueprint
❑ Process maturity—changes to executive role
❑ Expectations for Steering Team Review Number Eight

18

Week Sixteen: Level Four Process Development

Where the Process Rubber Hits the Implementation Road

The Supply Chain Operations Reference (SCOR) Level Three blueprint is complete, organization structural recommendations are under consideration, process performance targets are set, and RACI analyses for the Level Three elements are finalized. The team now starts to focus on implementation. In general language, there are five steps to process implementation: define high-level business requirements; complete detailed solution design for technology-enabled solutions; configure the software, test, or pilot; go live; and roll out. In Six Sigma language, this equates to the DMAIC steps of Define, Measure, Analyze, Improve, and Control

The SCOR Level Three blueprint is most often associated with high-level business (process) requirements and has been a staple of many projects. What many people refer to as SCOR Level Four processes seem to fit in as part of the detailed solution design and, in fact, are necessary for any kind of implementation activity to occur. This discussion is kind of a misnomer because the SCOR model doesn't have any standardized definition for Level Four processes (Figure 18-1); although the quick reference guide illustrates the relationship of Level Three to Level Four, there are no Level Four definitions to be found in the SCOR dictionary itself. This chapter, then, is dedicated to the concept of creating Level Four diagrams.

The question of how to build SCOR Level Four processes has been on the Supply-Chain Council's frequently asked questions list since 2000. Some argue there are no standard Level Four processes; some argue that one standard needs to be defined for all. The truth usually lies somewhere in the middle, balancing "standard" leading practice criteria with "custom" functionality found in the company's mix of information systems.

Constructing a SCOR Level 4 Process

There are eight steps to build a Level Four SCOR process; here is the list:

1. Find appropriate leading practice books that can guide you through best in class characteristics.
2. Map your company's "best practice" processes to SCOR Level Three processes (for those who readily admit that they have no leading practices, skip this step).
3. Cross-reference the processes as detailed in the book to appropriate SCOR Level 3 processes.
4. Identify the main system modules to be used, and cross-reference the transactions to the appropriate SCOR Level Three process; this will help with the inputs and outputs and names for the transactions.
5. Use information system resources to help create a "screen shot storyboard" that illustrates the different screens (features and functionality) from the beginning of its Level Three parent to

Figure 18-1.　Level four processes in relationship to the rest of the SCOR model.

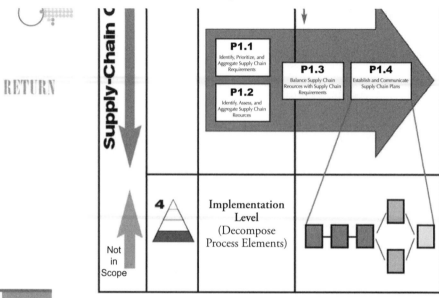

its end. The storyboard is relatively easy to produce; the "print screen" keys on the computer allow for easy capture. This is not intended to replace technical documentation; the goal is to provide the design and appropriate extended teams with a visual tour of the important functionality.

6. Use the storyboard and the leading practice book to create the first draft of your Level Four process.

7. By using a "conference room" pilot approach with appropriate design and extended team members, walk them through the process map and storyboard. Leverage the experience of the design and extended teams in refining the process and completing RACI analysis for each Level Four element; use information system resources in refining their storyboard (and ultimate detailed solution design).

8. If possible, set up an information system live test environment where company data can put the new processes and functionality to the test away from the actual live system. In many cases, these "sandboxes" were set up as part of a previous information system implementation effort.

Fowlers' P1 Plan Supply Chain Level Four processes

The team satisfied steps one, two, three, and six using Wallace's *Sales & Operations Planning* book (Figure 18-2). They were able to use the process details described in Wallace's fifth chapter to assemble the leading practice perspective of the P1 Plan Supply Chain Level Four process. Figures 18-3 to 18-6 illustrate the level process flows for demand planning (P1.1), supply planning (P1.2), reconciliation (P1.3), and senior leadership review (P1.4), respectively. As an added twist, the team put the Level Four processes in time-phased groupings. In each figure they placed the Level Four processes in one of four rows; each row relates to a week of a month (i.e., the first row contains all Week One activities for P1.1, P1.2, P1.3, and P1.4). That way, a new demand planner can look at Figure 18-3 and understand what work needs to be completed during

(text continues on page 227)

Figure 18-2.   Amazon.com book graphic and partial table of contents from leading practice book guiding the P1 plan supply chain level four process development.

Part Two — How to Make It Work

Figure 18-3. Fowlers' P1.1 Level Four process blueprint for demand planning. SKU, Stock Keeping Unit.

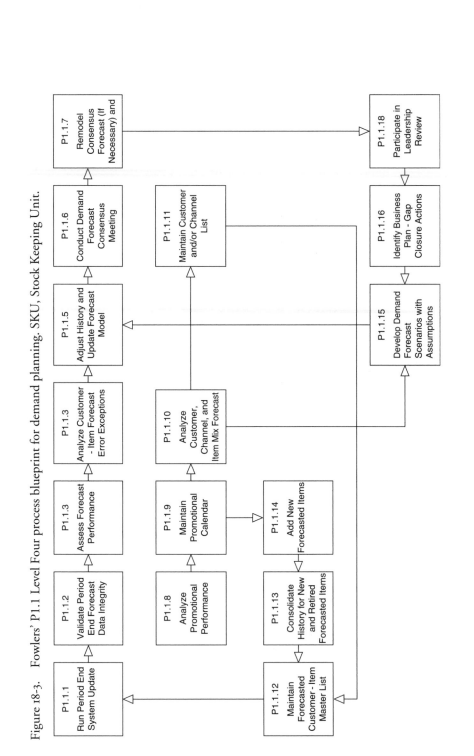

Figure 18-4.   Fowlers' P1.2 Level Four process blueprint for supply planning. SKU, Stock Keeping Unit.

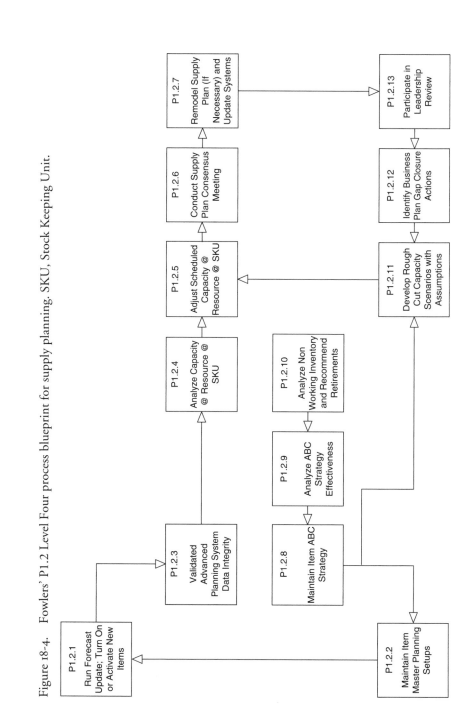

Figure 18-5. Fowlers' P1.3 Level Four process blueprint for reconciliation.

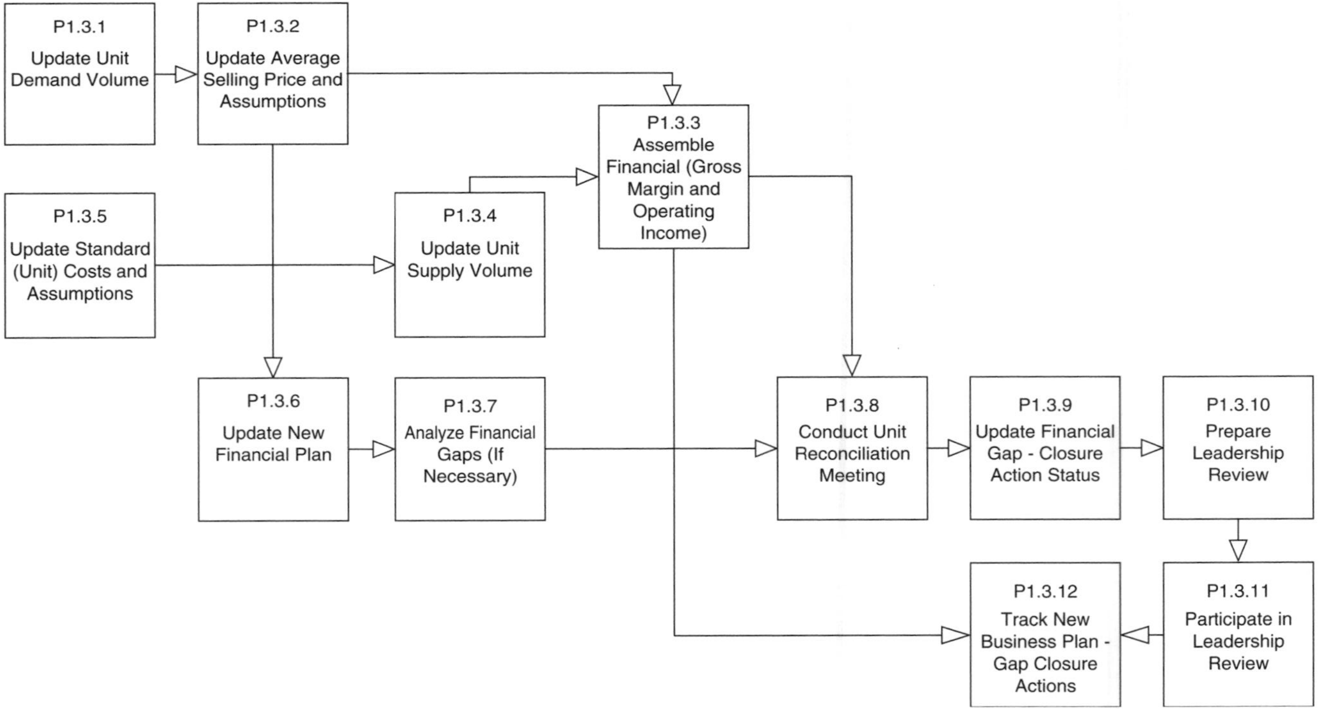

Figure 18-6.   Fowlers' P1.4 Level Four process blueprint for senior leadership review.

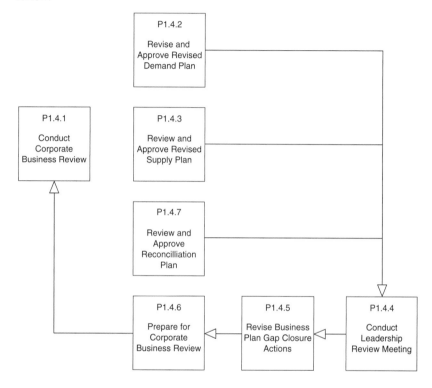

each week of the month. In completing steps four and five, the team cross-referenced the "forecast to plan" module of the software with the P1 Plan Supply Chain processes. Figure 18-7 is a screen shot taken from the P1.1 storyboard that illustrates where the analytical effort from P1.1.4, P1.1.5, P1.1.7, and P1.1.8 (Figure 18-3) would be entered. The shot also illustrates the set of new names for minor transactions, that is, order forecast, marketing adjustment percentage, marketing/sales events, and so on.

Because the "forecast to plan" functionality was a planned replacement for the current demand planning tool, the information systems design and extended team members already had a head start on setting the conference room pilot using a sandbox test environment (steps seven and eight). They had selected sample data from the last twelve months to help assess some of the forecasting algorithms (i.e., seasonality) and more sophisticated product-customer forecast aggregations (i.e., forecasts by Stock Keeping Unit and by customer). The team would get their first view of the sandbox during the next two weeks.

Figure 18-7.   Sample of one screen shot from the Fowlers' storyboard.

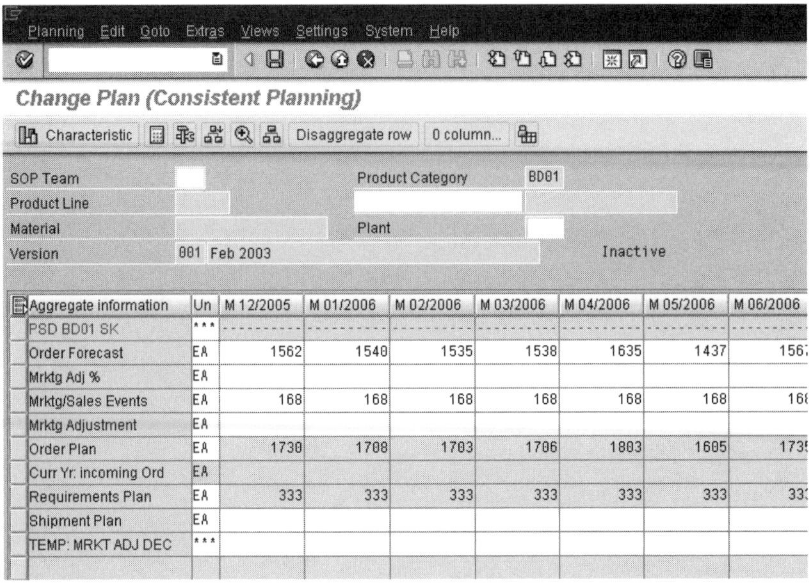

■ Applications of SCOR Level Four Processes

Seeing future supply chain processes in action through simulation truly gives the team a glimpse of the future; this shared vision of what the TO BE picture looks like is a powerful educational process and acts as a magnet for the rest of the organization. The Fowlers' design and extended team members were so enamored with the process, they brainstormed some other ways this process could help Fowlers.

1. For those using Lean Six Sigma to implement supply chain process improvements, the process could be incorporated as part of the Six Sigma DMAIC process steps.
2. For those in some phase of software implementation, the process could provide a consistent requirements guideline for software demonstrations in selection, defining detail business requirements before configuration, and organizing sandbox configuration test scripts.

3. For others using the Supply Chain Excellence approach to implement a project portfolio, the Level Four processes could provide a more detailed foundation for the corporate process management framework and a means to audit current practices.

The next—and last design session—summarizes benefits, updates the project portfolio, assembles implementation plans, and previews a new organization to support the longer-term business process management needs.

19

Week Seventeen: Implementation Planning, Program Management, and Steering Team Review Number Eight

Organizing Supply Chain Improvement as Part of Daily Life

The finish line! Or is it? After one of the toughest graduate classes at the University of Minnesota, as Professor Richard Swanson handed out the final exam, he said, "True learning is a painful experience . . . I can see that all of you have learned a great deal in this course." As the last of the students left the room at the end of the hour, he offered one more piece of advice: "Remember," he said, "that the road never ends. It's the journey that must be your home."

Design teams end this sixteen-week process weary, but also transformed, enlightened, broadened, deepened . . . changed. In many respects individuals knew the answers to the problems the very first day. When asked why they still needed sixteen weeks, most would summarize it something like this: "Each of us had our own biases, ideas, and agendas. The sixteen weeks helped us put data behind the ideas, replace individual agendas with a shared vision, document every assumption, educate our leaders on the real issues and gain support for some tough changes. Our company is about to undergo massive transformation, the time was necessary to change us, the foundation, first."

The final week of the project called for the team to build an effective implementation plan, paying attention to both critical details and long-term vision. Details include polishing up the project portfolio based on the work and information flow analysis, developing a preliminary return-on-investment analysis, and assembling an implementation timeline. The visionary part focuses on architecting a program management process and organization to help sustain the current list, strategically select and facilitate similar design efforts, and integrate nearer term projects with the Lean Six Sigma program.

Fowlers' Project Portfolio and Projected Return on Investment

On Day One, the Fowlers design team met to review the project portfolio and projected return on investment (Figure 19-1). The numbers provided some surprises. The first was in Project No. Three: Improve Information Technology Effectiveness. Nearly everyone had fit into one of two camps at the start of the project. The "rose-colored glasses" group saw the new Tier One Enterprise Resource Planning system as having achieved all that it was engineered to achieve; it was in and that was the goal, right? Those in the "system is the problem" group viewed the Enterprise Resource Planning system's implementation over the last couple of years as the main reason the company wasn't as successful as it had once been. But now, looking at the project portfolio, both groups agreed that to improve performance, more investment was needed to use the system to its fullest. The return on investment value of Project

Figure 19-1. Fowlers' final project portfolio and projected three-year return on investment.

Fowlers' Project Portfolio

Gross EVA Benefit ($ in 000s)	1st-Year Cost Investment	3-Year Benefit			3-YR ROI
% of Annualized Benefit Achieved	100%	FY 1	FY 2	FY 3	
		25%	40%	100%	
1 Improve Demand Management and Forecasting	$ (250)	$ 75	$ 120	$ 300	1.98
2 Optimize Supply Management Practices	$ —	$ —	$ —	$ —	—
3 Improve Information Technology Effectiveness	$ (6,500)	$ 625	$ 1,000	$ 2,500	0.63
4 Improve Data Integrity	$ —	$ —	$ —	$ —	—
5 Improve Supplier Flexibility	$ (1,800)	$ 1,400	$ 2,240	$ 5,600	5.13
6 Implement Formal Product Life Cycle Management Process	$ (1,100)	$ 625	$ 1,000	$ 2,500	3.75
7 Engineer an Integrated Tactical Planning Process	$ (250)	$ 1,250	$ 2,000	$ 5,000	33.00
8 Implement Sales and Operations Planning	$ (2,200)	$ 2,826	$ 4,521	$ 11,303	8.48
9 Improve Efficiency and Effectiveness of the Physical Supply Chain Network	$ (2,250)	$ 4,375	$ 7,000	$ 17,500	12.83
10 Tighten Up Order Management Discipline	$ —	$ —	$ —	$ —	—
11 Establish Formal Return Management	$ (750)	$ 775	$ 1,240	$ 3,100	6.82
12 Eliminate Poor Inventory Control Practices	$ (125)	$ 75	$ 120	$ 300	3.96
Grand Total	$ (15,225)	$ 12,026	$ 19,241	$ 48,103	

Number Three was low (0.63)—particularly in relation to the high level of first-year investment. This helped bring the camps together on prioritizing supply chain improvement elsewhere before putting more money into the system.

Another surprise had to do with Projects Seven and Eight: Engineer an Integrated Tactical Planning Process and Implement Sales and Operations Planning. Nobody had realized the tremendous cost of poor planning; fixing it offered the second biggest opportunity for profit improvement. The entire company had practiced execution and fire fighting until it was an art form. In fact, service awards were given to Fowlers' employees who effectively responded to the most crises in a quarter. All of that could now change. Even though the processes to be implemented that would improve the company's planning efforts were leading practices, the implementation approach was not rocket science. Of more concern was the human discipline needed to make, follow, and appropriately adjust plans. There were a thousand-and-one behaviors to change—from the executive team all the way to the manufacturing scheduler. Only a third of the cost for this project actually went to improving planning functionality; the rest was process and change management.

The third surprise was in Project Number Eleven: Establish Formal Return Management. The financial impact of poor product return is the first low-hanging fruit of the Twenty-First Century. Accruals, obsolescence, return policy, reverse logistics, customer service, technical support, inventory disposition, product recall, and consigned excess inventory have all evolved to a point where a well-designed RETURN element can deliver significant financial impact on every income statement and balance sheet.

The fourth surprise was in Projects One, Two, Four, Ten, and Twelve. These offered little to no operating income financial return; their focus was on the customer. A need to improve delivery reliability, order cycle time, and flexibility to respond to unplanned demand were all things that had shown up on customer satisfaction surveys. Although no one in sales and marketing would commit to an increase in revenue from addressing these issues, the team thought there were several benefits. First, the process performance analysis indicated that these projects would free up non-value-added time from DELIVER and SOURCE resources. Second, data from lost opportunity and canceled sales orders suggested that delivery reliability could provide positive revenue impact. Third, these projects were foundational to supply chain excellence; other projects were dependent on them.

The fifth observation was no surprise; the physical supply chain network was extremely inefficient—both from the supply base and within the distribution network. Projects Five and Nine combined to offer the biggest operating income opportunity. The sixth surprise was

Project Six: Implement Formal Product Life Cycle Management Process. It was the first time that the interdependency was recognized among marketing, product development, and supply chain. For years, obsolete and excess inventory, new product shortages, and engineering changes were shouldered by the supply chain team.

Implementation Timeline

The Fowlers' team viewed the implementation in four phases (Figure 19-2). Phase One initiated "foundational" projects (one, two, four, ten, and twelve) that would make customers happy while improving productivity and freeing up resources to help with Phase Two. Phase One assumptions included the following: uses Lean Six Sigma implementation tools and resources, improves customer facing measures, raises process performance at least one grade, starts immediately, and requires no or low capital investment.

Phase Two initiated the "planning" projects (six, seven, and eight). Scheduled to start six months after Phase One, this group's job was to drive both internal and external facing measures, infusing the company with the first significant operating income benefit. Phase Two assumptions included the following: drive significant operating income and deliver next wave of customer improvements, drive at least 50 percent of the benefit, and force integration between sales, marketing, and operations.

Phase Three initiated the "network" projects (five, nine, and eleven). Scheduled to start three months after Phase Two, this group's job was to engineer an efficient distribution and supply network to support strategic growth and drive significant operating income benefit. Phase Three assumptions included the following: drive significant operating income benefit; and plants, warehouses, sources of supply, and transportation were all open for change. Phase Four initiated the "system" project (three). Scheduled to initiate three months after Phase Three, this group's job was to identify necessary technical requirements from the *new* Fowlers and assemble technology use-migration strategy. Phase Four assumptions included the following: Fowlers is using legacy information systems to their potential, collaboration with suppliers and customers is paramount, accelerated business intelligence is a competitive advantage, and so forth.

▌Program Management

Companies that have had the most success transitioning their Supply Chain Excellence project from an event into a way of life have two

Figure 19-2.   Fowlers' high-level implementation timeline.

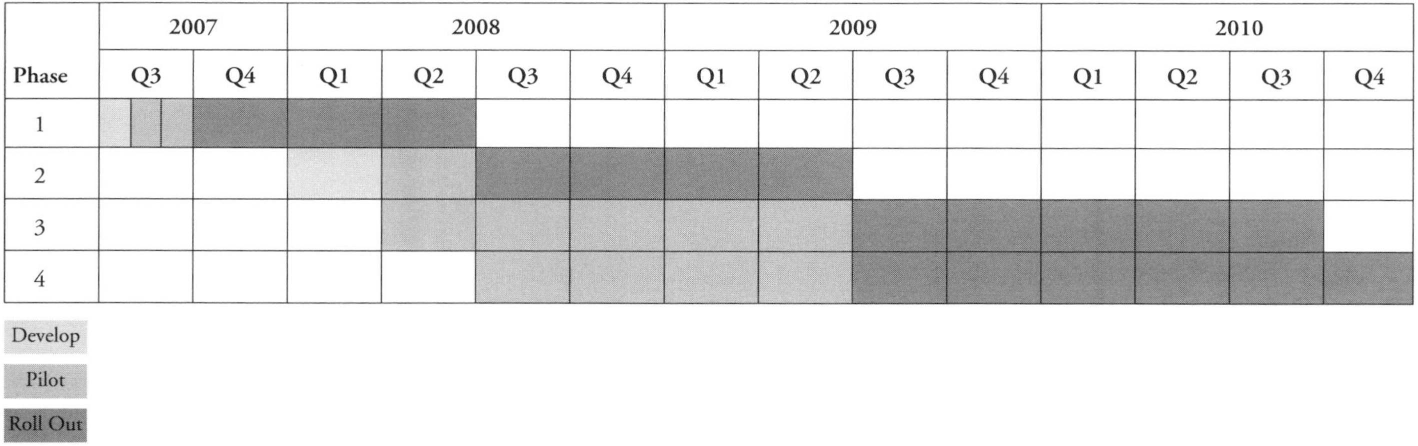

Phase	2007 Q3	2007 Q4	2008 Q1	2008 Q2	2008 Q3	2008 Q4	2009 Q1	2009 Q2	2009 Q3	2009 Q4	2010 Q1	2010 Q2	2010 Q3	2010 Q4
1	Develop	Roll Out	Roll Out	Roll Out										
2			Develop	Pilot	Roll Out	Roll Out								
3					Develop	Develop	Pilot	Pilot	Roll Out	Roll Out	Roll Out	Roll Out	Roll Out	
4							Develop	Develop	Roll Out	Roll Out	Roll Out	Roll Out	Roll Out	Roll Out

Develop
Pilot
Roll Out

things in common. They learned how to manage processes effectively, and they put an organization in place to focus just on that. With that kind of success in mind the Fowlers' team's next task was to put together a vision of how they would support sustaining efforts in Supply Chain Excellence. They agree that the vision needed to include effective process management methodology and a dedicated organization.

Supply Chain Process Management

The Fowlers' process management approach had to address the integration of activity in three different time horizons (Figure 19-3). The first horizon—immediate—needed to address unplanned performance issues and align to the methods (Lean Six Sigma) and resource pools (e.g., green belts, black belts, Lean master) developed through the continuous improvement program. The second time horizon—rolling twelve months—needed to coordinate planned Supply Chain Excellence deployments and support portfolio implementation efforts from previous efforts. The third horizon—strategic—needed to address the annual alignment of process strategy with business direction, including setting process goals and objectives, refreshing the three-year process excellence plans, and gaining executive support for

Figure 19-3.   High-level process management framework.

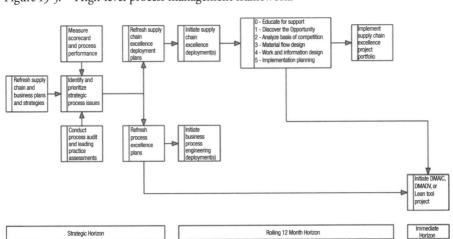

future Supply Chain Excellence deployments. To keep things simple, the graphic illustrates one cycle with no return loops.

Organization

It seems that the degree of centralization swings like a pendulum over time. Companies that have achieved high-performance supply chains seem to look at it more like a teeter-totter using effective process management as the fulcrum to balance work between business units and corporate roles. Figure 19-4 illustrates the concept that many supply chain excellent companies have used as a model. The columns are defined by business units or entities and represent the decentralized part of the equation. They execute supply chain

Figure 19-4.   Centralized versus decentralized concept.

		Business A	Business B	Business C	Business D	Business E
		Decentralized Resources Deployed in Business Units to Operate Processes to Drive Business Results				
	Plan Process Owner					
	Source Process Owner					
Centralized Resources Deployed in Process Roles to Drive Process Excellence Throughout the Enterprise	Make Process Owner					
	Deliver Process Owner					
	Return Process Owner					
	Enable Process Owners					

Figure 19-5. Supply chain organization scenario with matrix reporting. CEO, Chief Executive Officer; VP, Vice President; CIO, Chief Information Officer; CFO, Chief Financial Officer; R&D, research and development; HR, Human Resources.

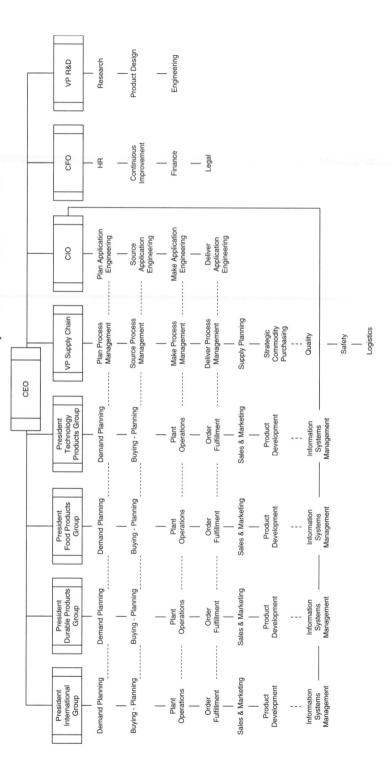

processes to drive business results. The rows are defined by centralized resources deployed in process roles to drive process excellence throughout the enterprise. Process standardization, efficiency, and effectiveness are the priority. ENABLE processes include things such as information systems, project management, and finance.

Reporting relationships—dotted line versus solid line—can vary depending on the business models, autonomy, and global nature of locations. Figure 19-5 illustrates one of the leading scenarios for Fowlers. Assumptions behind this scenario include business unit product development, sales, marketing, manufacturing plants, order fulfillment, purchasing buyer/planners, and demand planning. Central roles included supply planning, strategic commodity purchasing, quality, safety, and logistics.

▪ The Final Steering Team Review

The day is finished with the eighth steering team review, with the following agenda:

- ❏ Project roadmap status.
- ❏ Review the project portfolio and return-on-investment profile.
- ❏ Discuss risk for each project.
- ❏ Expectations for transition to implementation.

20

Extending Excellence Beyond the Supply Chain

Improving the Value Chain by Analyzing Barriers to Profitable Growth

There is a limit to the amount of change that anyone can handle at one time. Individual changes, organizational changes, and more macro or global changes can fill up capacity. By integrating supply chain changes into operational strategy, material flow, and work and information flow, the Supply Chain Excellence process results in fewer but deeper projects that ultimately produce bigger and faster returns, in other words, a manageable amount of change designed to be measurable and meaningful.

That's why the best part of a project is often the final review, where the design team presents its TO BE design, project list, and associated assumptions. To watch each team member speak to both strategy and tactics in the same conversation and understand the thread that ties it all together is worth the pain of the previous weeks.

Joe Farelong, president of the Durable Products Group, was speechless after the design team's final steering team review. He had just seen the future leadership of the company collectively present an organized, customer-focused, financially sound plan to drive supply chain performance. The presentation showed passion, conviction, and confidence. It was the first time he had seen anything like it at Fowlers.

The Durable Products Group had a different set of challenges, and he wondered, "How do I take this approach into my business?"

The Durable Products Group was developing a reputation of leaving money on the table. It had premium brands that commanded premium prices, but profits were average at best. Unlike any other operation in the company, its business model was primarily make-to-order and engineer-to-order. Although his business was routinely touted as the future growth driver for the company, Joe lacked confidence in his ability to hit sales projections because there didn't seem to be any "science" behind the numbers.

Further, as sales, order fulfillment, manufacturing, sourcing, planning, and product design teams worked to get product introduced and out the door, they all had their own ways of getting the work done, and "exceptions" were the norm. In one plant tour he had received from a shift foreman, he counted forty-five instances in which he was told, "...it works like this except when...."

For a long time, the Durable Products Group had been an early innovator in quick response and flexibility to customer demands for both new and existing products. But Joe knew that competitors were catching up—and no one seemed to own "the plan" to take it to the next level. Finally, he was under pressure from Lisa Booker, the Chief Financial Officer, to commit to a plan to improve return on sales. Analysts were not being kind to Fowlers' stock price, and this measure was a significant factor.

With all this on his mind, Joe pulled the coach aside and shared his thoughts. The coach was planning to stay an extra day—so he could join the design team's scheduled celebration. The two agreed to use the full day before the final party to discuss how they might tweak the Supply Chain Excellence approach using Supply Chain Operations Reference (SCOR), Demand Chain Operations

Reference (DCOR), and Customer Chain Operations Reference (CCOR) models. Brian and David caught wind of the meeting and asked if they could join as well.

▪ Value Chain Excellence

The concept of value chain is not new. Both Michael Porter (*Competitive Advantage: Creating and Sustaining Superior Performance.* New York: The Free Press; 1985) and W. Edwards Deming (*Out of Crisis.* Cambridge, MA: Massachusetts Institute of Technology Center for Advanced Engineering Study; 1986) had developed process frameworks that depicted the entire system of value creation. The derivative, supply chain, was not new in 1996 when the Supply-Chain Council released version 1.0 of SCOR. It was introduced then to provide more detail around common definition, metrics, and practices with the goal that companies could use the framework to improve supply chain performance across industries and trading partners. As has been demonstrated, Supply Chain Excellence describes a project approach to identifying a strategic project list to help drive sustainable improvement.

With the introduction of the CCOR and DCOR processes, the Supply Chain Council is again positioned to support value chain performance improvement through common process definition, metrics framework, and leading practices. The question is how to use these models in a project.

That's the question that Joe asked to start his meeting. Figure 20-1 illustrates how Joe, Brian, and David adapted the major phases of Supply Chain Excellence to the extended value chain. Their next challenge was to figure out how to adapt the major deliverables. Fresh off the supply chain project, the team was familiar with each week's key deliverables. They wrote a list and then, for each supply chain deliverable, asked two questions:

❑ Is it necessary for a value chain assessment?
❑ What is the estimated degree of adaptation?

Figure 20-1.   Project phases adapted for the value chain.

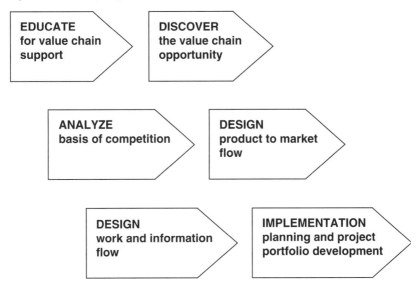

Figure 20-2 summarizes their descriptions of key value chain tasks by phase; the rest of this chapter will summarize the team's discussion highlighting the adaptations for value chain.

▪ Educate for Value Chain Support

The team agreed to describe the deliverables from this phase as (1) identify value chain improvement roles, evangelists, active executive sponsor(s), core steering team, and design team; (2) assemble and deliver appropriate educational content; and (3) gain consensus for a pilot project.

Identify Value Chain Improvement Roles, Evangelists, Active Executive Sponsor(s), Core Steering, and Design Teams

This task would use the same steps (Chapter 2) as used in Fowlers' supply chain project. As the discussion turned more philosophical, the coach described the concept of Learning Quotient (LQ)—an or-

Figure 20-2. Value Chain Excellence project phases and key deliverables.

Value Chain Excellence Project Phases	
Educate for Value Chain Support	• Identify Value Chain Improvement roles, Evangelist(s), Active Executive Sponsor(s), and Core Steering Team • Assemble and Deliver Appropriate Educational Content • Gain Consensus for Pilot Project
Discover Value Chain Opportunity	• Define Big Business Question(s) and Summarize Business Background • Calculate the Number of Value Chains • Assemble High Level Industry Comparison • Decide the Scope of the Project and Finalize Project Charter
Analyze Value Chain Basis of Competition	• Identify Appropriate Value Chain Performance Metrics • Complete a Metric Defect Analysis • Assemble Appropriate Benchmark Comparisons • Assess and Prioritize Competitive Requirements
Design Value Chain Product to Market Flow	• Using AS IS, Disconnect, and TO BE Product—Market Analysis • Identify Sales Region Growth Barriers • Identify Product Profit Barriers • Identify Potential Quick Hit Improvements
Design Value Chain Work and Information Flow	• Using AS IS, Disconnect, and TO BE Process Analysis • Identify Value Chain Transactional Productivity Barriers • Conduct Value Chain Leading Practice Gap Assessment • Identify Value Chain Strategic Process Barriers
Implement Value Chain Improvements	• Assemble Value Chain Improvement Opportunity Effort—Impact • Develop Value Chain Improvement Project Portfolio • Identify Appropriate Project Implementation Approaches • Create 18- to 24-month Implementation Plan

Source © Copyright 2006 SCE Limited. Used with permission.

ganization's ability to acquire knowledge and adapt behavior in response to changes in the business environment. A low organizational LQ (poor adaptability) is like a perpetual "Go to Jail" card in Monopoly. You never pass Go and are stuck watching the game from behind bars unless you get a lucky roll of the dice. The Evangelist,

Active Executive Sponsor, Core Steering, and Design teams are four key roles that will set the pace of the organization's LQ in relation to value chain improvement; all four roles must be in place to pass GO.

Assemble and Deliver Appropriate Educational Content and Gain Consensus for a Pilot Project

The team reflected on how they progressed from knowing nothing about SCOR and Supply Chain Excellence to the final steering team in six months: light speed compared with other major initiatives. They defined three stages to their organizational learning and agreed that each must occur to move on to the next one. They substituted the word "Value" for "Supply" and agreed that Durable Products would need to follow the same path.

Initial Exposure was the first stage; the objective was to investigate the Value Chain Excellence framework and the fit of the process models of SCOR, DCOR, and CCOR. The educational content of this phase would be characterized by the phrase "short and sweet." This is the stage at which Evangelists and Active Executive Sponsor(s) evaluate the fit of the method and the process frameworks with their business needs.

Learn How to Sell is the second stage; the objective of Evangelists and Active Executive Sponsor(s) is to sell Core Steering Team members on the benefits of *Value Chain Excellence* and prepare them to sponsor a pilot project. The educational content of this phase takes the overview content style of the first phase and incorporates real company data in as many places as possible to give the leadership team the best vision of a project in their own business language.

Implement a Pilot Project is the third stage; the object for the Project Team—including the Evangelists, Active Executive Sponsor(s), Core Steering, and Design Teams—is to develop the knowledge, skill, and motivation to successfully execute a project. The educational content in this phase is a mix of detailed "how to" templates and anecdotes that take theory to practice.

The amount of time spent in each phase depends on the organization's LQ. Companies with low LQ spend a lot of time in the first phase, often kicking tires until they're flat. High LQ companies can advance to the last phase in as little as three months; the typical duration is four to six months.

Durable Products Group Challenges

Joe Farelong summarized three challenges Durable Products would need to address as part of this phase. First was to identify the right evangelist (and ultimate project leader) for an initiative that would cross multiple processes and trading partner boundaries. To make matters complicated, the *product design* role on the new chart reported to a corporate function, and the formal *product development* role reported directly to Joe (Figure 19-5).

The theory was sound, but Durable Products would have to learn how to operate in the new world. Joe's short list of candidates included the Director of Product Development and his best Regional Sales Manager.

The second challenge was to identify a core steering team that ultimately would be in charge of implementing the value chain changes. This would be the first time that Durable Products' sales, marketing, product development, and supply chain would jointly sponsor anything—and two of the four roles had no experience with process improvement. His first draft included the Vice President Supply Chain, Vice President Research and Development, Durable Products' Director of Sales and Marketing, Chief Financial Officer, and Chief Information Officer

■ Discover Value Chain Opportunity

The team described the deliverables from this second phase as follows: (1) Define the business objective and summarize business background, (2) calculate the number of value chains, (3) assemble high-level industry comparison, and (4) decide the scope of the pilot project and finalize project charter.

Calculate the Number of Value Chains

Defining the number of company value chains requires the same technique as that of defining the number of supply chains (Chapter 3). Figure 20-3 illustrates the Durable Products Group's adaptations. As in the supply chain, the rows represent lines of business or product families, and the lowest level of the row hierarchy is an item or Stock Keeping Unit. The columns represent customers or customer segments, and the lowest level of the column hierarchy is a customer "ship to" location. The "X" indicates a product or service that is delivered to a customer; the number of X's provides a first draft of the number of company value chains. One adaptation also included "F"—future value chains that would evolve as part of the

Figure 20-3.   Adaptations for the Durable Product's value chain definition matrix where data represents growth versus prior period.

Durable Products Group			U.S. Customer/Market Channels		
			Direct-to-Consumer	Home Delivery	OEM-Key Accounts
U.S. Lines of Business	Product Family A	Revenue	5.6%		
		Unit	10.0%	X	F
		Gross Margin	−2.5%		
	Product Family B	Revenue			
		Unit	X	X	
		Gross Margin			
	Product Family C	Revenue			
		Unit			F
		Gross Margin			
	Product Family D	Revenue			
		Unit	X	X	F
		Gross Margin			

strategic plan. A second adaptation includes growth rate (revenue, unit volume, and gross margin) data for each value chain. Durable Products has six current and three future value chains.

Assemble High-Level Industry Comparison

The industry comparison is assembled using the same steps as for the supply chain (Chapter 4), with five new data comparisons focused on the rate of growth from the prior period. These categories are revenue; sales, general, and administration expense; gross margin; operating income; and net income.

Deciding on Your Project Scope

The phrase "think big, act small, and scale fast..." still works for value chain analysis. The value chain priority matrix is assembled in the same fashion as for supply chains (Table 3-5). The team brainstormed other categories (columns) to consider, including revenue growth rate, percent of new product revenue, and return on sales.

Durable Products Group challenges

Without data, the conversation was mostly theoretical, but it migrated around three important points. First, in assembling the priority matrix, the weighting needed to emphasize both current and projected growth, and return on sales. Second, because most of the Durable Products Group's competitors were private, the industry comparison would need to include companies in similar industries. Third, it would take some minor wizardry to gather the unit, revenue, and margin growth rates for the current value chains—and major wizardry to project numbers for the future value chains.

■ Analyze Value Chain Basis of Competition

The team listed four deliverables for this phase: (1) identify appropriate value chain performance metrics, (2) assemble appropriate benchmark comparisons, and (3) assess and prioritize competitive requirements.

Identify Appropriate Value Chain Performance Metrics and Assemble Appropriate Benchmark Comparisons (Combined Steps 1 and 2)

Although the previous scorecard (Chapter 4) provides a proven baseline to measure supply chain performance, it does not include measures for the other business processes. The coach suggested the team use a Balanced Scorecard (The Balanced Scorecard Institute, Cary, NC, and Rockville, MD; www.balancedscorecard.org), an approach to strategic management developed in the early 1990s by Dr. Robert Kaplan and Dr. David Norton. The basic idea is that an organization should measure its performance from a balanced view against its goals as established in its vision and strategy. The Balanced Scorecard has four measurement categories: customer facing, internal process, financial, and individual employee.

The challenge for Joe, Brian, and David was to pick the right metrics for each category. The coach discussed two methods to generate the list. The first starts with a blank sheet of paper; we've all been through that method. The second—which the team ultimately picked—is to identify relevant metrics from a pool of readily available benchmark sources. The coach suggested some of the same sources used in the supply chain project (Figure 4-11). They include the following: The Supply-Chain Council (www.supply-chain.org), The Performance Measurement Group (www.pmgbenchmarking.com), Hoovers (www.hoovers.com), APQC—formerly the American Productivity & Quality Center (www.apqc.org), and Manufacturing Performance Institute Benchmark Toolkit (www.mpi-group.net). Figure 20-4 is the list that the team generated. Each metric was assigned to a Balanced Scorecard category; the team decided not to cre-

(text continues on page 252)

Figure 20-4. List of value chain level one metrics and benchmark sources; the SCOR metrics are highlighted in gray.

Benchmark Source	Level One Value Chain Metrics	Customer Facing			Process				Financial		Employee	
		Reliability	Responsiveness	Flexibility	Supply Chain	Design Chain	Customer Chain	Aggregate	Profit	Growth	Performance	Development
APQC PMG	Perfect Order Fulfillment	X										
PMG	Warranty Fulfillment	X										
PMG	Service Order Fulfillment	X										
MPI APQC	Product Quality	X										
APQC PMG	Order Fulfillment Cycle Time		X									
APQC	New Product Development Cycle Time		X									
Data GAP	Selling Process Cycle Time		X									
APQC	Return Process Cycle Time		X									
PMG	Upside Supply Chain Flexibility			X								
PMG	Engineering Change Order Flexibility			X								
PMG	Design Reuse Flexibility			X								

Source	Metric						
APQC	Total Returns Management Cost			X			
Data GAP	Total Customer Chain Management Cost			X			
ALL	Days Sales Outstanding			X			
PMG APQC	Total Supply Chain Management Costs	X					
ALL	Inventory Days of Supply	X					
APQC PMG	Total Design Chain Management Cost		X				
APQC	Total Warranty Cost		X				
APQC PMG	New Product Revenue				X		
ALL	Cost of Goods Sold				X		
APQC PMG Hoovers	Sales, General, and Administrative Cost				X		
ALL	Cash-to-Cash Cycle Time				X		
PMG Hoovers	Asset Turns				X		
Hoovers	Return on Assets				X		
ALL	Gross Profit Margin					X	
ALL	Operating Margin					X	
Hoovers	Net Profit Margin					X	
Hoovers	Revenue Growth						X
Hoovers	Gross Profit Growth						X
Hoovers	Operating Margin Growth						X

ate employee metrics before brainstorming with a larger group. Figure 20-5 is a sample of some of the benchmark data available for select value chain metrics.

Assess and Prioritize Competitive Requirements

With respect to value chain competitive requirements, the team agreed that a broader framework was needed to assess overall business strategy. The coach suggested a modification of a Michael Porter (Competitive Advantage: Creating and Sustaining Superior Performance) concept, which describes two basic strategies of competitive advantage: Low Cost or Differentiation. These two strategies, when applied to a narrowly defined industry segment, create Porter's third generic strategy: Focus. Put another way, a company must answer two questions; "Will I focus on a broad industry or a narrowly defined segment?" and then, "Will I achieve competitive advantage through Low Cost or Differentiation?" Porter describes companies that try to represent all strategies to all customers as being "stuck in the middle"—and they generally perform at or below parity in all dimensions.

The team also was enamored with the simple assembly and the large impact of the supply chain competitive requirements (Figure 5-2) exercise. The concept was easy to explain: A company must decide on a supply chain strategy to achieve superior and advantage positions in some metric categories, while maintaining at least parity in others.

So how can the concepts of Porter and SCOR be brought together? Figure 20-6 represents the team's best attempt to mock up an example using the Durable Products Group. The left arrow represents performance in the "cost" strategy, and the right arrow represents performance in the "differentiation" strategy. Specifically, they related the left arrow with process measures and the right arrow with customer-facing measures. The base of the arrow is actual performance, the end of the arrow is target performance.

(text continues on page 255)

Figure 20-5. Sample benchmark data for select value chain metrics.[1,2]

| Process Model | Metric & Benchmark Source | Sample of Level One Value Chain Metrics | Value Chain Benchmark | | |
| | | | Performance Versus Comparison Population | | |
			Parity 50th Percentile	Advantage 70th Percentile	Superior 90th Percentile
DCOR	APQC	New Product Development Cycle Time[1]	245 days	186 days	99 days
DCOR	APQC	Total R&D cost as a percentage of revenue (current reporting period)[1]	17.41%	10.00%	3.04%
DCOR	APQC	Total R&D cost as a percentage of revenue (three reporting periods ago)[1]	16.81%	7.99%	3.44%
DCOR	APQC	Design cycle time in days from start to design, build, and evaluate through completion of test market product/service for new product/ service development projects[1]	720.0	437.4	334.5
DCOR	APQC	Total cost of the development cycle as a percentage of revenue[1]	13.00%	11.13%	4.13%
DCOR	APQC	Percentage of sales which is a result of products/services launched during the most recently completed 12 month reporting period[1]	16.50%	25.20%	50.00%
DCOR	PMG	Design Reuse Flexibility[2]	9.50%	8.49%	7.47%

(continues)

Figure 20-5. (*continued*)

Process Model	Metric & Benchmark Source	Sample of Level One Value Chain Metrics	Value Chain Benchmark Performance Versus Comparison Population		
			Parity 50th Percentile	Advantage 70th Percentile	Superior 90th Percentile
DCOR	PMG	Total Design Chain Management Cost[2]	9.50%	8.49%	7.47%
DCOR	PMG	New Product Revenue[2]	22.50%	39.20%	55.90%
ALL	Hoovers	Sales, General, and Administrative Cost	19.45%	13.00%	9.06%
ALL	Hoovers	Revenue Growth	13.94%	18.99%	31.31%
ALL	Hoovers	Gross Profit Growth	18.01%	31.55%	39.66%
ALL	Hoovers	Operating Margin Growth	34.29%	63.55%	165.95%

[1]APQC is reporting this data on the assumption that lower R&D costs, lower cycle time, lower product development costs, and higher sales due to recent product launches represent superior performance. APQC acknowledges that correlating these measures to various outcomes may support a different perspective. Mr. Bolstroff has APQC's permission to present the perspective that best fits his current needs. © Copyright 2007 APQC. All Rights Reserved. Used with permission.

[2]Data Reuse Flexibility, Total Design Chain Management Cost (PLM Operating Cost), and New Product Revenue data © Copyright 2003 The Performance Measurement Group, LLC, subsidiary of management consultants PRTM. All Rights Reserved. Used with permission.

Figure 20-6.   Sample of Durable Products' value chain scorecard with 2007 estimate performance, benchmark comparisons, and competitive requirements.

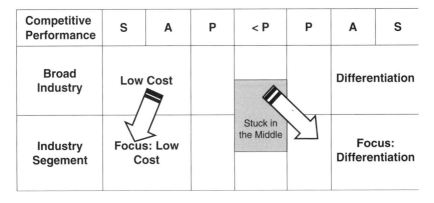

Joe talked through one possible strategic scenario: by focusing on niche markets the Durable Products Group could adopt both cost *and* differentiation tactics to put itself into a better market position. The direction of the arrows suggests that Durable Products narrow its products and customer focus from "Broad Industry" to a narrow industry niche and that it pursue superior cost performance within that niche, while customer-facing metrics operate at parity.

In value chain metric terms, process measures need to move toward the 90th percentile, and the customer-facing measures need to move toward at least the 50th percentile. They all agreed this chart needed more work, but that the concepts made sense. They recognized that if both arrows are in the shaded portion, action is required.

Durable Products Group challenges

By lunchtime, the team felt a need to draw closure on this phase; completing the scorecard would satisfy that desire. Figure 20-7 represents their output; not all metrics were included; 2007 actual performance was an estimate; and parity, advantage, and superior competitive requirements needed some work. Some obvious themes were already emerging: Although spend was comparable to other competitors, new-product cycle time was far below parity, due in part to poor design reuse. Revenue from new products lagged accordingly.

Figure 20-7. Sample of Durable Products value chain scorecard with 2007 estimate performance, benchmark comparisons, and competitive requirements (highlighted in gray).

	Metric Categories	Metrics	Fowlers—Durable Products Group 2007 Estimate	Benchmark Comparison Parity	Advantage	Superior	Parity Gap	Source
Customer Facing	Responsiveness	New Product Development Cycle Time	325 days	245 days	186 days	99 days	-80 days	APQC
Customer Facing	Flexibility	Design Reuse Flexibility	18.0%	22.0%	37.2%	42.3%	-4.0%	PMG
Process	Design Chain	Total Design Chain Management Cost	9.4%	9.5%	8.5%	7.5%	-0.1%	PMG
Process		New Product Revenue	15.0%	22.5%	39.2%	55.9%	-7.5%	PMG
Process	Aggregate	Cost of Goods	87.7%	72.9%	69.6%	58.1%	-14.8%	Hoovers
Process	Aggregate	Cash-to-Cash Cycle Time	80.2	81.3	62.6	26.1	1.1	Hoovers
Process	Aggregate	Inventory Days of Supply	55.5	33.5	25.1	19.7	-22.0	Hoovers
Process	Aggregate	Asset Turns	0.8	1.2	1.7	3.0	-0.4	Hoovers
Financial	Growth	Revenue Growth % to prev Year	11.0%	13.9%	19.0%	31.3%	-2.9%	Hoovers
Financial	Growth	GP Growth % to prev Year	9.0%	18.0%	31.6%	39.7%	-9.0%	Hoovers
Financial	Growth	OM Growth % to prev Year	28.0%	34.3%	63.5%	165.9%	-6.3%	Hoovers
Financial	Profitability	Gross Profit Margin	12.3%	27.1%	30.4%	41.9%	-14.8%	Hoovers
Financial	Profitability	Operating Margin	3.8%	2.7%	5.7%	12.2%	1.1%	Hoovers
Financial	Profitability	Net Profit Margin	1.8%	1.9%	3.5%	7.3%	-0.1%	Hoovers

Further, sales growth lagged compared with others in the industry, and although operating income was a little better than parity, year-to-year growth in operating income was below parity—and less than half that of companies in the 70th percentile. Joe sat down, rubbed his face, and put his elbows on the table. Even imperfect data validated what he and his staff had been feeling. His next question was "How do we turn the ship?" The afternoon would detail and adapt the next two phases.

▪ Design Product-to-Market Flow

The team discussed four types of deliverables for this phase: (1) Metric Defect Analysis, (2) Product-to-Market Map, both AS IS and TO BE, (3) Process Thread Diagram, both AS IS and TO BE, and (4) Disconnect and Opportunity Analysis.

Metric Defect Analysis

The team agreed that the disconnect analysis was critical to uncovering the issues related to performance. Although some templates would need to be created for the new metrics, the steps (Chapter 8) were identical to the supply chain project.

Product-to-Market Maps

This set of deliverables was the most difficult to adapt. In the supply chain project, the geographic map was an easy concept to grasp; even applying the SCOR Level Two strategies (Chapter 7) was pretty straightforward. Although there is a material movement piece to value chain, the team discussed two other layers that needed to be considered as part of the analysis as well.

First, it would be necessary to understand sales by region, as the sales-and-marketing team views it. Figure 20-8 illustrates the three regions of U.S. sales for Durable Products. Layering the geographic map on top of the sales-by-region map was both intuitive and logical for the team.

Figure 20-8.   Durable Products' U.S. sales by region map.

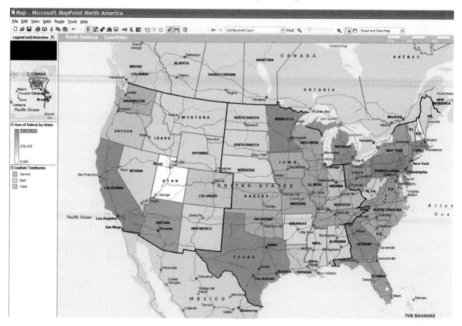

The third layer was not as simple. In fact, a spreadsheet was a better tool than a picture. The concept the team was after was to understand the rate of growth in each sales region between new and existing products, and among new and existing customers. Figure 20-9 is a mock-up of the concept, which the team eventually labeled Value Chain Growth Analysis. The analysis attempts to calculate growth rates for revenue, gross margin, and unit volume for each cell in the matrix. With the use of predetermined criteria, a cell (product and customer) is graded red, yellow, or green. The results helped the team understand the issues behind growth. For example, Product Family B has growth issues across the board, whereas Product Family A has particular trouble building sales of existing products to new customers.

The benefit of this perspective is that next set of "why" questions are not just aimed at supply. Marketing campaigns, pricing strategy, product quality, product life cycle management, sales incentives, and so forth are all in the mix of potential root causes and ultimate projects.

Figure 20-9. Durable Products U.S. growth rate analysis. +, positive growth; -, negative growth; and 0, neutral growth.

Durable Products—U.S. Value Chain			Western US Sales Territory					
			New Customers			Existing Customers		
			Revenue	Gross Margin	Unit	Revenue	Gross Margin	Unit
North America Lines of Business	Product Family A	New Products	+	+	+	+	+	+
		Existing Products	−	−	−	+	+	+
	Product Family B	New Products	−	−	−	0	0	0
		Existing Products	−	−	−	−	−	−
	Product Family C	New Products	−	−	−	+	+	+
		Existing Products	−	−	−	−	−	+
	Product Family D	New Products	−	−	−	+	+	+
		Existing Products	+	+	+	−	−	−

Process Thread Diagrams

As in the supply chain project, the preparation required to create a process thread diagram (Chapter 8) involved identifying the appropriate Level Two processes for each location. Figure 20-10 is a partial list of the choices for each location; one necessary adaptation is the small-letter designation in front of the Level Two ID; "c" is CCOR, "d" is DCOR, and "s" is SCOR.

Figure 20-11 illustrates the team's work assembling a logical Durable Products flow. The dotted lines represent information; the solid lines represent product flow. As with any concept drawing, the team had a tough time differentiating "the should be" from "the AS IS." Joe, David, and Brian also realized they would need to get signed

Figure 20-10.   Demand chain operations reference, customer chain operations reference, and supply chain operations reference level two process categories.

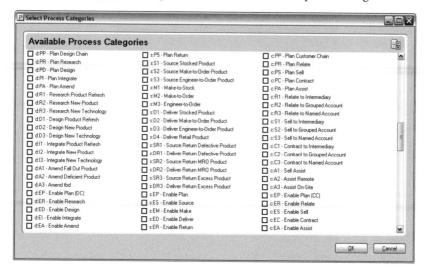

Figure 20-11.   Demand chain operations reference, customer chain operations reference, and supply chain operations reference level two process categories by location.

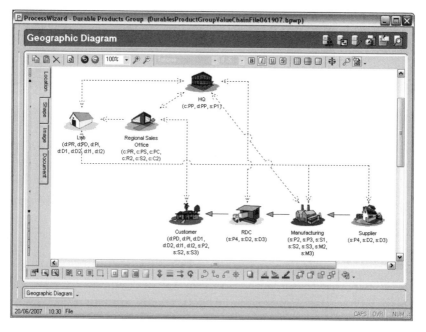

up for DCOR and CCOR framework classes. They needed to affirm their intuitions about the difference between design classifications of "product refresh," "new product," and "new technology," as well as between the customer classifications of sell to "intermediary," "grouped account," and "named account." For the mock-up, they used both refreshed (new and improved) and the traditional new-product categories for design. For customer categories, they used grouped account (direct-to-consumer). Figure 20-12 is the first draft of the process thread diagram, with few connection rules. The team decided that one of the necessary adaptations would be to create a set of primary and secondary connection rules among DCOR, CCOR, and SCOR Level Two process elements. They also considered substituting Lean Valve Stream maps for this particular deliverable.

Disconnect and Opportunity Analysis

The team agreed that this foundational supply chain deliverable would be necessary to help dissect the issues, build projects, and quantify the improvement (Chapters 9, 10, and 11). They thought the defect analysis value chain growth analysis, and enterprise value stream maps would be candidates for the brainstorm categories. No other adaptations were necessary.

Durable Products Group challenges

In addition to getting acclimated to the new process categories, the primary challenges for Durable Products would be the introduction of this high level of rigor, data and analysis to sales, marketing, and design—corners of the organization that had never been part of a large-scale process-improvement initiative. As for putting revenue estimates against projects, it wouldn't be any easier than it was in the supply chain project.

▪ Design Work and Information Flow

The team discussed four types of deliverables for this phase: (1) Staple Yourself Interviews, (2) Level Three process, functional areas,

Figure 20-12. Durable Products' process thread diagram.

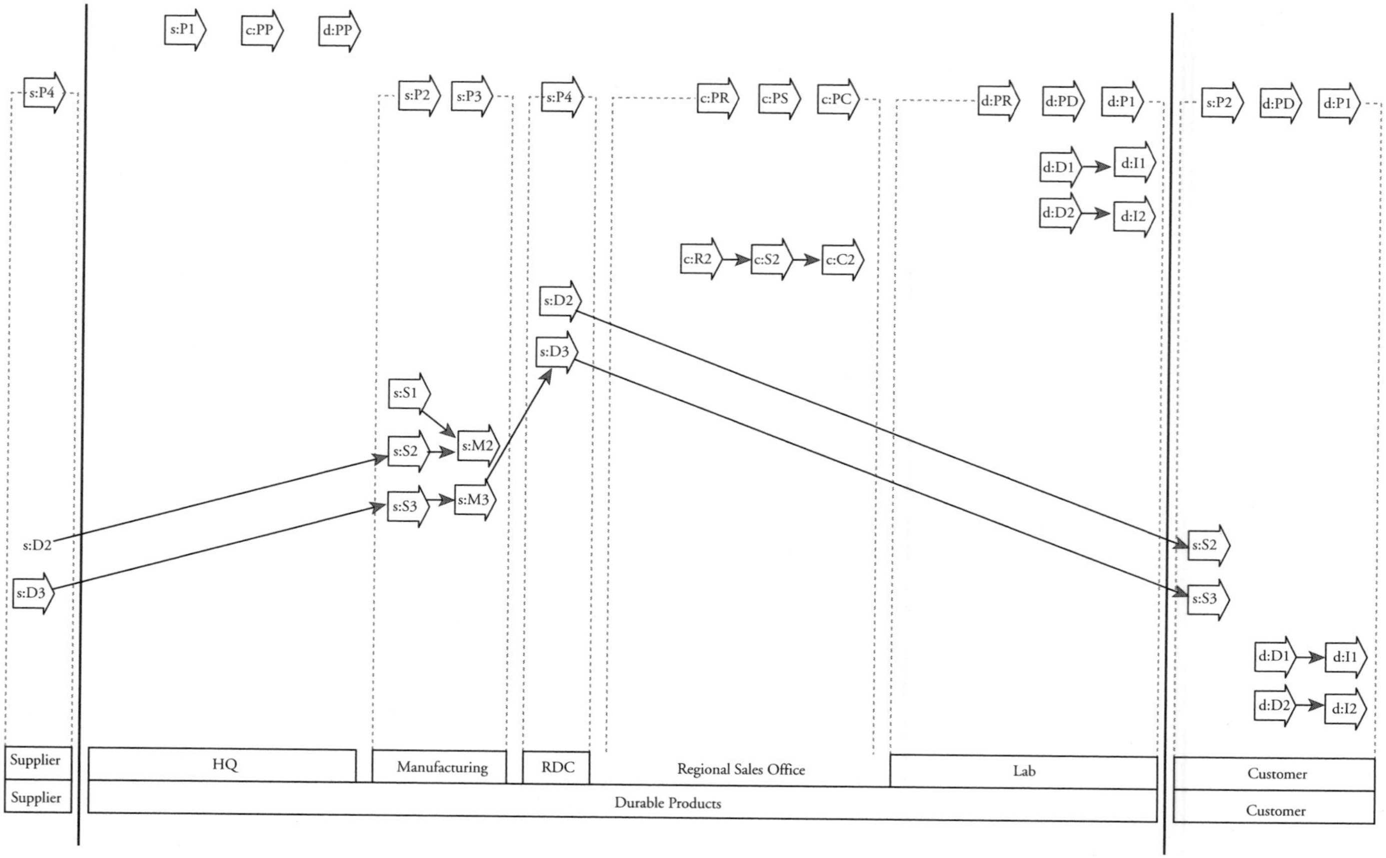

and responsibilities diagrams, both AS IS and TO BE, (3) process performance summaries, and (4) TO BE Level Four process diagrams with information system storyboards.

Staple Yourself Interviews

The team decided that the steps in preparing and conducting the staple yourself interviews would be identical (Chapter 14). The only necessary adaptation was to brainstorm major transactions for CCOR and DCOR. Here is their first draft list:

Supply Chain
- ❏ Purchase Order
- ❏ Work Order
- ❏ Sales Order
- ❏ Return Authorization
- ❏ Forecast
- ❏ Replenishment Order

Customer Chain
- ❏ Customer Profile
- ❏ Sales Call to Contract
- ❏ Quote/Proposal
- ❏ Service Request
- ❏ Sales $ Forecast
- ❏ Quota

Design Chain
- ❏ Engineering Change Request
- ❏ Product Design Specification
- ❏ Manufacturing Qualification "Certificate"
- ❏ New Product Introduction Plan

Level Three Process, Functional Areas, and Responsibilities Diagrams

As in the interview deliverables, the team agreed that the steps in building process diagrams, conducting the RACI analysis, and documenting the functional areas and responsibilities diagrams would be identical to that of the supply chain project (Chapter 15).

Process Performance Summaries

Here too, the steps involved in creating process performance summaries for the major transactions were identical to those of the supply chain project (Chapter 16). The team did have two potential adaptations. First, they were unsure of which leading practice assessment would be appropriate for sales and product design; more research would be necessary. Second, they needed input from the information systems team regarding the minor transactions for sales and design. Supply chain transactions garnered most of the attention at Fowlers.

TO BE Level Four Process Diagrams with Information System Storyboards

As with a broken record, the team found the steps to build level four processes and educate team members through the information system storyboards were a direct application to value chain (Chapter 18). No additional adaptations were deemed necessary.

Durable Products Group challenges

Joe discussed two big challenges with this phase. First, there would be a learning curve in his organization relative to the new organizational chart (Figure 19-5). His hope was that bad habits, brick walls, and work-arounds wouldn't become the norm before the project initiating. His largest concerns were how a central research and product design team would work with his product development team, and how his product development team would cooperate with his sales-and-marketing group. Second, his business unit did not have many resident software experts relating to the design and sales tools; the Chief Information Officer would have to provide that expertise, and there would be a steep learning curve as that executive learned the Durable Products' make-to-order and engineer-to-order business.

Implementing Value Chain Improvements

The team discussed two types of deliverables for this phase: (1) project return on investment summary and (2) program management process and supporting organization. In both cases, the team agreed that the same steps, processes, and supporting organization would be directly applied to the value chain initiative (Chapter 19). The only adaptations would be formalizing process manager roles for the customer sales and design processes. The question is whether to organize around the Level One processes, that is, plan, research, design, integrate, amend, relate, sell, contract, and assist. If the answer is yes, then the main issue is establishment of formal reporting relationships.

Value Chain Conclusions

The clock was pointing to 5:30 P.M., and the foursome sat around the conference table, exhausted. They were already a half-hour late leaving for the party that the supply chain design team was holding, but they had that satisfied, head-spinning feeling that a well-studied college student gets at the end of final exams. Nobody seemed quite ready to move.

Surrounding them were three 12-foot whiteboards full of diagrams, notes, and numbers—each with a great big "SAVE" scribbled in the corner. In one day, they had outlined how to stretch the Supply Chain Excellence approach to cover the value chain requirements in Joe's very different business. They were confident it would work—and just realistic enough to know the method would have to be adjusted as they progressed.

David and Brian felt as though they'd just gotten two process improvements for the price of one. Joe felt that great sense of being unburdened from the quiet troubles that had been building within his business.

"When can we get started?" Joe asked.

Brian smiled and replied, "Can we wait until after the party?"

Index